BRITISH VIOLIN MAKERS

QUARTET OF OLD ENGLISH INSTRUMENTS.

Frontispiece.

BRITISH VIOLIN MAKERS

A Biographical Dictionary of British Makers of
Stringed Instruments and Bows and a
Critical Description of their Work

WITH INTRODUCTORY CHAPTERS, AND NUMEROUS
PORTRAITS AND ILLUSTRATIONS

BY THE
Rev. W. MEREDITH MORRIS, B.A.

FOREWORD BY
BENJAMIN HEBBERT

PELICAN PUBLISHING COMPANY
Gretna 2006

Copyright © 2006
By Pelican Publishing Company, Inc.
All rights reserved

First edition, 1904
Second edition, revised and enlarged, 1920
Third edition, 2006

The word "Pelican" and the depiction of a pelican are trademarks of Pelican Publishing Company, Inc., and are registered in the U.S. Patent and Trademark Office.

ISBN-13: 978-1-58980-431-9
ISBN-13: 978-1-58980-220-9 (pbk.)

Printed in the United States of America

Published by Pelican Publishing Company, Inc.
1000 Burmaster Street, Gretna, Louisiana 70053

FOREWORD

When William Meredith Morris first published *British Violin Makers* in 1904, it was at a point when he was able to contend that the best living violin makers, as opposed to the best makers of the past, were British. The time would come, or so he thought, when older Italian and French instruments would be worn out by age, and instruments by the British makers who had emerged after the 1880s would be the choice tools of the great musicians of the future. Morris does not make clear why he was so forthright in his opinions. Indeed, the present-day commentator on violins might be tempted almost to bypass the vibrant living school that Morris describes with such passion, or at least acknowledge it in a way that does not leave it in such a prominent position. Therefore, it seems prudent to supply the reader with some of the history and context in which this book was written.

In 1904, Britain was at the height of its power, commanding an empire that stretched across the globe and enjoying the wealth to go with it. The possibilities open to the newly fledged English school of violin making were endless, and with the judicious coaching that Morris felt qualified to provide, English violin making could perhaps become everything that he dreamed. A decade later, the First World War had begun, and the halcyon days of the British Empire were over. Before Morris died in 1921, he had issued his second edition of *British Violin Makers,* from which this edition is reprinted. The work is partially revised, with extra biographies in the main text, but a series of appendices reveal that it was not finished the way he would have intended had he lived a few years more. The world was already changing, and his dreams would be shattered. Britain plunged into economic and social turmoil, and very few violin makers sustained themselves. At the same time in Italy, where fine makers such as Leandro Bisiach were already carving a career for themselves, a new school of violin making became increasingly important as Benito Mussolini's newly installed Fascist government became more interested in sustaining Italy's ancient national traditions.

The violin's history had begun in Italy four centuries before, and the city of Cremona owed its reputation at the forefront of violin making to successive generations of makers who had worked in its close-knit community. In the 1560s, King Charles IX of France had commissioned violins to be made for his court by Andrea Amati, the earliest of the known Cremonese violin makers. Surviving examples from this set of instruments represent the earliest violins, violas, and violoncellos known to us that are made in effectively modern form. Eventually all the major courts of Europe would be populated with Cremonese stringed instruments. By the time that Antonio Stradivari had assumed the position of patriarch over Cremonese violin making in the 1680s, at least three generations of the Amati family had preceded him. Yet the community that had defined the best violins in the

FOREWORD

world had its Achilles heel, for while their instruments were highly prized, were perfectly crafted, and commanded heavy premiums above any of their competitors' work, they were also durable and adaptable to change, so that periodic renewal was not needed. By the 1740s, demand for newly made Cremonese violins had run dry because everyone who needed one had one, and with the death of the last generation of classical makers (Stradivari in 1737, Giuseppe Guarneri del Gesu in 1745), the community who had defined the violin had become a spent force. The romantic contends that their secrets were taken to the grave, but likely as not the simple traditions by which they worked became worthless and forgotten.

The end of the eighteenth century had seen remarkable revolutions in musical culture: the dawn of the classical era, new public concert halls, and the cult of the virtuoso. The violins of Stradivari and Guarneri del Gesu were perfectly suited to these conditions, not only because of their sound properties, but because of what they represented as rare and ultimately valuable objects of art. The first modern affirmation of the importance of Cremonese instruments came in 1781 when Viotti made his debut performance at the Concert Spirituel in Paris. His success was instantaneous, placing him in the top rank of all violinists, but he attributed much of his success to the properties of the Stradivari violin that he played. Some years later in 1806, similar circumstances surrounding Niccolo Paganini after he was given the *Canon* violin (1742) would place the violins of Guarneri del Gesu in the same limelight. In Paris, from the 1780s, the sort of "Golden Period" Stradivari violin that had been promoted by Viotti seems to have been a rarity, promoting the particular need for modern copies to be made in a most exacting fashion. Among the leading musicians of the time, Ole Bull conducted a lengthy concert tour using a violin by Francois Pique, and Louis Spohr wrote in praise of violins by Nicolas Lupot. Although these violins did not perform as well as a genuine "Strad," they were at least a magnificent improvement upon the entrenched vernacular designs that had been propagated in France and other parts of Europe throughout the eighteenth century.

Paris remained the dominant marketplace for old instruments and a center in which the best new instruments were made. In contrast to the gradual accumulation of old Italian masterpieces made by English gentlemen over the seventeenth and eighteenth centuries, promoting a sedate market in which they were traded in London, after France had recovered from its Revolution, the insatiable appetite of its newly arisen bourgeoisie for high culture led to an unprecedented pillage of great instruments from mainland Europe. Legend has it that the Stradivari *Duport* violoncello still bears Napoleon's spur marks on its bottom ribs, while a host of other violins have provenances that began in Napoleon's army. Among them, the violin by Guarneri del Gesu that became known as the *Kemp* (1738) belonged to General Ernouf, and the *Kreisler* (1733) was once the property of Marshal Andoche Junot before his ship was lost to British privateers. Amidst France's economic recovery from military defeat, music became an ever more important signifier of cultural identity among the bourgeois. The market for fine Cremonese instruments

FOREWORD

boomed, and with it the market for modern substitutes. The history of the market for violins in Paris after the Napoleonic wars rests solely on the shoulders of Jean Baptist-Vuillaume, a maker and dealer of singular genius who instigated the commercial forces from which the modern-day market takes its origins. From the middle of the 1820s, he had applied the already well established rules of the antique furniture trade to violins. The effects of his strategy inflated the prices of original antiques—the "Strads," Amatis, and those of "del Gesu"—and at the same time his careful facsimiles, antiqued to look original, commanded premium prices above those of ordinary new violins. His asking price for his own work was always a tenth of the price of the instrument that he was copying, but the better his facsimiles became, and the more competition he incited among his colleagues, the greater the sums he was able to charge for his own work. Yet it was *always* a tenth of the price he would conceive of for the original. The market worked because consumers accepted the prices that they were expected to pay. Classical violins flooded into Paris, exposing makers to the best examples of violin making while providing a ready market for their painstakingly fastidious copies of Cremonese workmanship.

Meanwhile, the British violin makers had been overshadowed by their French contemporaries. At the beginning of the nineteenth century, several makers working in London had acted in a manner that was influenced by the French. Thomas Dodd claimed to be the only possessor of the true Cremonese varnish (which, unlike the real stuff, blackens over time). Likewise, John Betts and William

Forster were heavily influenced by the classical instruments that passed through their hands, though not to the same extent as Lupot and Pique in Paris, and they retained a good dose of English vernacular character in their work. But by the middle of the nineteenth century, except for a few excellent restorers and forgers, Jack Lott and Bernhard Simon Fendt among them, Britain was suffering under a flood of German- and French-made factory instruments, so that one commentator wrote that the English school was practically extinct: "The unfortunate English fiddle maker has been slowly starved to death by a grinding competition he has been unable to meet" (Balfour & Co., *How to Tell the Nationality of Old Violins* [London: 1901], 1).

Formerly, a fine Italian violin had been an obligatory acquisition of the gentleman or aristocrat on the Grand Tour. As Britain redefined itself in light of its vast industrial and imperial economy, the nouveau riche attempted to seek cultural legitimacy along the lines of the old aristocracy. Great red-brick country houses sprang up along the railway lines that served London, while every sort of pastime—especially those that required intellect, elitism, and disposable income—enjoyed a heyday. By the 1880s, the rarest postage stamps were changing hands among philatelists for hundreds of pounds, though the very concept of stamps, let alone the idea of collecting them, had only come into being forty years before. In the first years of the twentieth century, during evenings at Buckingham Palace, swapping stamps with the king of England became central to the transatlantic identity and legitimacy of Lord Duveen, "the greatest art dealer of all time." Natural history became equally venerated through the hobby of entomology, by which the luckiest collectors could stick a pin through the rarest of beetles or butterflies from the farthest-flung corner of the remotest island in the British Empire, but only if their luck was backed by riches to afford those specimens. Most English collecting fads were based upon utterly mundane objects. Anybody could own a dead beetle, a used postage stamp, a piece of old crockery, a chair, a clock, or a violin, and anybody could amass a collection of any size based on worthless examples of any of these. Those who collected could dream of having something extraordinary thanks to a chance encounter. The difference was if it was a genuine Penny Black, a piece of Sevres, a Chippendale, a Tompion, or a Stradivari. The rich and cultured had the distinct advantage of being able to buy the envy of others for a thousand pounds, rather than depending on chance encounters or time-consuming searches. While many could afford to pay prices for one or two of the best violins, collectors and connoisseurs of rare violins became an exclusive clique within English collecting society. Very few people engaged in this elite activity due to the cost, but the finer points of violin connoisseurship were well respected among the public at large, who knew that a profound understanding had to be attained to tell a cheap factory fiddle apart from the greatest work of art. A central characteristic among Victorian Britain's greatest minds was the attention paid to all aspects of the violin, causing Dr. Watson to grumble bitterly in Sir Arthur Conan Doyle's novels when Sherlock Holmes "prattled on about the differences between a Stradivari and Amati violin" (*A Study in Scarlet*). In real-life circles, few seem to have been immune to the violin's allure. Prime Minister William Gladstone remarked that "even the Locomotive is not a greater marvel of mechanism than the violin."

Before the death knell of Parisian violin dealing had sounded, Vuillaume was already dealing strongly in old and new instruments within the English market through his London agent, Robert Cocks, and he colluded with many of the major London dealers. The British public may have been content to live under the shadow of France, a nation to which Britain had long been a cultural dependency. But the reality of the French market was that it only survived for as long as Vuillaume was at its head. The abundance of violin makers and dealers who shared his Parisian address did little other than prosper under the wave of fortune that he had brought. Vuillaume's egotism prevented him from grooming a successor, and the fact that he had only daughters meant that his name would be lost forever even if he kept his business within the family. He jealously guarded his violin-making secrets, even from his own workmen. For example, after varnishing instruments alone in his summer house, he would cover himself in aniseed so that his workers would not deduce the ingredients of his varnish from the smells on his clothes. With no French rivals in the same league as Vuillaume, just as he had established Parisian dominance of the violin world within a few years of his arrival in 1818, so Vuillaume orchestrated its ending as well. A short time after his retirement in 1858 to Les Ternes, the Parisian market was playing second fiddle to London.

London's position at the center of the violin world was almost a gift from Vuillaume. The firm of W. E. Hill & Sons

FOREWORD

became the world leaders in violin dealing, and Georges Chanot, from a respected and long-established violin-making family for whom Vuillaume had briefly worked at the dawn of his career, left Paris for London. Not long afterwards, the crown jewel of the violin world, Stradivari's *Le Messie* of 1716, owned by Vuillaume since it had been brought from Italy in 1856, became *The Messiah* under British ownership by the Hills. Violin making in France retreated mostly to its traditional home of Mirecourt in Les Vosges, many miles from anywhere where fine violins took the concert-hall stage, and where the industry was directed towards factory-like mass production for the lower end of the market. France was not devoid of good violin makers. Nestor Audinot in Paris, Pierre Hel in Lille, and Honore Derazey in Mirecourt were among those who kept to a standard that resembled that of the earlier Parisian makers, but the glory days of French lutherie were over.

British violin makers were fundamentally different from those from almost any other country, since they did not rely on the training grounds of Mirecourt, Mittenwald, and Markneukirchen, nor were they bound by ancient guild regulations. One of the features of French work is that almost every maker of violins worked for a while in Mirecourt and followed the same dogma in their making. Throughout the nineteenth century, most makers were following the same ideas with such precision that, while their violins are reliable and consistent, they lack any personal character and are often indistinguishable from one another. But worse than that, having arrived at a moderately successful product, they stopped thinking for themselves. For better or worse, British violin makers had no overarching regulations to command their work. Most came to violin making from other professions and were exposed to musical instruments by violin shops or willing owners. Just as earlier French makers had been influenced by the market in antique violins when it was strongest in Paris, as the market came to Britain, demand for new instruments and exposure to old ones benefited and encouraged British makers. Moreover, British collecting fetishes transformed themselves into the written word, with more books published on the violin in English than in any other language, thereby providing unprecedented direction to the British maker.

In 1885, having appeared as a series of articles, *Violin Making as It Is and Was*, by Edward Heron-Allen, was first published. Though a lawyer by profession, the author had taken instruction on violin making from Georges Chanot at his London shop and turned his experiences into a comprehensive manual on violin making, complete with full-scale plans of the preferred models of Stradivari and Guarneri del Gesu instruments. The book received high praise by Morris, and his appreciation for Chanot's role in its creation even led to the almost unprecedented inclusion of this ethnically French violin maker into the second edition of a work about "British" makers. The consequences of *Violin Making as It Is and Was* are varied. There was a time when it could be found on the shelves of most public libraries in Britain, and it arguably remains to this day the most accessible work on the subject. Many people appear to have made only a handful of violins by its instructions, Morris among them, who never claims to have made a single instrument, though an example from 1904 is known and another is in the National Museum of Wales. Others made fewer than one before giving up, and even those who became proficient by the book created instruments that are sterile of Cremonese finesse. Yet the same criticism may be made of professionally trained Continental makers, who were also largely incapable of following the finer points of classical ideals without direct access to original instruments. Many of the violins made according to Heron-Allen's instructions lack the same sort of exposure, so that it is fair to assert that no violin maker made a successful career solely by following Heron-Allen's advice.

On the other hand, many who used the book were already advanced woodworkers or engineers. In making their first violins according to the book, they learned to adapt their skills towards violin making. And in discovering the shortcomings of their work when they presented it to the critical eye of the violin dealer or connoisseur, over time they gained the experience and exposure to create truly excellent instruments. Among the best British makers, Frederick Channon had enjoyed a prodigious career in cabinetmaking, becoming foreman of one of the largest cabinet shops in Devonport (now a part of Plymouth) at the age of twenty-one. He commenced violin making in 1887 as a hobby during his spare time, but within two years he had turned professional. Arthur Richardson apprenticed to the woodcarving and patternmaking trades; William Hamilton was a consulting engineer; and William Robinson, who spent his childhood converting empty boxes into rustic fiddles, became apprenticed to the saddlery trade and was known in the violin world for his beautiful leather-bound cases before instrument making became his primary occupation.

Morris both documents and adjudicates the modern British school that formed out of the pages of Heron-Allen's book. A reference work for this school of violin making, Morris's remarkable book is punctuated by first-hand accounts by the makers he writes about and pithy criticism where he feels it is due. However, his overall aim is to assert the supremacy of the modern British makers who understood Cremonese ideals, something he achieves by throwing considerable caution to the wind. Few makers have lived up to the reputations that he promises for them, yet he would probably argue that their time is yet to come. It is certainly the case that all early-twentieth-century violins have been overshadowed by the cachet of the rival Italian school, which Morris would have had scant information about in his lifetime, yet the best of the British school provide formidable competition.

Morris's book is also extraordinarily useful to the modern violin maker. His work is an attempt to preach to a flock of self-taught violin makers the wisdom he had gathered from seeing over a thousand new instruments by British makers. Within his introductory chapters and among his biographies, the practices and tendencies perpetrated by makers with whom he disagrees do not escape careful scrutiny. He does not offer solutions of his own, perhaps understanding that they would fuel debates further, but makes a point of exposing nonsense when he sees it. Morris was clearly appalled at the time and money spent by makers in pursuit of the mysteries of Stradivari's varnish, something that had aroused the curiosity and obsessions of generations of violin makers and chemists before 1904, and yet they had arrived at nothing. Why did makers continue to waste their lives painting their instruments with varnish preparations that would chip to pieces, when fine and enduring commercial preparations could easily be had by mail?

In other areas, he directs makers towards proven standards of making: "The woods used by the leading makers are imported from the Cantons of Schwytz and Lucerne. Our amateurs are not always so careful about the quality of wood as they might be. The idea has got abroad that old wood is the best, and very often the wood used by them has been pulverised by age."

Today's violin maker fits more closely the profile of Morris's British school than that of any other. Makers often work in near isolation, dispersed among towns and cities all over the world in order to serve a local clientele. The literature at their disposal owes its origins to the British traditions of the late nineteenth century, and for these reasons the same questions and problems recur with every generation. There is something timeless in the futile quest for Stradivari's varnish. Morris estimated that thousands of pounds had been spent in search of it. Now the sum is in the millions, but the answer remains solidly the same.

One area where Morris deserves criticism is in his approach to makers of the past. In holding to the idea that Cremonese ideals ruled supreme, he is unable to attach much reverence to the makers of the seventeenth and eighteenth centuries, except the select few who receive canonisation in the early part of his text. Occasional comments indicate that he was writing against his better nature, forcibly undermining the reputation of old makers who worked to other patterns just as much as he overpromoted the makers of whom he approved. But in a Britain where old Italian and French instruments were abundant, and modern makers commanded higher prices, his views may seem reasonable. In a global market where these instruments are more valuable and dispersed, a century later, it is harder to be dismissive of the early British makers, and these opinions are wholly outdated. He is also a poor historian. At times, such as his entry on Barak Norman, he has the wisdom not to interfere with historical record, and states as much, but other instrument makers may be judged on a single example. In the case of John Barrett, he fixates upon an uncommonly bad example of the poor man's work without giving him the credit that a wider survey of his instruments would provide. He also uses formulaic assumptions that have no basis in fact; "chiefly a maker of viols" and similar statements are employed at times with excruciating effect.

Morris ultimately deserves censure for serving an unbalanced nationalistic agenda. Many of the greatest contributions to British violin making have been made by foreigners. Morris explains that his dictionary is "exclusive of dealers in factory-fiddles, Anglo-French makers, &c., all of which classes have no claim to consideration in a work dealing purely with British violin-making."

While one has to have some sympathy for his ideas, given that they are consistent with the times, his position to judge who was British and who was not is questionable. Morris was unaware that the earliest-known violin maker working in London, Jacob Rayman, was in fact from Fussen in Germany; otherwise he would have omitted him. Bernhard Simon Fendt, who also came from Fussen,

FOREWORD

may have wished that Morris had known this about him, since he becomes the focus of Morris's rage against fakers. Vincenzo Panormo, who came from Sicily, is considered to be one of the greatest influences on British violin making, and his name appears in relation to other makers, but neither he nor his sons are entered in the dictionary. Other examples will become apparent to readers as they dip into the pages of this book.

At the end of the nineteenth century, Mirecourt-trained makers were being brought to England to work in the workshops of W. E. Hill & Sons. Their traditional training, combined with the exposure to old instruments they worked alongside, produced (not in all cases) some of the finest violins of the period, with a lasting influence on British violin making. Morris's prejudice seems to be based on ethnic lines rather than national ones, and siblings of foreign makers who were born or spent all of their lives in Britain, such as George and Louis Panormo, are also excluded from the dictionary. The inconsistency of his approach is borne out by the aforementioned inclusion of Georges Chanot in his second edition. One other break from this rule worth highlighting involves the touching circumstances of the Foucher family. Felix Foucher was killed in action in France on 24 August 1917, as a member of the British Expeditionary Force, serving as a private in the East Surrey Regiment. The inclusion of the Foucher family for this reason and his portrait in military dress show how much the world had changed in the last years of Morris's life, and how the certainties of the past were no longer there. An unfinished manuscript by the firm of W. E. Hill & Sons exists that was begun around the time that

Morris died, supplying positive biographies of the early British violin makers and celebrating the foreign influences that benefited them so greatly. *British Violin Makers* is neither an accurate nor a complete account of the history of violin making. However, as an investigation of those violin makers who happened to be born in Britain and worked during the nineteenth century it is an invaluable resource. It provides delightful accounts of the makers whose works are now in the hands of countless musicians worldwide. Its commentary is also frequently as pertinent now as it was when Morris put pen to paper, for which reason alone it deserves to be a ready resource on every violin maker's bookshelf.

BENJAMIN HEBBERT
St. Cross College, University of Oxford

PREFACE

THE first edition of this work was published in 1904. Its splendid reception, the ready sale it obtained, and the fact that it has long been out of print, encourage me in the hope that a new edition may find favour with the public. The title of the present edition differs slightly from that of the first, and the book has been partly re-written, thoroughly revised, and considerably enlarged. The present effort is, I hope, an improvement in every way upon the first ; for one thing, it shows a better sense of proportion and a truer appreciation of the relative merits of makers, past and present. The list of makers has been extended by the addition of about a hundred and fifty new names, and the extension made it necessary to condense the matter of the first edition wherever possible. The work would extend to twice its present length if it included the name of every one in this country who has dabbled with violin making, but I have rigorously excluded all who have not made at least half-a-dozen instruments. The line had to be drawn somewhere. I regret that a few names are unavoidably omitted which it had been my desire to include : these are the names of makers working in London, and two or three of the principal towns, who are employed in making for music shops and wholesale houses, and who therefore are not in a position to allow their names to be published. Among these are a few clever craftsmen who, if the Fates were only more propitious to them, would be reaping the reward of public recognition.

I need hardly say that I have never missed an opportunity since the first appearance of the book of extending my acquaintance with violin makers and violins, and of deepening my knowledge of the fascinating art of violin making. Within the last few years I have visited nearly all the fiddle workshops in Great Britain, and have examined thousands of instruments, new and old.

The fiddle has been the companion of my spare moments (too few alas!) for thirty-five years, and if I have laid myself open to the charge of having written too enthusiastically about it, my apology is that I could not write coldly about a dear, blessed little "creature" that has been of untold comfort to me. When I have had to wrestle (often unsuccessfully) with the difficulties of a large industrial parish, I have not lacked cheer with my fiddle at hand.

My sincere thanks are due to all violin makers who have furnished me with biographical and other particulars, and to all who have helped in a variety of ways to make the work a success. I am specially indebted to the following gentlemen for much valuable assistance: the Rev. Father A. L. Greaven, B.A., C.C., parish priest of S. Paul's, Belfast; J. Michie, Esq., of Brechin, N.B.; Charles Challenger,

Esq., of Tiverton Villa, St. Andrew's, Bristol ; W. M. Groundwater Esq., of Salford ; James Atkins, Esq., of Cork ; Count G. N. Plunkett, F.S.A., etc., Director of the National Museum of Science and Art, Dublin ; the Messrs. W. E. Hill & Sons, New Bond Street ; the Messrs. G. Hart & Son, Wardour Street, W. ; the Messrs. G. Withers & Sons, Leicester Square ; and W. W. Cobbett, Esq., 34 Avenue Road, London, N.W. I must also acknowledge the assistance of my wife, who has been good enough to correct the proofs, and of Mrs. Matthew Lewis, who kindly furnished some of the illustrations. The authors whom I have consulted are acknowledged in the text.

CLYDACH VALE VICARAGE,
S. WALES.

CONTENTS

	PAGE
PREFACE	xxi

PART I
INTRODUCTORY

I.	THE OLD SCHOOL	3
II.	THE MODERN SCHOOL	21
III.	BRIDGES: OLD AND MODERN	33
IV.	STRING MANUFACTURE IN ENGLAND	38
V.	LEGEND, ART, AND STORY	48
VI.	THEORIES ABOUT THE ITALIAN TONE	62
VII.	MISCELLANEA	72

PART II

A DICTIONARY OF VIOLIN AND BOW MAKERS . . . 89

PART III

A DICTIONARY OF VIOLIN AND BOW MAKERS (*continued*) . 261

APPENDICES 297

LIST OF PLATES

QUARTET OF OLD ENGLISH INSTRUMENTS	*Frontispiece*	
VIOLIN BY ATKINSON	*To face page*	94
VIOLA BY BANKS	,, ,,	99
VIOLINS BY BANKS	,, ,,	100
F. W. CHANNON	,, ,,	118
G. A. CHANOT	,, ,,	120
GEORGES CHANOT	,, ,,	122
GEORGE DARBEY	,, ,,	128
VIOLIN BY DUKE	,, ,,	137
G. L. DYKES	,, ,,	140
VIOLONCELLO BY " OLD " FORSTER	,, ,,	150
VIOLIN BY GILBERT	,, ,,	156
GEORGE HART	,, ,,	171
WILLIAM EBSWORTH HILL	,, ,,	179
VIOLIN BY MAYSON	,, ,,	198
VIOLIN BY OWEN	,, ,,	212
VIOLA BY PARKER	,, ,,	215
VIOLIN BY PARKER	,, ,,	216
VIOLIN BY PERRY	,, ,,	218

LIST OF PLATES

VIOLIN BY TOBIN	*To face page*	239
JAMES TUBBS	,, ,,	241
EDWARD WITHERS (Père)	,, ,,	253
EDWARD WITHERS (Fils)	,, ,,	254
FELIX FOUCHER	,, ,,	269
EDWARD KEENAN	,, ,,	277
VIOL D'AMOUR BY LEE	,, ,,	280

PART I
INTRODUCTORY

BRITISH VIOLIN MAKERS

I.—THE OLD SCHOOL

THE period embraced by what may be termed the "Old School" of British violin making is almost conterminous with the eighteenth century, and includes the work of Banks, Forster, Duke, Parker, Hill, Wamsley, Betts, Hart, and a number of other men of equal or less note. It is advantageous to review its remains from the point of view of model, material, varnish, workmanship, and tone.

A.—THE MODEL

In contemplating the model adopted by our old makers, two features alone seem to stand out sufficiently prominent to arrest the attention of the connoisseur, viz. the absence of originality and the inferiority of the type adopted. The manifest poverty of idea is very extraordinary when we bear in mind that the English excelled as makers of the lute and viol. There can be no doubt that viols of British manufacture were *facile princeps* among instruments of that type. We gather as much from a work by Jean Rousseau entitled *Traité de la Viole*, which was published in Paris in 1687; from numerous statements on the subject in Mace's *Musick's Monument,* and from other works dealing with the history of music. So extraordinary are the above features considered to be that most writers on the subject have thought it necessary to endeavour to account for them. Hart, in his standard work, *The Violin : Its Famous Makers and their Imitators,* offers the following explanation : " It may be that Continental connoisseurs have credited themselves with the works of our best makers, and expatriated them, while they have inexorably allowed bad English fiddles to retain their nationality."

This is possible but hardly probable. Some connoisseurs are blessed with an easy mind and an elastic conscience, we know, but we doubt whether, apart from their tonal qualities, there be sufficient merit in our old instruments to tempt dealers to "expatriate" them. Instruments that are "faked" are, as a rule, such as are meant to be purchased by the eye and not by the ear. If lack of originality had been the only defect of our old instruments, the explanation would be plausible, but there is beyond that the further defect of inferiority of model.

The British copied, and in numerous instances exaggerated, the high arch of Stainer. Doubtless there are reasons, and cogent reasons. We are not for a moment to conclude that British artists have at all times been unequal to the higher flights of art. I hazard the following explanation. There was—

(1) *A want of stimulus.*—During the greater part

of the eighteenth century the intellectual world passed through the chill cloud of (what Sir Leslie Stephen terms) "otiosity." If British violin makers were possessed of the necessary talent, the means were wanting to call it forth. Healthy environment is as much a condition of life as is healthy organism. The glories of the Elizabethan age were past and gone. Reaction—that principle which runs like an undercurrent through the waters of universal history—was already in motion. The force was even now at work which eventually culminated in the production of Latitudinarianism in ecclesiastical polity, of pamphleteering in literature, of artificiality in poetry, of Epicureanism in morals, and of mechanical servility in art. Ennui was in the air, and the nation, from Parnassus down to Bedlam, caught the infection. There were sporadic efforts at originality in some departments, but periodical intellectual gushes are not to be mistaken for the persistent and even flow of true genius. The social conditions of Britain in the eighteenth century were not favourable, I certainly think, to the production of original work in the branch of art which we have under consideration here. It has been objected that social conditions have nothing to do with literary or art activities, but I think the intelligent reader will be more likely to agree with Sir Leslie Stephen, who says: "To my mind . . . the philosophy of an age is in itself determined to a very great extent by the social position. It gives the solutions of the problems forced upon the reasoner by the practical conditions of his time. To understand why certain ideas become current, we have to consider not merely the ostensible logic but all the motives which led men to investigate the most pressing difficulties suggested by the social development. Obvious principles are always ready, like germs, to come to life when the congenial soil is provided. And what is true of the philosophy is equally, and perhaps more conspicuously, true of the artistic and literary embodiment of the dominant ideas which are correlated with the social environment " (*English Literature and Society in the Eighteenth Century*, p. 3).

(2) *Musical conservatism was a potent factor.*—The viol enjoyed a monopoly of public favour, and the upstart violin in its battle for the possession of the British music world, or for a share of its patronage, had to contest every inch of the ground. This is painfully if amusingly evident from the vituperations of old Thomas Mace, whose "doleful jeremiad" over the intrusions of the "scoulding violins" are familiar to every student of violin literature. The viol held its ground more or less down till about 1650, and perhaps even later. In spite of Court and other influences the "French fashion" (as the cult of the fiddle was called) was looked upon by the public as "a giddy and impudent intruder." Even when modified by the "Italian fashion" it found its path strewn with many thorns. Very timely was the arrival of Thomas Balzar in 1656, and of Nicola Matteis in 1672. Their wielding of the magic wand it was that proved the principal means in undoing the conser-

THE OLD SCHOOL 7

vative spell. By the time the strife had fully ended the eighteenth century had dawned. The art of violin making in Italy was then at its zenith, and Cremona stood unrivalled in the production of the "King of instruments." Age and use had done much for the Brescian, early Cremonese, and Tyrolese instruments, and those which found their way into this country were incomparably superior to the raw material produced by the native makers. Even as the demand on the Continent a hundred years previously had been for the splendidly-made and well-matured English viol, so now in England (that had at length awakened to the superiority of the violin) the demand was for the unrivalled instruments of Italian and especially of Tyrolese manufacture.

Owing to a constitutional abhorrence of innovation we started a hundred years late, and we of necessity lost the race.

(3) *Puritan fanaticism.*—The furious bigotry of Anabaptists, Levellers, and Fifth-monarchy men had placed music under a ban, and the gentle voice of melody had been drowned in the hoarse battle-cry of the "saints." In the fanatical days of "Praise-God-Barebones" many and many a precious old viol shared the fate of the stained glass and carved work of our cathedrals. Puritan England was the Patmos of art. Nearly a century elapsed before the muses ventured forth to fan art into a flame out of the embers of its dead self.

If some of my readers should think (as some of my critics have thought) that I am over-stating the case against the Puritans, let them consult such a work as *The Building of Britain and the Empire*, edited by H. D. Traill, D.C.L., and J. E. Mann, M.A., where we read that "During the troubles which followed the death of King Charles I. the cultivation of English music was utterly extinguished. Not only was progress impossible : it was equally impossible, in face of the open hostility of the Puritans, to maintain the high level that had already been attained. The cathedral and collegiate libraries were sacked by the Roundheads, the great organs were destroyed, all singing worthy of the name was prohibited in the desecrated churches, and dramatic music was publicly condemned as a snare of the Evil one" (*vide* vol. iv. pp. 548-9).

So much for the absence of originality. As to the other characteristic, the inferiority of type, I fear no explanation or apology can be offered. It shows lack of discrimination. The old makers adopted the model of Stainer and followed it with but few departures for the greater part of a hundred years. In following those who had gone before they unwittingly showed a predilection for the least worthy. Something may be said for the copyist who, conscious of his inability to create, assiduously sets about to copy that which is best and noblest in art, but apology becomes difficult in the case of the man who deliberately copies an inferior model. The British in their choice of type showed inability to differentiate tone nuances, and lack of artistic feeling in the matter of form and proportion. That they sinned without excuse is

THE OLD SCHOOL

perfectly certain. They were acquainted with Brescian and early Cremonese instruments as well as with those of the Tyrol. They were in a position to make a choice, and their choice fell upon the inferior model. I am aware that the truth of the last statement has been denied by certain writers, and it will be well perhaps to bring forward the evidence upon which it rests :—

(1) There were numerous Italian instruments brought into this country about this time. William Corbett, who resided for some years in Italy, brought back a rare collection—" A Gallery of Cremonys and Stainers." These were bequeathed by him to Gresham College, and handed over to the authorities on the death of the collector in 1748, with the proviso that they were to remain open for inspection. Soon after the death of the donor the college authorities disposed of the " gallery " by auction (it is supposed), and the instruments became the property of dealers and private collectors. The Duke of Hamilton, the Duke of Cambridge, the Earl of Falmouth, and others, also formed collections of Italian instruments.

(2) That Italian models were known in this country is proved by the fact that they were occasionally copied ; *e.g.* :—

(α) Richard Meares (1680) adopted the Brescian model, and made excellent violins on the lines of Maggini. This old maker probably made the first English violoncello.

(β) Barak Norman (1683–1744) ornamented his instruments in the Maggini style, and used labels which are no doubt in conscious imitation of those used by Del Gesù.

(γ) An undoubtedly genuine violin by Christopher Wise (1656) is on the Maggini model.

(δ) Peter Wamsley (1715-51) is admitted by most experts to have made several copies of Stradivari, and to have followed that *maestro* closely except in the matter of graduating the thicknesses. He spoilt his work in attempting to produce the Italian tone by over-thinning the plates.

(ε) Cuthbert (1700). An admittedly genuine example of this maker is on the Maggini model.

(ζ) Matthew Hardie made many violins on the Stradivari model towards the end of the eighteenth century, and that at a time when the Amati model was the vogue.

(3) There is further the fact that several eminent Italian *virtuosi* visited this country from time to time. The performances of these must, one would naturally think, have drawn attention to their instruments.

(α) Francesco Geminiani came to England between 1709-14, and met with a great success. Here he remained and published his works, making a few tours on the Continent and again returning.

(β) Veracini came to London in 1714, and led the Italian Opera Band there.

(γ) Gaetano Pugnani (1727-1803) visited London more than once, and stayed there on one of these visits for nearly two years.

THE OLD SCHOOL

(δ) Giardini came to London in 1744 and remained there for two years.

(4) Somewhere about 1686 the banker Michele Monzi, of Venice, sent a set of Stradivari violins, altos, and violoncellos, as a present to King James of England. In this connection it may be remembered that, according to Sandys and Forster, a consignment of new Strad instruments sent to this country on approval could not be disposed of at six pounds apiece!

Thus there is not a shadow of doubt that Italian models were known in this country early in the eighteenth century, and there is not a shadow of doubt that the best models were deliberately set aside in favour of an inferior type.

B.—THE MATERIAL

The wood used by our old makers is for the most part maple and pine of the orthodox kind, but various other woods were occasionally used, either by way of experiment, or because there was a scarcity of the right sort. Benjamin Banks used plain English sycamore for the back of some of his violins, and red pine for the front tables of a few of his violas. "Old" Forster used common deal for the table of many of his second-class instruments. Richard Duke and Daniel Parker were usually very particular about their wood, and the latter ranks with the most careful of our native makers in this respect. Would that we had many more examples of his art left us! Duke's maple is mostly plain, but is invariably good acoustically. Matthew

Hardie used anything that came to hand for his second-class instruments, though he generally used excellent wood for his Stradivari copies. A "Long-Strad" copy of his make now in the possession of the Messrs. Hill is made of very fine wood. Edward Withers, the elder, whose instruments are rising in value, was very careful in the selection of his material. The wood in instruments bearing the label of John Betts is usually good, but mostly plain. Tobin, one of the very best of our British makers, was very particular about his wood when circumstances allowed him the free exercise of his will, but he often was obliged to use indifferent material. These are isolated examples, and the departures from the traditional rule are neither numerous nor important. One thing to be noted in particular about the pine used is that it shows a general preference on the part of the makers for wood with a medium "reed," or grain. Very close or very wide grained wood seems to have been systematically avoided. Some of the best examples of "Old" Forster are an exception to the rule, but many of these have common English deal, and not Swiss pine.

C.—THE VARNISH

The varnish is excellent as regards elasticity and adhesiveness. The oil varnish of our old makers will probably wear better than that of even the great classical makers themselves. I have seen many a battered old Duke and Forster with the varnish still plentiful and "defiant." Of but few Italian instruments can this be said: the majority

THE OLD SCHOOL

of the best of them are quite bare. Nothing short of a serious accident will damage the English varnish. I have seen a Dodd's 'cello varnished with the celebrated "original Cremona varnish," which had a hole knocked in one of the bouts, and the varnish around the scraggy edges had parted "clean." There was not a suspicion of "chip" or transversal cracks. In this respect the varnish of our old makers contrasts favourably with some of the best varnishes on the market to-day. One drawback, *e.g.*, of Whitelaw's varnish is that it is brittle, and that it chips in a most provoking manner. In other respects the modern varnish is far superior to the old. The varnish of most of our old makers lacks colour and brilliancy: that is the rule, but there are notable exceptions.

Colour and transparency, however, are not so important as elasticity and adhesiveness. In its bearing upon tone, elasticity is perhaps the most important of all the *known* qualities of varnish. I say "known," because it is highly probable that the varnish has a subtle influence upon the colour of the tone, the nature of which is not yet precisely understood. Long experience and innumerable experiments compel me to think with the Messrs. Hill (*vide* their *Life of Stradivari*) that varnish plays a much more important part in the evolution of tone nuance than is usually admitted.

It is remarkable that so few authentic recipes of old varnishes have been handed down to us. This is a fact which militates against the opinion that the nature of the ingredients and the method of making them into a varnish were regarded as a trade or professional secret. "Secrets" were generally confided to "black and white," paradoxical as it might seem. The secret of many a long-lost art consists in the fact that at the time it was practised it was no secret at all. If the art of embalming had been regarded as a mystery, known only to a small inner circle of hierophants in ancient Egypt, we should probably know more than we do about it to-day. At one time everybody in the land of the Pharaohs knew how the mighty Cheops was built, and how the stones were quarried and conveyed, and the fact that everybody knew then is one of the reasons why nobody knows to-day. The masters of painting had no darkened chambers wherein they ground their pigments and mixed their oils: it would be better for modern artists if they had. On the other hand, make a mystery of an art, and you thereby secure for it a niche in one of the safest recesses of Walhalla. The art of the magician in the days of Aaron was a secret, but the pundits of India practise it to-day. Archimedes enshrouded with a veil of mystery the discovery of the principle which is named after him, and, thanks to the fact, the world has not had to re-discover the law of specific gravity.

Innumerable instances might be quoted in support of my contention, but sufficient has been said to illustrate the point. The inference is this: the varnish of Stradivari, Guarneri, and other Cremonese, was no professional secret; if it had been such we should be familiar with its composition to-day. Dodd guarded the secret of his mixture with a jealous eye, but his varnish has been applied to many an instrument since he laid his brush to rest.

Our old makers used both oil and spirit varnishes. The gums, resins, etc., which entered into their composition are perfectly familiar to us. One thing alone is doubtful, viz., whether or not in these sinful days we get the pure and unadulterated article. A list of these substances is given in a useful appendix to the valuable work of Mr. Edward Heron-Allen, *Violin Making, as it Was and Is*, and the reader who wishes for full information on the subject is referred to that book.

I do not think our older makers, or at least a number of them, varnished in the same way as modern makers do, and as the Italian masters undoubtedly did. Their varnish appears to be perfectly homogeneous, that is to say, there is no sizing of colourless or yellow varnish, with subsequent coats of colour varnish. There is no foil of golden sheen to etherealize the fire of the varnish. All that was probably done in the majority of instances was the mere rubbing of a little oil into the wood, followed by the application of varnish in the usual way. A few instruments, it may be, show evidence of some such sizing as that of gamboge, notably amongst the examples of Parker, Forster, Tobin, Dodd, Fendt, and a few others.

D.—THE WORKMANSHIP

The distinguishing feature of the workmanship is its solidity. Some of the greatest of our old makers at their best produced work which may justly be described as beautifully finished and graceful, but "solidity" is a word that generally applies to all. A typical maker is Daniel Parker. Here we have plenty of timber, careful workmanship on the whole, with sometimes an absence of regard for finesse, and something which impresses one with a sense of unconcerned self-reliance and freedom. If there is no evidence of laborious finish, there is certainly nothing even remotely connected with the vulgar or grotesque.

Many of our second-rate and inferior instruments were probably built without a mould. So were a large number of the Italian ones; but there is generally this difference in the result: the latter are often crude and sadly out of line; the former, at the worst, are only a little rough and quaint looking. Our average British luthier may not be highly artistic, but he is certainly never truly barbarous.

Generally speaking, the part of the work which is most frequently deserving of censure is the scroll. Old British scrolls not infrequently show some strength and decision of character, but the curves are inclined to be stiff, and the heads a trifle flat. The throat of the scroll is usually somewhat thick, and the head in consequence appears diminutive. Almost invariably the back of the peg-box diminishes rapidly right away from the scollop down to the first turn, where the volute begins. This is so persistent a characteristic of old English scrolls that an expert could pick one out from among a dozen others with his eyes shut. In all Italian fiddles of the first water, the width of the back of

THE OLD SCHOOL

the peg-box diminishes almost imperceptibly until it reaches the throat, where it diminishes much more rapidly : this arrangement of lines and curves gives the whole scroll a feeling of majesty combined with simplicity—a feeling wholly lacking in all but the very best of our old English fiddles.

Richard Tobin was the best scroll carver that Britain has ever produced. I do not hesitate to say that his finer scrolls vie with the best work of Stradivari. It is a sin and a shame that the poor man has been robbed of his due by an unscrupulous posterity. The heads have been removed from many of his best violins, and grafted (I more than suspect) on the bodies of nondescripts which have, perhaps, sold again and again as " Italians."

Curiously enough, Benjamin Banks, our English " Amati," has left some scrolls which are rather feeble in design and execution.

The interior of our old instruments is often rough and unfinished, the marks of the chisel and gouge being discernible ; especially is this the case with the end blocks, which are rounded off in a more or less haphazard fashion with the chisel. In the larger instruments the blocks are often shaped by a few applications of the tool. I do not think our old makers troubled much about glass-paper and its uses, either in the finishing of the interior or exterior. They handled their scraper very nattily, and were content with the result. Nor were they at all times particular about matching their wood. I have seen fine examples of Duke and Forster with an odd rib, cut the wrong way of the grain to match the other ribs : I have also seen a Banks viola with ribs cut from three different pieces of timber varying in width of curl. It is a common occurrence to meet with a fiddle with the head cut from a differently figured maple from that of the back and ribs.

There is one point more in the general character of the workmanship which calls for remark, and that is the absence of purfling in a large number of instruments of the poorer class, and in not a few of those of the better class.

Ink-lines as a substitute are but an eyesore and a sham, and are further to be deprecated as affording no protection to the exposed edges.

E.—THE TONE

An extraordinary thing about the tone of our old violins, and one which has, apparently, escaped the attention of all connoisseurs, is that it is very different from the tone of Stainer's violins, which our luthiers copied so slavishly for three-quarters of a century. Our artists followed the contour and arching of Stainer, but they gave us a tone approximating to that of the Amatis. The best description of the Stainer tone that I have read is that given by the Rev. H. R. Haweis, who says it is "a loud, piercing, and pungent" tone. "A violinist," he remarks, " in the orchestra could make his Stainer cut through all the first fiddles, and once the taste for that sort of tone was excited, it would be to the ear what curry, or vinegar, or quinine bitter, or absinthe is to the palate. The Stainer tone is a sort of drastic, stinging stimulant to the ear, almost an intoxication; and the ear that has once been caught by it craves for it, and misses it even in the loud richness of Joseph, the exquisite velvety timbre of Amati, or the superb ringing brightness of the great Antonio." (*Old Violins*, p. 99.) That description, as any one knows who knows anything about fiddles, cannot be applied to the tone of any English instrument of the old school. There were hundreds of Stainer copies produced in this country in the eighteenth century, some of them very exact in the matters of outline, arching, thicknessing, etc., but I have never come across a single instrument of that period the tone of which could be said to have the slightest resemblance to the tone of Stainer. The tone of old English fiddles is neither loud nor piercing: it is rather small, but bright, silvery, and responsive.

I do not at all know how to account for this rather remarkable fact, but I would point out that it has its modern counterpart. Many makers who have copied Stradivari and Guarneri more recently have given us a sufficiently piercing, pungent, Stainer-like tone!

I fully agree with those writers who aver that the qualities of our old instruments have been much under-rated. The very best work of Banks, Forster, Duke, Parker, and a few others, rivals all but the very best Italian work, and I submit that in this supremely important matter of tone production, our old makers take rank next to the Italians. There are one or two old French makers who may be superior to our best artists, but only one or two;

the rank and file of French luthiers are not fit to hold a rushlight to our old makers. Stainer is, of course, head and shoulders above us, but one man does not constitute a school.

The tone of our old fiddles is not powerful, and it may not fill our large modern music halls, but it carries well, and ought to win, where it fails to conquer, by its purity and sweetness.

II.—THE MODERN SCHOOL

A.—THE REVIVAL OF VIOLIN-MAKING

IT has been said that the art and craft of violin-making is dead in Britain since about the middle of the nineteenth century, but the fact is that it never was more alive than it is at the present day. There are fifty to sixty professional luthiers now living and working, and at least ten times that number of amateur and occasional makers. This number is exclusive of dealers in factory fiddles, foreign makers living in this country, and firms who employ merely repairers. Since about the year 1850 the British School of Violin-making may truly be said to have accomplished the most complete of its *avatāra*, or incarnations : it has been born again—born, I verily believe, to a higher and fuller manifestation of life. We have now working amongst us Atkinson, Byrom, Channon, Chanot, Darbey, Gilbert, Hesketh, Keenan, Owen, Richardson, Withers, etc., much of whose work will, I venture to think, be highly esteemed a century hence. Some of these have struck out a path for themselves, and the British school promises to justify its claims to the highest honours for the production of first-class instruments. Material, varnish, workmanship, and tone place the work of our best artists in the front rank.

The renewed interest in the art of violin-making is due in part to the general activity in the world of art and letters of the last three decades of the Victorian era. Such works as *Violin Making, as it Was and Is* (Heron-Allen), *The Violin : Its Famous Makers and their Imitators* (Hart), *Old Violins and their Makers* (Fleming), *Old Violins* (Haweis), *Antonio Stradivari* (Hill), and other good books, have also materially helped to foster the love of the " King of instruments." Greater than all has been the impetus given to the study of the violin by the bewitching charm of the playing of such *virtuosi* as Joachim, Sarasate, Ysaye, Wilhelmj, Wieniawski, Dunn, Lady Hallé, Kubelik, Kriesler, and others.

B.—CHARACTERISTICS OF MODERN WORK AND MATERIAL

The salient features of modern work demand close attention. The models mostly adopted are those of Stradivari and Guarneri. It is rather curious that English, Irish, and Welsh makers have a decided preference for the Strad model, whereas Scottish makers seem to prefer the Joseph model. Maggini, Gasparo da Salò, Amati, Bergonzi, and Gagliano are also copied, but not so often nor, I think, so carefully.

Atkinson, Channon, Gilbert, and one or two others among professional makers, mostly work on models of their own. The late Walter H. Mayson, of Manchester, who made over eight hundred instruments, also made nearly all his violins on a model which was decidedly original. The wood used by

THE MODERN SCHOOL

our leading makers is of the traditional kind and quality, and is frequently of exceptionally beautiful texture and figure. Our amateur fiddle makers are not always as careful about the quality of their wood as they might be; the idea having got abroad that old wood is the best, and very often they use timber which has been almost pulverized by age. The instruments made of such wood cannot live long. And here I would utter a note of warning : it is possible to ride a hobby-horse too far ; that is, being interpreted, it is possible to make too much of the old wood theory.

The right sort of timber, cut at the right time of the year (in winter), and naturally seasoned in blocks for about ten to fifteen years, or twenty at the outside, is what is required. Some makers ransack the land, hole and corner, for wood which is two or three hundred years old, but they could well spend their time more profitably. The tone obtained from extremely old wood is not a whit better than that got from wood which has been seasoned for a reasonable number of years ; and in a hundred or more years hence, when fiddles made from fresh and properly seasoned wood will be beginning to live, those made from very old wood will be ready to die. It is feared by some makers that instruments made from wood of only twenty years' seasoning will shrink ; but what about the instruments of the old masters ? These, if they have shrunk at all, have not done so to any appreciable extent, and they were made from wood seasoned by them in their own lifetime.

My readers will remember that most Continental authorities agree with me on this point. August Riechers in *The Violin and its Construction* (p. 11) says: "The age of the wood I consider of only very small importance; if it has been lying by for five years, ready cut or split, as the case may be, for the construction of a violin, it will then be sufficiently dry, and will need no further preparation. I have exactly ascertained the weight of wood which had been laid by for drying for five years, and then, having weighed it again at the end of twenty years, have found it had not become perceptibly lighter." I have not come across one Italian, French, or German writer on the subject who advocates the use of *very* old wood. This country has one advocate of old wood, Mr. W. C. Honeyman, the author of several popular works on the violin. Many Scottish makers are converts to his teaching, and use nothing but the oldest timber they can lay their hands on. I have had fiddles down from Scotland for inspection from time to time which were said to be made from wood which had been cut two or three hundred years ago. I can well believe some of them were made from wood which had been cut twice as long ago, for they seemed as brittle as a mummy, and ready to crumble at the slightest touch. One trembled to draw the bow across the strings lest the fiddle should vibrate into dust.

And just a word with regard to seasoning timber. It is much more difficult nowadays to obtain a block of old naturally seasoned wood than is usually imagined. It is usual to look for such in old build-

THE MODERN SCHOOL

ings, old furniture, etc., but it is not always borne in mind that the method almost universally adopted to season timber in days gone by was that of submersion under water for an extended period, followed by exposure to dry air for a similar or longer period. The newly-sawn planks were sunk in deep water for two years or thereabouts, and afterwards stowed away in open sheds.

My father (a Pembrokeshire yeoman), who had paid a great deal of attention to both the theory and practice of timber seasoning, always treated his oak, ash, beech, elm, and sycamore in this way, and held that that method had been in vogue in this country from the days of the Romans. The timber used in our cathedrals and ancient churches was all seasoned in this manner, he maintained. He explained that the submersion caused the permanent tissue of the wood to "pack," on account of the distension which took place in the cells of the meristem, and that the active cells themselves were made more susceptible to dessication. Thus there was secured a minimum of meristem and a maximum of density in the permanent tissue. He said the permanent tissues were to be regarded as the bones of the timber, and the meristem the flesh. The bones would last, but the flesh began to decay from the moment the tree was cut, and the important thing in seasoning timber was to over-rule or retard the process of decay as long as possible.

When violin makers talk about old, naturally seasoned wood, the question is : What do they mean by "naturally" in that connection ? Is the process described above a "natural" process? If not, then what is the "natural" process?

I have searched patiently and long for what I could accept with a degree of confidence as historical evidence of the exact method adopted by old Italian violin makers in seasoning their wood, but I have searched in vain. Modern writers say that Stradivari, *e.g.*, was wont to dry his timber in a kind of loft or open attic, having first cut it up from the trunk or balk into blocks of suitable dimensions. I should much like to know where they get their information from. It is so easy to suppose this or that, but what we want is plain, exact historical evidence.

The workmanship of our leading professional makers, and of many of our amateurs, is excellent. Careful attention is usually paid to every detail of the work. This is a feature worthy of commendation, as the British have in the past been somewhat impatient of detail. Even details which to the ordinary observer would appear as mere trifles are now finished artistically. And what a difference this attention to minutiæ makes to the completed article! An artistically finished violin is a poem, a painting, and a musical instrument combined in one object.

English makers somewhat lower down the rank have yet something to learn in the matter of inlaying the purfling, the proportion of widths, the arrangement of the curves, the treatment of the button, etc., and many Scottish makers are open to the charge of having exaggerated the peculiarities

THE MODERN SCHOOL

of Del Gesù, more especially in the outline and sound-holes. It is possible that young or inexperienced luthiers do not quite realize that it is much more difficult to make a faithful copy of Joseph than of Strad. The so-called Gothic arch of the former is a veritable *pons asinorum* to the modern copyist.

A large number of amateurs pay little attention to the proper length of the stop, and the majority of them ought to exercise more care in the working of the neck. A thick, clumsy neck at the shoulder is a severe tax on the patience of the player, for it impedes shifting. Many otherwise fine old instruments were a great deal too bulky about the shoulders, but they have been refitted with a new neck in accordance with modern requirements. In the calculation and working out of form and proportion, art and craft must go hand in hand and contrive to give us that which is both elegant and serviceable.

Modern varnishes claim a few paragraphs. I need hardly say that curious connoisseurs and anxious luthiers have devoted much time and thought to the fascinating but elusive problem of varnish making. Innumerable experiments have been made and much money sacrificed in the endeavour to re-discover the Italian varnish.

Whether the time and money thus expended have been utilised wisely is very problematical. It has been held by not a few chemists and writers on the subject that the basis of the Italian varnish was fossil amber. The late Mr. James Whitelaw, of Glasgow, the late Dr. George Dickson, of Edinburgh, Dr. Inglis Clark, of Edinburgh, and many others, have been advocates of the amber theory. I do not exactly know what the data are which these authorities adduce in support of their view : to me there does not appear to be the smallest grain of historical evidence to support the amber theory. I believe I have read everything that has ever been written on this interesting subject, and I have hunted up old documents and made laborious research, and I am bound to say that what little information I have thus gathered points away from the amber hypothesis.

This is not a treatise on Italian Varnish, and I must not allow myself to run away after that *ignis fatuus* : I am writing of *modern* varnish. Whilst I am thoroughly convinced that amber varnish is not identical with, nor even distantly related to, Italian varnish, it is not to be inferred that I am insensible to its many good qualities : I think it an excellent substitute. I would not be disposed to quarrel with those who think that for brilliancy and transparency it is equal to the old Italian varnish. I think that, on the whole, it is the best covering we possibly can apply to our instruments to-day. I must make it clear, however, that by *amber varnish* I mean varnish which has real fossil amber for its basis, and not *oleum succinis*, commonly called oil of amber. A number of varnishes which are sold as *amber varnish* to-day do not contain the actual gum : they are usually made of much softer and less durable gums. It needs a knowledge of chemistry to solve fossil amber successfully, and especially to develop the deeper colours.

THE MODERN SCHOOL

The following varnishes, most if not all of them on the market, are made from genuine fossil amber, in solution in oil.

(1) Whitelaw's varnish. This has been on the market for many years, and is now very well known, and its excellency generally admitted. It is beautifully transparent, elastic, and fiery. It is easily applied, and does not take a long time to dry. It has one drawback: when hard set it is rather brittle and inclined to chip.

(2) Dr. Inglis Clark's varnish. The varnish of W. Inglis Clark, D.Sc., had been known to a few experts and a small circle of friends for several years before the inventor decided to put it on the market. It may now be obtained of Messrs. Duncan, Flockhart, & Co., manufacturing chemists, 104–108 Holyrood Road, Edinburgh. It is made in the following colours:—golden yellow, pale brown, orange brown, dark brown, orange red, and ruby red. It is transparent and elastic, and possesses a depth and richness of colour quite equal to the best of the old varnishes. It does not crack or chip, but it takes a considerable time to dry.

(3) Anderson's varnish. This is manufactured by Mr. Walter Anderson, of 4 Kildonan Terrace, Ibrox, Glasgow. With the use of this varnish the maker recommends that raw linseed oil, or other specially prepared oil, be rubbed into the wood first, day after day, till the wood can absorb no more, when the instrument must be allowed to dry thoroughly, and the varnish applied thereafter. It is made in various colours, but, as far as my experi-

ence of it goes, it is more successful in the lighter than it is in the darker shades.

(4) Harris' varnish, made by Mr. J. E. Harris, violin maker, 37 Nile street, Gateshead-on-Tyne. It is made, I believe, in all the usual shades, and is said to be of good quality. A number of makers have used it with good results.

(5) Walker's varnish. Made by Mr. John Walker, violin maker, 8 Broomfields, Solihull, Birmingham. It is soft, elastic, and transparent. I have tried it in the golden orange colour, which was very beautiful when laid on, but the colour had slightly faded in a year's time. No doubt I had exposed the varnish too much to the direct rays of the sun. It may be remarked here that varnish makers generally claim that their colours are lasting, but nearly all varnishes, I think, fade a little in the direct light and heat of the sun. This was a failing of even the otherwise perfect Italian varnish. Charles Reade, in his second letter on *A Lost Art Revived*, first published in the *Pall-Mall Gazette*, August 24, 1872, observes that "the sun will take all the colour out of that maker's [Stradivari's] varnish," and he knew more about the Italian varnish than anybody ever did, barring Luigi Tarisio.

I dare say there are many more amber varnishes on the market, but I think I have named most of the better known ones. Professional violin makers for the most part eschew amber varnish—at least the market article—and use varnish of their own make, but I cannot help thinking that it would be more to the interest of their art if a goodly number

THE MODERN SCHOOL

of them used Clark's, or Whitelaw's, or some other reliable varnish that has been produced by the assiduous application of scientific knowledge and a long experience in the laboratory. My remarks do not apply to the best of our makers of course, who are presumed to know at least as much about chemistry as the old Italian violin makers did.

A very beautiful varnish is produced by Mr. F. W. Channon, a clever and well-known professional violin maker, of London. Unlike the majority of professional makers, he does not attempt to make a mystery of its composition or of the method of its preparation; on the other hand, he readily reveals both. With his kind permission I am allowed to say here that he is prepared to furnish his formulæ with full instructions to any *bonâ fide* violin maker.

I cannot conclude my remarks on varnish without urging upon all violin makers the great importance of this branch of the subject. I reiterate the conviction that varnish has a very considerable effect upon the tone. I am not prepared to go so far as the Messrs. Hill, who say that of the factors that go to make a scientifically constructed fiddle which shall give the best possible tonal results, varnish is to be put down first in the order of importance. That, I think, puts the case too strongly. On the other hand I certainly cannot agree with a well-known writer who says that "Varnish has little or no effect upon tone." Only a man with no actual experience of violin making could write that. To cite the instances of old Italian violins which have been denuded of their varnish in proof of the contention that varnish has nothing to do with tone is beside the mark, for such violins have been robbed of only their surface varnish. All the instruments of the masters may be said to be embalmed bodies, the varnish having permeated their whole fabric, so that now they are really neither wood nor varnish, but a sort of compound of both. Every fraction of a drop of the varnish which these instruments have absorbed has entered into indissoluble relationship with the molecules of the wood. The Rev. H. R. Haweis very pithily observes: "Time, that sometimes robs it [the violin] of a little varnish, has no power over its anointed fabric. The hard durable substance steeped in silicate-like varnish has well-nigh turned to stone, but without sacrificing a single quality of sweetness or resonance." (*Old Violins*, p. 13.)

Little can be said about the tone of modern instruments. Its qualities, unlike those of outline, model, and workmanship, can be fully known only in the future, when time and legitimate use have wrought their beneficial effect. It may be said, however, that it fully justifies the belief that violinists of the future will have cause to remember gratefully the names of the old artists who carved, and varnished, and took thought for the morrow.

Note. An important contribution to the literature of the violin appeared some few years back, entitled: "The Varnishes of the Italian Violin Makers of the Sixteenth, Seventeenth, and Eighteenth Centuries, and their Influence on Tone," by George Fry, F.L.S., F.C.S. London: Stevens & Sons, Limited. The author has a wide knowledge of the chemistry of varnishes and of vegetable life.

III.—BRIDGES : OLD AND MODERN

BRIDGE manufacture in our days is a distinct branch of industry, and even as there is a factory fiddle, so also is there a factory bridge, the one lacking in merit as often as does the other. Very few luthiers make their own fiddle accessories nowadays. A gross of factory bridges can be purchased at less than it costs in time and energy to make a dozen artistic or "hand-made" ones. In the good old days a maker of violins was also the maker of all the various fittings required for the instrument. The importance of the bridge cannot well be over-estimated, since a bad one will infallibly spoil the tone of an instrument, however good the latter may be. It has ever been a matter of surprise to me how few makers, and how few players for that matter, appear to know this simple fact. It is quite the exception to find a good bridge on a modern fiddle. The tailpiece, which is of little or no importance acoustically, is often made with the utmost care and elaborate finish, whereas the cheapest bridge made of green wood, or baked wood, high and thick, is clamped on the suffering fiddle. A good instrument is very exacting in its demands upon the bridge, and the finer its qualities, the finer also must be those of the bridge. A fact worth remembering is that fiddle and bridge, once mated, should never be divorced. They must be allowed to live their existence together in indissoluble unity, for there is a sort of psychic bond between them which cannot be broken with impunity. If a bridge which has been on an instrument for a length of time should get damaged it ought to be carefully repaired, and not thrown away as a worthless trifle. I believe there are one or two somewhere in the country who make a speciality of this class of repair.

The present design of bridge is supposed to have originated with Stradivari. Our early makers were either unacquainted with it, or did not consider it the best, as they adhered to the quasi-viol and other forms of bridge down till well-nigh the end of the eighteenth century. Very few bridges of the Stradivari pattern were made in England, I think, before the beginning of last century.

FIG. 1.—(Daniel Parker).

Fig. 1 is an illustration of an authentic specimen of a Daniel Parker bridge, and is typical of the work of the period, which was neither geometrically precise nor highly finished. Fig. 2 represents a bridge by the little-known maker Henry Whiteside, made somewhat later. The design is less archaic, and the workmanship a little more finished.

The claims of the modern bridge were advanced

BRIDGES : OLD AND MODERN

in this country chiefly by the labours of William Ebsworth Hill, who made hundreds of bridges, using only the very best wood, and finishing his

FIG. 2.—(H. Whiteside).

work with the utmost care. It is to be feared that time and more especially the carelessness of players have considerably reduced the number of Hill bridges. The Messrs. Hart, of Wardour Street, and the

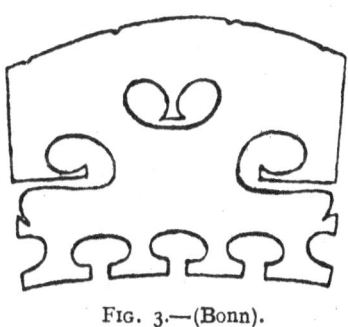

FIG. 3.—(Bonn).

Messrs. Withers, of Leicester Square, are makers of high-class bridges, which are of the finest, well-seasoned wood, and of simple but beautiful design.

Many innovations—" improvements," as they are called—have been put on the market during the last few years, only the more important or curious of which can be noticed here.

Mr. J. Edwin Bonn, of Brading, Isle of Wight, makes a four-footed bridge (fig. 3) for violin, viola, and violoncello. He thinks that four feet ensure a more energetic and regular communication of vibrations to the front table.

A rather pretty design, known as the sound-holes bridge, was introduced a while ago by the Messrs. Balfour (fig. 4). Its prettiness was not improved by the inevitable " Patent " writ large upon it.

A very curious, and, it must be admitted, ungainly bit of furniture is the bridge designed by a Mr. Edward Davies, of Cheltenham. It is made of two pieces of pine cut so that the grain runs at an angle of 45° to the perpendicular axis of the bridge, and which are glued together by means of two strips of wood placed between.

FIG. 4.—(Balfour).

Each piece, or half, has a protruding wing which reaches out nearly as far as the sound-hole. The inventor claims that the wood being pine, with the grain running nearly vertical, the re-inforcement of the vibrations of the strings is much more intense.

A new kind of bridge, recently put on the market, is called the *Gallrein Patent*. It is made of three

BRIDGES : OLD AND MODERN

pieces of wood, consisting of two outer layers of maple, with a layer of pine between.

There have been sundry other varieties, freaks, and "patents," all of which have "had their day and ceased to be." Many more may come, but the old pattern bridge is as little likely to be discarded as the old pattern violin.

IV.—STRING MANUFACTURE IN ENGLAND

WRITERS who pay attention to the subordinate but important subject of violin accessories are in the habit of telling us that strings of British manufacture are of no great account.

Haweis allows that "the English make a good, serviceable string," but adds that "English strings are only fit for rank-and-file orchestral fiddling, but not good enough for the leader" (*Old Violins*, p. 158). Other writers speak in much the same strain. I venture, with all due deference to these authorities, to take up the cudgels in defence of the English string, and I am glad of the opportunity to do so for more than one reason. First, my experience of violin strings of English manufacture enables me to say that they are by no means the comparatively worthless articles they are made out to be, and I am of the opinion that some, at least, of the people who condemn them have formed their conclusions too hastily. About ten years ago I resolved to discover the truth about strings for myself, and since then I have thoroughly tested in every possible way all the principal strings on the market, including those of Italian, French, German, American, English, and even of Russian and Indian manufacture. The result of these tests (conscientiously and systematically carried out) shows conclusively that the differences in the relative merits of strings of foreign and native manufacture are very slight indeed. Some of the finest Italian strings, notably those of Neapolitan manufacture, were admittedly more uniformly true, but, as a set-back, they were nearly always more brittle than those of English manufacture. The greater purity of Italian strings, when it exists (very often only in the imagination of the player) is of so small a degree and subtle a character as to be appreciable only to the highly trained ear. People who talk glibly about the "immense superiority" of foreign strings are, in nine cases out of ten, incapable of distinguishing differences in tone nuances. I have again and again come across people who boasted an advanced musical education, and who were certainly good violinists, who could not distinguish any difference between the tone of a first-class Italian string and that of an English string. I have repeatedly tried the experiment, and nearly always with the same result—neither player nor auditor knew for certain (that is, from the tone) which string was Italian and which English. I was not at all surprised, for what difference there was, if any, was really very slight.

But there is something more important to be said in favour of the native article. Strings of British manufacture are frequently "doctored up" a little, and sold as "Italians."

This fraudulent practice commenced on a small scale a good many years ago, and it has been going on at a rapidly increasing rate ever since, so that at the present time—it is no exaggeration to say—there is as much fraud in the string trade as there is in the fiddle trade itself. This may sound very startling in the ears of some, but if they will be at pains to ascertain the truth about string manufacture, as I have been, they will learn this and a great deal more. They will soon learn, at least, that they cannot *always* be certain that a string which is sold to them as " Italian " is of Italian manufacture.

Furthermore, it is not generally known, I imagine, that the finest gut in the world for the purpose of string manufacture is that obtained from English lambs, and that the Italians use no other for their finer strings. Haweis was assuredly ignorant of this fact (or he was romancing, as he was often wont to) when he said that the gut obtained from young Italian lambs killed in September was used for the best Italian strings.

It passes one's comprehension why the British public, or a large section thereof, should be for ever acclaiming everything of foreign origin and denouncing everything British. That sort of thing has too long been prevalent in Britain, and it is about time we had done with it.

The day was (and has not long passed the eventide) when an artist in order to succeed in this country had to go abroad to complete his studies. We used to be told years ago that a few second-rate artists had been known to drop their English names and to assume a grand-sounding foreign cognomen and foreign manners in order to enhance their chance with the English public. It seems incredible,

STRING MANUFACTURE IN ENGLAND 41

and it certainly is too contemptible for words. But matters will improve by-and-by. The British artist and the British fiddle are coming to their own, and British strings will not tarry long.

Many violin books give a very good account of the process of making strings abroad, it might be of some interest if I give here an account of how strings are made in England. I am indebted to Mr. G. A. Parker, of 94 Burghley Road, Kentish Town, London, N.W., for the information which follows. He very courteously allowed me to inspect his factory, and carefully explained to me every detail in the process of making strings, from the raw material to the finished article. I may mention here that only the very best strings are made in this factory, the gut and material used being the finest England can produce.

Before explaining the process of making, it will be well to describe the fixtures, tools, etc., used. The plant is by no means elaborate, and there is nothing striking about it except, perhaps, its almost primitive character. Here is a complete list of the articles (for they can hardly be termed anything else) used :

1. The bench. This rests on two trestles, one of which is a little higher than the other, and is made in two parts, each of which is about 8 feet long and 18 inches wide. The trestles are so constructed as to make the bench dip in the centre, to allow all water and other liquids to run off. On the trestles also is fixed, in the centre, a trough, or gutter, running the whole length of the bench. In the bench

are cut six holes, the first two being about 3 inches from the lower end, and 1 foot apart; the next two are 5 feet up the bench and the same distance apart; the remaining two are about a foot from the upper end, and also the same distance apart. The use of these holes will be described further on.

2. Iron bins, with lids, to hold water.

3. Enamelled bowls.

4. Metal scrapers, to clean the gut.

5. Loops. These are made of the finest hemp, each about 3 inches long. To these the strings are attached.

6. Splitting board. This is about 1 foot square. It has a hole in the centre, in which the knife is fixed, and a wooden peg on the left side, which acts as a guide for the gut. The knife has a blade about 10 inches long, and a long, tapering handle which fits into the hole. On the blade are fixed two or three bone guides, which are so constructed as to counteract the natural curve of the gut before it comes in contact with the knife. The point of the knife is upwards and the edge away from the operator.

7. Spinning wheel. This is made of wood, with iron axles, and consists of one large wheel connected to two small wheels by a gut band. To the small wheels are attached hooks, which enable the operator to spin two strings at a time.

8. Drying frames. These are of wood, with pegs fixed at both ends, and are of two lengths, 5 and 7 feet respectively, the shorter ones being

STRING MANUFACTURE IN ENGLAND

for E strings, and the longer ones for A, D, and 'cello strings.

9. Coiling table. A neat, simple but ingenious little machine used for coiling the string.

10. Sulphur box. This is a large wooden box with a tight-fitting lid, and is so carefully constructed that it is not only water-tight but also practically air-tight. Into this is put the sulphur lamp. Now for the process.

As soon as a lamb or a young sheep is killed the gut intended for strings is thoroughly cleansed. It is important that the cleansing be done almost immediately, otherwise the gut deteriorates, and its value for string making is lessened. It is then very carefully dried on frames, and is shortly ready for the string maker, to whom it is sent in bundles, called "shocks," weighing about 2 pounds each.

A shock of gut is taken and placed in a bath, and covered with water. (The water in this country has first to be chemically treated, as it is too hard in its natural state.) In about six hours the gut is thoroughly soaked, and is then turned out on the bench, when every strand is carefully pulled through the fingers to get out all tangles and knots. A shock is divided up into about seven parts, each part being placed in an enamelled bowl and covered with water and allowed to soak for about twelve hours, when the water is drained off. It is next scraped, every length of gut being scraped twice before it is split, first up, and then down. This removes anything that might be adhering to it, and it is very essential that the scraping be carefully and thoroughly done. When this is completed the gut is soaked again in water for a short time. It is now ready for splitting. A bowl of gut is taken and placed to the left of the splitting board, one end of the gut being taken out of the bowl, passed round the wooden peg, and split on the point of the knife. The gut is opened and fixed on the bone guide [the guides are of varying sizes, according to the width of the gut] and is then pulled by the operator towards him, being split as it comes in contact with the keen edge of the knife. Great care has to be exercised in this operation, to ensure that the strands are of uniform width. When all the gut is split, it is put in bowls, and is again carefully scraped in the same manner as before, this time to cleanse the *inside*. Another soaking in water follows, this time for four or five hours.

The gut is now turned out on the bench ready for spinning. The laying out looks an extremely easy matter, but is really very difficult, and is the most important and tricky part of the whole business, requiring great skill and a long experience for its proper manipulation. To make violin E strings three or four strands are used, violin A six to eight, violin D ten to twelve, etc., according to the width of the strands. Guts vary a great deal, some are hard, some soft; some are wide, others narrow; some are light, others dark. To make a string that is as near perfection as possible, it must be made of strands that are of the same texture, colour, and width, and it is in the correct and rapid selection of suitable strands that the skill of the workman comes

STRING MANUFACTURE IN ENGLAND 45

into evidence. The gut is laid out on the bench in the desired length, being carried backwards and forwards until the right gauge is obtained. The right thickness is ascertained by feeling, there being no gauge made to test the thickness at this stage, and great care has to be taken that the strands are perfectly even and straight, and that they do not cross each other.

Each string (or batch of strands which make the string) is now placed in a bowl, with the end hanging over the edge, the next string being then made and laid beside the first, and so the process continues till all the gut is used up.

The string (hemp) loops are now brought into use, the ends of gut resting over the brims of the bowls being attached to them, *i.e.* each batch of gut strands to one loop of hemp string. A wooden peg is inserted in the first hole of the bench and another peg at the other end. A bowl of strings is taken and all the strings are laid out on the bench with the loops at the first peg. One string is taken up at a time, the loop being placed over the peg, and the gut drawn down the bench between finger and thumb till it reaches the peg at the other end, when it is cut the desired length and the end attached to a loop placed over the second peg. This process continues until there is a sufficient number of strings on one set of pegs, when other pegs are brought into use.

When several pegs are thus made up, the spinning wheel is used. The wheel is placed at one end of the bench, and two strings are attached to the hooks, the handle turned about fifteen times, and the first spinning is done. One turn of the spinning wheel gives about twenty-five revolutions to the hooks, so that each string is twisted from 350 to about 370 times.

The pegs are now replaced by rods which are made to fit into the sulphur box, and the superfluous water being squeezed from the strings, the latter are carried to the sulphur box or chamber, and put in position. The lid of the box is closed down, and all cracks or crevices carefully sealed up. The lamp is now lit, a tin of sulphur placed over it, and both are inserted into a properly constructed closed chamber at the bottom of the box. This part of the work is usually done the last thing at night, and the strings are allowed to remain in the sulphur chamber until the following evening, when the lamp is again lit. Only a very small quantity of sulphur is used for the best quality string; but in making lower priced strings, and when cheap gut is used, a much larger quantity of sulphur is burnt, and it is often necessary to use bleaching water. The lovely white strings we get from the Continent are really of inferior quality, if the buyer only knew it. The strong bleaching impoverishes the gut, but the whiteness sells the string.

The strings are removed from the sulphur chamber into the drying-room, where they are stretched on drying-frames. The spinning wheel is again used, each string being given from 150 to 200 revolutions. When the strings are half dry, they are spun for the third and last time, being given about the same number of revolutions as before. Care has

STRING MANUFACTURE IN ENGLAND

to be taken at this stage that an even temperature is kept up in the drying-room, and that there is not a particle of dust about. When the strings are thoroughly dry they are polished. The polishing is done with specially selected pumice stones, in which grooves have been cut, six or seven strings being polished together in one groove. The strings are then dusted and oiled. Finally they are cut off the loops, coiled, and tied with silk or gut, and placed in bags and boxes ready to be dispatched to the wholesale houses and dealers. For covered strings the gut is not oiled. The process of covering the string with wire is a very simple one—so simple that I was able to learn it in about ten minutes, and to cover a G string for myself, which I keep as a memento of my visit to Mr. Parker's excellent factory.

V.—LEGEND, ART, AND STORY

(1) *LEGENDS.* Readers of violin literature are familiar with various legends and traditions relative to the origin and development of the fiddle and other stringed instruments, and it would be invidious to relate here tales that are already "grey with age." There are, however, two or three pretty legends which I have happened upon in my reading that have never, as far as I am aware, been related in any book on the violin : these are of some interest, I think, and may afford the reader a little entertainment.

One is a Keltic legend of the tenth century, related in "The Adventures of the Great Bardic Company." According to this story (which doubtless belongs to a much earlier mythology) the *cruit* or *cruidh* (= *crŵth*) is a metamorphosed mermaid. Thomas Moore has turned the legend into verse, substituting, however, *harp* for *cruit*, perhaps in accordance with a later version, or it may be on his own responsibility. This is how Moore puts it :—

The Origin of the Harp [*Cruit*].

" 'Tis believed that this harp, which I now wake for thee,
  Was a Siren of old, who sung under the sea ;
And who often, at eve, through the bright waters roved,
To meet on the green shore a youth whom she loved.

LEGEND, ART, AND STORY

But she loved him in vain, for he left her to weep,
And in tears, all the night, her gold tresses to steep,
Till Heaven looked with pity on true love so warm,
And changed to this soft harp the sea-maiden's form.

Still her bosom rose fair—still her cheeks smiled the same—
While her sea-beauties gracefully form'd the light frame;
And her hair, as, let loose, o'er her white arm it fell,
Was changed to bright chords, uttering melody's spell.

Hence it came, that this soft harp so long hath been known
To mingle love's language with sorrow's sad tone;
Till thou didst divide them, and teach the fond lay,
To speak love when I'm near thee, and grief when away!"

Here is another Keltic legend from the folk-lore of South Wales:—A huntsman once upon a time set out hunting in the forest of Nêdd [*dd* = *th* in thee], and chanced to put an arrow through the heart of a beautiful fawn. On lifting up the dead fawn to sling it over his shoulders it became a flute. The ancient huntsman played upon this flute daily, and its sweet tone gave him unbounded pleasure. But it chanced one day that he let fall the flute on the spot where he had slain the fawn, and the flute when it struck the ground changed into a serpent, which bit him, so that he died. His son passing that way found his father's corse, and surmising the cause of his death, hunted for the serpent a year and a day. He found it coiled up and basking in the sun. The serpent sprang at him, but he, being an agile youth, leapt aside, and struck the serpent a hard blow, so that it lay stretched out at his feet. On lifting its body up with his staff it changed into a lyre. The youth, not in the least alarmed at so wonderful a change, picked up the lyre, and bore it away with a glad heart, and it was his wont to play upon it daily, and his soul delighted in its charming sounds. But it chanced one day as he was roaming in the forest that he accidentally let fall the lyre on the very spot where he had slain the serpent, and the lyre upon striking against a stone was instantly changed into an eagle, which flew away to the heights of Ban. So great was the grief of the old man (for he was now stricken in years) at the loss of his lyre, that he shortly died of a broken heart. His son swore on his grave that he would avenge his father's death, and went hunting for the eagle a year and a day. He found its eyrie on the top of Mynydd Ban, and rested him on the heather till he should espy the eagle. When at length it flew close above the youth, a well-directed arrow brought its lifeless form down fluttering at his feet. He eagerly picked it up to examine the wound, when lo! no sooner had he lifted it from the ground than it changed into a musical instrument, the like of which he had never beheld before. Its form was like that of a fair maiden, and its tone like the notes of a nightingale. Each time he drew the bow across its strings it whispered:—

> "A fawn was I, my tale to tell;
> A fiddle am I till breaks the spell."

The word in the Welsh legend is *crwth*, which I have rendered *fiddle*, modern Welsh itself frequently preferring the latter word to the native and more ancient one. South Walians invariably call a violin

LEGEND, ART, AND STORY 51

ffidl, whereas North Walians have retained *crŵth*, using it as the equivalent of *fiddle*.

A very curious legend is current in certain parts of Poland. It says that the *goudok*, a kind of rustic fiddle, was invented and brought to Europe by The Old Wandering Man, and that from this the modern violin has been developed. The story of the Old Wandering Man looks like a variant of the legend of The Wandering Jew, but it has some peculiar features. The old man in this case is said to have invented, many centuries if not millenniums ago, a cabalistic magnet which possessed the extraordinary property of "secretly attracting the *aura*, or mysterious spirit of human efflorescence and prosperous bodily growth, out of young men, and to gather these benign and healthful springs of life and apply them to the person of the inventor, by inspiration and transudation, so that he was able to concentrate in himself, though waning in age, the accumulated rejuvenescence of many young people, who were consumed in proportion to the extent their vitality was extracted from them." The Old Wandering Man is believed by the Polish peasantry to be still living, and to be going to and fro, as devotedly attached as ever to his primitive fiddle, his only consolation in life.

(2) *Art.* The treatment of the violin in painting, wood carving, stained glass windows, etc., is a very wide subject, but I can touch only the fringe of it here, and that at only one point. Every lover of the leading instrument who is also a lover of truth cannot but be puzzled and pained by the persistence

of the badly painted and badly carved fiddle in modern art. Almost every year picture exhibitions, coloured windows, and decorative carving, more especially of the ecclesiastical class, furnish us with numerous examples of impossible fiddles. Why is this? And why is it tolerated? If a painter treated an ordinary article of furniture with the same liberty or indifference that he does the violin which he sometimes puts in the hand of his sitter he would be voted a mere dauber. What violin connoisseur is there that does not feel angry with the painting entitled *The Old Fiddler*, exhibited at one of the Art galleries a few years ago, and now owned by a rich collector? The picture depicts an old strolling fiddler crossing a bleak hill on a wintry day, carrying his fiddle in a green baize bag under his arm, with its head protruding. The picture was pronounced by the critics to be very fine, and so it would be but for one stupid blunder—the head of the fiddle is shown twisted round on a level with its sides!

But painters, great delinquents though they be, are eclipsed by stained glass artists and ecclesiastical wood carvers, especially the latter, who, I think, are the greatest sinners of all in this respect. Out of innumerable examples of bad carving which I could easily cite, I will take one example, which shall serve as a type of its class. It is that of the instruments on an elaborate and very expensive reredos put up in a large modern church where I officiated recently —a church which boasts an aristocratic and cultured congregation. The carving on that part of the

LEGEND, ART, AND STORY 53

reredos which lies immediately behind and above the altar depicts the "Heavenly Choir," led by a small orchestra of angels, who are playing upon various stringed instruments, all of a modern description. Of the two principal figures, which stand slightly in front of the group, and are in high relief, one plays upon an instrument that is perhaps intended for a banjo, but which looks more like a frying-pan than anything else. The other holds a tolerably decent fiddle, and a bow that might pass muster for a "Tourte," in an attitude which is intended to show that he is in the act of playing, but which really suggests that he has had a fiddle put in his hands for the first time, and is attempting to scrape out a few notes!

One often wonders what conclusions future musical historians, judging alone by such painting and carving as I have described, would form as to the shape, size, and proportion of the fiddle of the nineteenth and twentieth centuries, and as to the technique of violinists of that period. They would not be very flattering conclusions, I trow. It is a pity the ancient Greek law is not in force to-day which made it a punishable offence "for painters or other imitative artists to innovate or invent any forms different from those which were established," and "unlawful in painting, statuary, or any branches of music to make any alteration or false representation" (*Vide* Plato, *De Legibus*, liber II). For, assuredly, truth is as important a virtue in a work of art as it is in a business transaction, and art itself ceases to be of real value when it relinquishes its hold upon truth. Ruskin very justly observes that "there are some faults slight in the sight of love, some errors slight in the estimate of wisdom; but truth forgives no insult, and endures no stain." (*Vide The Seven Lamps of Architecture*, chap. on "The Lamp of Truth," par. 1).

It is no answer to the strictures made here (more especially on the carvings) to say that the artistic treatment of the violin in this case is to be considered as a mere abstraction—that sort of answer has been given from time to time. As a matter of fact it is not abstraction, and if it were, it would be illegitimate in these particular cases. That it is not abstraction is evident from the position of the carving and the attempted perfection of the form in almost all the instances that have come under my observation. In abstraction only a limited number of the qualities of a thing are represented, but in the carvings here considered an attempt is made to show all the essential qualities of the form of the instrument.

And if it were abstraction, it would be open to the still more serious charge of illegitimacy. It is a canon of architecture that abstraction is not legitimate where an object is to be closely seen, but only where it is to be viewed from a distance. The carvings in the examples reviewed here are in close proximity to the altar, choir stalls, etc., and are on a level with the eyes of the spectator, and only a few feet away from him. We may reasonably ask those who offer this kind of apology for bad art: Why— if the instruments put in the hands of angels, etc., are

LEGEND, ART, AND STORY 55

intended for mere abstractions—are not the figures themselves treated as mere abstractions?

Nor is it a good defence of bad painting and carving to quote the example of certain masters who have given us false or imperfect representations of the violin. To such a shallow defence I would reply in the words of Landor: " I dare not defend myself behind the bad example of any man, and the bad example of a good man is the worst defence of all " (*Pentameron*).

(3) *Story*. The violin has an *olla podrida* of romance, anecdote, song, proverb, nursery rhyme, and what not, all its own, quite apart from its more formal literature. I can only indicate in a general sort of way, with no attempt at classification, the character and extent of this class of writings. Charles Reade's " Jack of all Trades " and " Christie Johnstone " are familiar to most readers. These tales, written as they are by one of the first connoisseurs of Europe, and by a master of English literature, are rather disappointing. If " Thomas Harvey " is a thin disguise for Thomas Hardie, the son of Matthew Hardie—and there is not much doubt about it—then the writer has exaggerated the importance of Hardie as a violin maker. Reade says that Harvey, or Harvie (= Hardie), was " remarkably successful in insuring that which had been too hastily ascribed to accident—a fine tone " : as a matter of fact the tone of Thomas Hardie's instruments is almost always poor and often positively bad. Honeyman is of the opinion, having regard to Reade's great knowledge of the violin and his

passion for truth, that Hardie's violins must have originally had a good tone, but that they have gradually deteriorated owing to the wood having been artificially seasoned. Some scores of novels have appeared since Reade wrote these two tales, in which a violin maker or player is the hero, or an important character; many of them are of considerable merit, and a few very instructive and interesting. A really clever and fascinating book is "Interplay," by Beatrice Harraden, in which one of the minor characters is a violin maker, bearing the rather commonplace name of Paul Stilling, whose imbecile innocence of the world and its affairs is eclipsed only by his phenomenal ability and skill as a fiddle maker and repairer. He is described as one who makes great fiddles by intuition, and as "an absolutely entrancing companion in his own realm." The authoress—evidently a "modern woman"—has a thorough knowledge of the subject of violin making and repairing, and has produced something worth reading.

Of interesting violin anecdotes there is no end. Hart, in his book, has a choice selection, to which may be added many more equally entertaining from "Some Early Musical Recollections of George Haddock," the numerous publications of the late Dr. T. L. Phipson; "The Fiddle in Scotland," by A. G. Murdoch—a little work which contains several quaint stories of old Scottish fiddlers and fiddle makers—and from other books and periodicals. To the particularly pleasing and amusing stories of Gainsborough (related by Hart) may be added others about Romney, and one or two other great painters, who " found inspiration and solace in the sweets of the fiddle." Painters and *littérateurs* as a rule are musical, and are able to appreciate the difference between beautiful and commonplace music, but there are exceptions, and Ruskin was one. In the " Life and Letters of Sir Charles Hallé," Mr. C. E. Hallé in a passage relating to certain musical incidents at a house party, where several celebrities had gathered, including Tennyson, Swinburne, Burne Jones, Rossetti, Watts, Browning, Leighton, Millais, Fred Walker, Doyle, and several other poets and painters, says : " My father was always delighted in having such men to play to ; with painters, as he has himself said, he was always safe—with *littérateurs* he was occasionally not quite so fortunate. They were fond of talking and found it difficult to sit long and listen, whatever other sounds were being made, and at times matters fared even worse. Some years ago, in 1864, Professor Ruskin asked him to come and play to a school of young girls in whom he was greatly interested. My father readily consented, and as the Professor was there himself, and it was the first time he had played to him, he was careful to select what was most great and beautiful, and played his very best. When it was all over and my father was about to leave, one of the girls told him she had been practising Thalberg's arrangement of 'Home, Sweet Home,' and would very much like to hear my father play it before he went away. He told her it was a pity they should listen to a trivial thing like that after the beautiful music they had just heard, but as she appeared disappointed and some other girls came forward with the same request, he gave way, sat down, and played it. To his chagrin, Ruskin, who had been politely appreciative, now became enthusiastic, and told him *that* was the piece he liked best far and away!"

Mr. Heron-Allen has told us all about nursery rhymes connected with the fiddle, it only remains for me to give a few proverbs I have heard in different parts of the country.

"Drunk as a fiddler" is an expression which is often heard, and is common to all parts. It is rather hard on the poor fiddler, who would doubtless break his heart but for the knowledge that he sins in good company—so at least another proverb, "Drunk as a lord," tells him.

"Fiddler's pence," a collection of small coin.

"Fiddle-sticks!" expressive of contempt, etc.

"Mending his fiddle" (S. Pembrokeshire), trying to recover lost ground, retrieve his position, and a variety of meanings.

"Playing her fiddle," Welsh "*Canu ei chrŵth*," said of a cat purring, and metaphorically of a woman humming a tune pleasantly while at work. "Digon o grŵth a thelyn" (Welsh), which means literally, enough of a fiddle and harp, said of one who can sing a good song, tell a good tale, play an instrument, or anything to entertain a company; who is, in fact, an entertainment in himself.

"Playing the fiddle," is an expression applied by Welsh people to a preacher who has "more sound than sense," referring, of course, to the peculiar style of oratory known as Welsh *hŵyl*.

" Yea canna vettle shoon with a viddle stick " (S. Pembrokeshire) = you cannot repair shoes with a fiddle stick.

" I wunna crowdy to norra one " (S. Pembs) = I will not play the fiddle to any one, that is, I will not fawn upon any one.

" To play second fiddle to " = to act a minor part, to take a back seat, etc.

" Playing the fiddle to the devil."

" Many a good tune is played on an old fiddle."

" A dry fiddler makes a dry fiddle."

> " There are three won't work without a stick,
> An ass, a fiddler, and gentleman Dick."

" You grease the fiddler, he'll grease the fiddle " ; " greased " in the second instance, of course, referring to the popular error that grease or some such lubricant is applied to the bow.

" The fiddler blaming the fiddle, and the fiddle blaming the stick," *i.e.* saddling the blame on another, and he on somebody else.

> " Three guests who never miss a feast,
> The fiddler, beggar, and the priest."

" Fit as a fiddle."

" As taut as a fiddle string."

" Fiddling with it " = trifling with it, a common expression.

" Like fiddle and fiddle-stick " ; *i.e.* inseparable, or indispensable to one another.

"Got it all in his head like a fiddler." This may refer to the music, which the old time fiddler usually committed to memory, or to the miscellanea he carried in his top hat in the shape of strings, ballads, spare neck-bands, resin, etc.

"A face like a fiddle, and a tongue like a fiddle-stick."

"As busy as a fiddle-stick."

"Tickle your strings!" Meaning: "Be up and doing!" Fiddlers at a country dance when their enthusiasm flagged were encouraged by the crowd who shouted, "Tickle your strings, ye merry fiddlers!" The expression now has a variety of applications.

"Fiddling money out of people" is an expression frequently heard in S. Wales.

"Drawing the long bow," exaggerating, finessing, putting too fine a point to a story, etc.

"Talking and fiddling," a common expression.

"Talking and fiddling with their hats and feathers" (Pepys).

"Every fiddle to its faddle," equivalent to "every man to his own trade"; cf. "Let the shoemaker stick to his last."

"Call the fiddlers!" When an altercation threatens to become serious the more placable portion of a drinking company cry "Call the fiddlers!" to show their disapproval of the noise, and their desire for order and peace. This proverb is a testimony to the power of the wee fiddle as a peacemaker, for it points back to the good old time when the fiddle was the one indispensable thing at country weddings,

LEGEND, ART, AND STORY

fairs, village green gatherings, wakes, etc., where its strains often hushed an angry dispute.

"He has more than one string to his bow." This proverb has two or three variants.

"Tighten your strings!" Pluck up courage.

"Leaning on the fiddle," concentrating energy and attention upon anything; derived perhaps from the habit of old fiddlers of bending forward and leaning their heads on their fiddles when playing earnestly and—it must be added—furiously.

"Mae e' wedi hongian 'i grŵth" (North Pembrokeshire) = he has hung up his fiddle; said of one who has failed in an enterprise, or given anything up in despair; *cf.* "We hanged our harps upon the willows" (Ps. cxxxvii., v. 2).

"A Two-penny fiddler" (S. Pembs.), one who is a mere dabbler at a thing, not at all limited to the violin, or to music. The recognized fiddlers in olden times charged each couple the sum of threepence for a "round" of dancing; the less capable fiddlers who charged only twopence were looked upon with contempt, hence the expression.

"Feathering the bow," "Feathering the strings," "Feathering the notes," and other similar expressions, have a variety of metaphorical applications. There are, doubtless, many more fiddle proverbs and colloquial expressions, some of them I dare say quaint and expressive, and concealing little bits of interesting history. A complete collection of these, with explanatory notes and comments, would be of value to the antiquarian.

VI.—THEORIES ABOUT THE ITALIAN TONE

THE Italian tone ! What is it ? And what its *raison d'être ?* Simple though these questions appear to be, they are by no means easy to answer. Indeed, I do not think the second can be satisfactorily answered at all.

To the question : what is the Italian tone ? there is given a diversity of answers, and it is difficult to say which exactly is the best. The answers are all of a more or less rhetorical character, and I am not aware that anybody has ever attempted to give us an exact scientific description of it, couched in the phraseology of acoustics. Nor do I think such a description easy to give. The epithets "sweet," "clear," "bright," "rich," "mellow," "silvery," "sonorous," "responsive," "bell-like," and such like, are applied to the Italian tone, all of them correct enough when they are used to describe the tone of the best instruments made by the great masters ; but I think the quality *par excellence* which distinguishes the Italian tone is—what I may figuratively call—its liquidity. It has a kind of oily smoothness which mollifies and pleases the ear in a manner that words fail to describe. It is a tone, then, produced by stringed instruments of the violin family which

THE ITALIAN TONE

has a peculiar liquidity in addition to other good qualities. It is a kind of tone, I need hardly say, which is not possessed by every instrument made by the old Italians, and not always by instruments made by even the masters. And I will add (what to some will appear rank heresy) a tone which is sometimes possessed by instruments made neither in Italy nor by the masters.

The fact is, the term *Italian tone* is much of a misnomer, leading to wrong inferences rather than to a right judgment.

Connoisseurs of ripe experience, and whose perceptive faculties have not been warped by prejudice, will agree with me that a great deal of nonsense has been written about Italian instruments and the Italian tone. Without a doubt, the finest of the old Italian fiddles are superior to all others, but there were great fiddles made outside Italy.

Mr. W. C. Honeyman appears to me to take a pretty sane view of the matter. He writes: " ' Are Italian violins superior to all others ? ' is a question frequently asked by the puzzled chooser of a violin. It is not easy to answer this question in an off-hand manner, players differ so much in opinion as to what is ' superior ' ; but no one of experience and proper training can deny that the best of the old Italian violins have a subtle and thrilling sweetness of quality of tone which is *rarely* found in those of any other country. . . . All Italian violins have not this quality. . . . If a skilled violin maker would but use the best Italian wood of matured growth, seasoned for years in the warm dry air of Italy, and make a good instrument, and cover it with a fine amber oil varnish and expose that violin for a year to warm dry air, I have not a shadow of a doubt that that violin would have the Italian tone, no matter where it were made." (*The Violin: How to Choose One*, p. 45.)

What is the *raison d'être* of the Italian tone? In other words, what was the secret of Stradivari, Guarneri, Amati, Bergonzi, Maggini, and other great Italians, and—I may add—of a few great makers outside Italy?

Connoisseurs differ widely in their opinions. Indeed, out of the small army of fiddle experts, past and present, hardly any two men will be found to have exactly the same opinion.

I think it might be of some interest, and perhaps of some value, if I put down here as concisely and clearly as possible the opinions—*theories* I had better call them—of some of the more important writers on the subject, and at the same time point out what I consider to be their defects.

A.—THE AIR MASS THEORY

The gist of this theory may be stated thus: The cubic capacity of the best Italian instruments (more especially of Stradivari's) is such as ensures the exact mass of air required by the tonal basis of construction. This theory has two fatal defects:

(1) It is well-nigh impossible to secure the required exact mass of air. The mass of air in the chamber of the violin is not identical at any two consecutive moments of time. Air is highly elastic, and its

THE ITALIAN TONE 65

density at any particular moment depends upon temperature and atmospheric pressure. And the quantity of reinforcement of vibration by a volume of air depends upon the density of the air at the time. (*Vide* Helmholtz : *Sensations of Tone*, and other works.)

(2) The present cubic capacity of many of the best Italian fiddles is not what it was when the instruments were new. Nearly all these old fiddles have been refitted with a larger bass bar and end blocks, which means a slight decrease in the cubic capacity. A large number of them have been opened time and again for repair, with the result that the ribs are not always quite as deep as they originally were. Others are indented here and there, especially around the bridge.

B.—THE RELATIVE PITCH OF THE PLATES

This theory was broached by M. Savart as a result of his researches on the acoustics of Italian violins, with special reference to those of Stradivari. It holds that the quality known as Italian tone is due to the relative pitch of the fundamental tones of the back and front plates of the violin, the pitch of the back being a tone lower than that of the front. (*Vide* Fetis : *Notice of Stradivarius*, p. 83.)

I observe (1) That this theory rests on the logical fallacy of non-observation. Savart does not tell us that he tested the plates of any violin intact, as it had left the hands of the maker, but he constructed a fiddle, or some sort of musical box, the plates of which he graduated to produce the required tonal difference, with the result that he obtained what he conceived to be the Italian tone.

The clue which set him on the right track he says he got by discovering that rods of maple and pine cut from shipwrecked Strads were found when thrown into vibration to give exactly the same relative pitch.

(2) I submit that we have no evidence that the plates of any great Italian instrument, much less an instrument by Stradivari, *in their original condition*, have ever been tested with a view of ascertaining their tonal pitch.

(3) I submit further that there is not a fiddle in existence, made by any of the masters, with its plates in their original condition. The fixing of a stronger bass bar has necessarily altered the pitch of the table. The use of glue in repairing is another little factor to be considered. A rod of glue would give a very different note from a rod of pine, and although the quantity of glue used in repairing be exceedingly small, still it has to be taken into account. And the majority of old Italian fiddles have some little glue in their flesh by now.

(4) It does not seem to have occurred to those who hold this theory that varnished plates of wood give out a different note from the same plates in the white. There is a slight difference of thickness to take into account, but more important is the alteration in density. Oil varnishes penetrate the wood and increase the specific gravity of the plates.

Presuming that the old makers worked their plates to produce a certain tonal difference, why should it

THE ITALIAN TONE

be supposed that that difference would be maintained after varnishing?

C.—RELATIVE DENSITY

Different pieces of timber differ in density. The great Italian makers had exact knowledge of the degree of density required in the back and front plates to produce what they term "the necessary acoustic accord." This appears to be the view of the Rev. H. R. Haweis, who says: "Charles Reade was napping when he expressed a hope that a certain Stradivari back, mated with a new belly, might some day be united to *some* Stradivari belly of which he knew; but unless it happened to be *the* belly Strad had selected for that particular back, what reason is there to suppose that the result would be satisfactory?"

Plausible as it appears, this theory will not bear much weight, for—

(1) The only method of determining the exact density of timber is by the use of the hydrostatic balance; and he would be a rash writer, indeed, who would venture to credit the old luthiers with a knowledge of hydrostatics. No doubt the great makers, particularly Stradivari, Guarneri, and a few others, were cunning craftsmen, endowed with intuitive powers beyond the average craftsman, still they had their limitations, and they were very ignorant, the majority of them, of book learning.

(2) The specific gravity of different pieces of maple and pine of the same dimensions varies infinitely. For example, ten pieces of pine of exactly the same

measurements, cut from the same log, and from the same side of it, if you like, would be found to give, if accurately tested, ten different specific gravities.

(3) By the mathematical theory of chance it is impossible that Stradivari or anybody else should succeed in fortuitously hitting upon a uniform ratio of density between the plates of a large number of instruments.

D.—QUALITY OF WOOD

This theory holds that the peculiar timbre of the tone is due to the kind and quality of wood used.

Mr. Honeyman says that nothing but Italian wood will give the Italian tone. Another says it must be cut from this, that, or the other locality, and a third that it must be from a particular part of the tree.

Now there can be no question that it is a matter of supreme importance to use the right kind of wood, and the very best of that kind, but that a fiddle made of such timber will necessarily yield the Italian tone we know is not the case. There are hundreds of fiddles made of Italian wood which have not the Italian tone. Curiously enough, the old Italian makers used wood of foreign growth for their better class instruments. We have it on the authority of the Messrs. Hill that all the finer figured maple of Stradivari was of foreign (*i.e.* non-Italian) growth. (*Vide Antonio Stradivari*, p. 169, 2nd Ed.)

E.—THE VARNISH

This theory holds that the Italian tone is to be attributed to the old Italian varnish absolutely.

THE ITALIAN TONE

The Messrs. Hill, whilst not going quite that length, perhaps, maintain that the varnish was the first and most important factor in the construction of Strad instruments.

But I quite fail to see why, if the secret of the Italian tone is in the varnish, so many Italian instruments of the classical period do not possess it.

There is genuine enough Italian varnish, I should imagine, on all instruments made in Italy from 1650 till about 1750, but a considerable number of these old relics can lay no pretence whatever to the Italian tone.

These do not exhaust the list of theories, there are many more. There is the plate tension theory of L. H. Hall, of Hartford, Conn., the natural varnishing theory of Otto Migge, the harmonic proportion theory of Carl Schulze, etc. I am not sure that I quite understand some of these theories, but I have a suspicion that if I did I should not be very much wiser.

I have not a pet theory of my own to offer my readers, and if I had, I should be exceedingly chary of putting it before them. In sooth I must confess that I know very little more about the mysteries of the Italian tone now than I did thirty-five years ago when I first took up the study of the subject.

I have thought about this mystery so long, pondered over it, and carried it about with me in all my daily rounds, that I verily believe I should not care to have it solved. There is a subtle charm about all mystery, and about this one in particular.

F

I do not think there would be half the number of violin makers to-day but for this mystery of the Italian tone. It is the magnetic pole of the fiddle world, which makes the gauges and callipers of a thousand craftsmen to point all in the same direction. I may express my meaning in the homely language of Bolingbroke, who said that "plain truth will influence half a score men at most in a nation, or an age, while mystery will lead millions of men by the nose."

I may in concluding these few and scattered remarks on the Italian tone point out briefly what theory and practice have taught me to regard as important factors in the construction of a good fiddle. They are:—

(1) The quality of the wood.
(2) The outline and model.
(3) The graduation of the thicknesses.
(4) Good varnish.
(5) Accurate workmanship.

I think the curves of the plates, especially of the back, have an important bearing on both the quantity and the quality of the tone, and I think also great care should be exercised to make the plates fit true on the ribs, to ensure their perfect freedom from torsional strain when glued on. It is needless to add that I consider it very desirable that the instrument should be finished in as artistic a manner as possible.

Stringent attention to all these points may or may not result in the production of an instrument which has the Italian tone. May or may not;

which of the twain is largely a matter of chance. This much is certain, however, to neglect these factors is to court failure, ending in disappointment and vexation of spirit.

VII.—MISCELLANEA

THE more important matters have been touched upon, it only remains to say something about those of minor interest.

And first, as to vagaries. By this term I mean departures from the traditional type of violin, and I would include under one head all modifications, varieties, and freaks, whether presented as " improvements " and trotted out under the aegis of the Patents Act, or otherwise.

No man who loves truth will deprecate scientific investigation and experiment, and the discovery of a new law, a new fact, a new element, or a new anything, will be hailed with delight by the thinking section of the community. The fiddle world would appreciate any real discovery or invention of undoubted worth ; but unfortunately the majority of violin vagaries can claim to be neither inventions nor discoveries : they are mostly eccentricities or absurdities.

Thus it stands with the fiddle, I believe : it has a long ancestry, reaching back thousands of years, but it appears to have entered upon its last cycle of evolution during the Renaissance, and to have reached the full measure of its stature early in the eighteenth century. Further it cannot go. Heron-

MISCELLANEA

Allen observes that "The violin ... is perhaps the only human contrivance which, taken as a whole, may be pronounced to be perfect. ... This exquisite machine, standing apart in its mysterious simplicity from the vulgar herd of instruments of melody and harmony, is capable of expressing more by its unaided voice than all the rest put together; and when this has been said, are we not perfectly justified in ascribing to it the attribute of perfection? And is it extraordinary that any attempted improvement only proves to be a deterioration ...?"

This is the unanimous verdict of experts, at least. It is manifest, then, that all attempts at improvements are a waste of time and energy. But hardly a year passes but that we read of the advent of one or more rivals to the traditional type.

Mr. Heron-Allen in his well-known work devotes a chapter to the description of some of the principal vagaries that had appeared up to about 1880: it only remains for me to mention those that have appeared since. For obvious reasons I omit the names of the inventors, patentees, etc.

(1) The aluminium violin. There have been several attempts made within recent years to introduce violins, and especially violas, made of this metal. I saw quite recently a viola made of what is known as aluminium gold, an alloy consisting of one part of aluminium to nine parts of copper. It was more of a curiosity than anything else, and the tone was small and harsh.

(2) Duple, triple, and sextuple barred fiddles.

These are fiddles with two, three, or six bass bars. I also saw recently a freak which, if I remember rightly, the maker named the cellular fiddle. In this instrument little cells or pits were carved all over on the inside of the back and front table, so that the surface appeared like a honeycomb. It looked curious, and must have cost an immense amount of labour, and that is about all that could be said in its favour. The makers of these vagaries appear to be labouring under the delusion that an increase of the interior vibrating surface of the instrument ensures a corresponding improvement in its tone-producing qualities.

(3) The radiophone fiddle. The back and front of this instrument are each made of twelve pieces of wood, which are so arranged that the grain runs radially from a common centre located mid-way between the sound-holes at the front, and from a corresponding point at the back. These pieces are not only glued together, but are tenoned and mortised—a method which involves the expenditure of time and energy sufficient to produce three or four violins of the orthodox pattern. This fiddle is fitted with a bridge made of six pieces put together on the same principle.

(4) The plated fiddle. This has two sympathetic plates fixed to the end blocks inside the instrument, consisting of laminae of pine about one-sixteenth of an inch thick, and extending about one-third of the length of the body of the fiddle from either end. The plates follow the lines of the upper and lower bouts, but stand away about half-an-inch from

MISCELLANEA

the ribs. Here again the idea seems to be that by an increase of the vibrating surface it is possible to obtain an increase of the volume of tone.

(5) The acute angled violin. In this device the back of the instrument is made slightly larger than the front, so that the ribs stand at an acute angle to it. Why it should be named an acute angled fiddle rather than an obtuse angled one is not quite clear, for since the ribs form an acute angle with the back, they must necessarily form an obtuse angle with the front. There would appear to me to be greater propriety in naming the invention after the larger angle. Great merits are claimed for this " patent " variety. The inventor in a letter under date of April 4, 1914, writes : " Violinists of great renown have tried them, some of whom say the angular violins are better than those of the old masters, and I know that I have a dozen of them here in my house, the like of which for tone have never passed through the hands of the Messrs. Hill & Sons." Possibly not !

(6) The rib sound holes. I have seen three varieties of this kind of fiddle ; one was such a beautifully made instrument that it seemed a pity it was not more conformable to " the traditions of the fathers." The inventor (evidently a scholarly man and a fine artist) in a pamphlet explanatory of the principles of this new departure says that " there is, aside from the absence of sound-holes in the top, no change from the well-known and orthodox pattern. The sound-holes have been removed because they destroy the continuity of the fine grain and fibre in

a table which, experience has shown, is delicately sensible to defects. In this table the sound-hole is but a decorative crack, and just as detrimental to the expression of full and perfect tone as any other crack. The old violins with really fine tone (and they are fewer than is generally supposed) possess this tone-quality in spite of their sound-holes—not because of them."

There are numerous other vagaries of recent introduction, some of them being revivals of forgotten freaks, such as the patent leather fiddle, the one-table fiddle, the reversed head fiddle, etc. There are patent finger-boards, tail pieces, tail-pegs, key pegs, and what not.

* * * * *

The factory fiddle claims a paragraph or two. This ubiquitous intruder came among us long ago, and when it did it evidently had made up its mind to come to stay. Decry it as we will, it is determined never to shake off from its varnish the dust of British resin. I am not sure that its advent was altogether such a bad event as we are wont to picture it. We know that it unfortunately helped to kill the home-made and hand-made article, but then we also know that it has helped to popularize the " King of instruments " in a country and among a people which are said to be not over-musical. The high-class, hand-made, artistic violin can never be produced at a price which brings it within the reach of the poorest of the people. Some violin makers claim that they can complete an instrument in the white in one week, but it is not possible that they can within that period give their work the degree of finish it should have. He is a very smart worker who can finish a fiddle in a fortnight, and keep on producing work at that rate. Long days and fine work demand a big price. No! we must not unreservedly condemn the little factory intruder ; he has a few points in his favour which help considerably to counter-balance his defects. One of our leading professional makers once remarked to me that he owed a great deal to the cheap fiddle. Put in the hands of a beginner it sufficed up to a certain point, but when that point was reached it quietly and without a murmur made way to its aristocratic brother, the artistic instrument. Once the love of the instrument is created within him, the student will not long rest content with an inferior or indifferent fiddle.

It is impossible that an artist, or even a player of merely respectable proficiency, should be anchored to earth by a factory fiddle.

A machine-made fiddle has no soul, and therefore no individuality.

It is a fiddle, that is to say, to which the player cannot impart his own individuality, and thus make it the medium of expressing his highest thoughts and deepest feelings. With his usual philosophic insight Haweis remarks that " when Balzac tells us of a man who had imprisoned the soul of his mother in a violin, he was nearer a certain truth than some of his readers fancy. The soul that is imprisoned in your violin is not your mother's, it is your own soul, seeking and finding through the most sensitive of all musical instruments an utterance such as the human voice alone can equal, but not excel." (*Vide My Musical Life*, p. 288.)

* * * * *

On the subject of the relative worth of old and new fiddles a great deal might be said. It has been my conviction for many years, and the conviction is growing with the growing years, that the penchant for old instruments is largely a matter of sentiment —is, in fact, a craze. I know it is heresy of an unpardonable nature to say so, and that the anathemas of a thousand-and-one devotees of the old cult will come down on my unfortunate head, but what advantageth it to hide a conviction ? Providing one has spared no effort in endeavouring to master his subject, and that he has not been slow to profit by experience, surely he has a right to express an honest opinion. Let it at once be admitted that a good old instrument, in a good, or at least very fair state of preservation, is indisputably superior to a new instrument —and I know not of an expert who would not readily grant as much—and all is admitted that is justly warranted by the case. As to the bulk of old fiddles, and all the wretched nondescripts which are masqueraded as old fiddles, the pity is they are not gathered into one pile, set fire to, and offered up as a holocaust to Zethus, or some other vengeful god. I am quite certain that a new fiddle, made of good material, scientifically constructed, and covered patiently with a good oil varnish, if played skilfully and given a few years to mature, will be superior in every way to seventy out of every hundred old fiddles which flood the market to-day. The truth is, half the number of these old fiddles were poor, cracked-voiced things when they were new, and no length of time nor any amount of playing *could* ever improve them, and as to the other half—well, about fifty per cent. of them have been spoilt by quack repairers and "patent" improvement maniacs. In believing and expressing myself thus, I am not alone and unsupported, as my critic of *The Athenaeum* wished his readers to think; I am abundantly borne out by the opinion of experts of long standing and good repute. For instance, Mr. J. M. Fleming (in a passage which I must beg leave to condense) says: "It is, undoubtedly, a general opinion current among professional and amateur players that new violins are usually *new* in the matter of tone. That means that the tone is 'woody,' 'hard,' or 'metallic.' These are really the only terms that may properly describe the supposed defect. Now, that opinion is, in regard to the vast bulk of ordinary trade violins, perfectly sound, and these three terms very accurately portray the kinds of tone which new violins of the trade class possess. Curiously enough, the same three terms will exactly describe the tones of ninety out of every hundred of the *old* type to be found in the market at the present time. . . . The reader will observe that I have said ninety out of every hundred—a rough and ready way of indicating the proportion of bad to good instruments. And by 'bad' I mean not intrinsically bad, but bad by comparison with new instruments at equal prices.

It is now going on for half a century since I began to take an interest in violins, and few aspects of the subject have caused me more surprise from time to time than the apparently fixed determination of people to have an *old* fiddle at all hazards. . . . Age guarantees nothing, except the possibility that there will be a few cracks . . . nothing with regard to excellence of manufacture or quality of tone." (*Vide The Fiddle Fancier's Guide*, p. 25.) Mr. W. C. Honeyman, the well-known Scottish expert, expresses himself much to the same effect, and even goes so far as to maintain that " good new violins entirely put out of court the majority of old ones." (*Vide The Violin: How to Choose One.*) Mr. Edward Heron-Allen observes : " No one who has seen the magnificent new instruments of Chanot, of Hill, of Boullangier, of Simontre, of Gand and Bernardel, and of many other living makers, can possibly deny that these instruments will be, when a little matured by age, far sweeter and finer than any of the time-withered, tampered-with, over-repaired, and dilapidated instruments which flood the market under the names of Stradivari, of Guarneri, of Amati, of Ruggerius, of Stainer, of Bergonzi, and a hundred lesser names "—(*Violin making: As it Was and Is*, p. 19). And Charles Reade, very pertinently, and in his own inimitable style, remarks that if you " take a hundred violins by Stradiuarius and open them ; you find about ninety-five patched in the centre with new wood. The connecting link is a sheet of glue. And is glue a fine resonant substance ? And are the glue and the new wood of

John Bull and Jean Crapaud transmogrified into the wood of Stradiuarius by merely sticking on to it ? Is it not extravagant to quote patched violins as beyond rivalry in all the qualities of sound ? " (*Vide* Fourth Letter in the *Pall-Mall Gazette*, Aug. 31, 1872.)

The testimony of many more competent witnesses might be given, but it is not necessary to belabour the point. I am not quarrelling with my critics : they have as good a right to their own opinions as I have to mine, but I think if they had been better informed on the subject they would not have said the foolish things they did about the comparative merits of old and new fiddles.

It is my earnest advice to players of moderate means, professional and amateur alike, who require a good fiddle, to spend their money wisely on a sound new instrument, made by some artist of recognized ability.

* * * * *

Repairing does not come within the scope of this work, but a few words on the sister craft will not be out of place. Good repairers are like gold, often scarce, always wanted, and much abused. They are often abused, forsooth, because they cannot perform miracles, and transform wretched old fiddles with broken voices into seraphic Cremonas.

Repairing, I need hardly tell my readers, is a special art, requiring much skill, great patience, and a double portion of the spirit of self-effacement and of reverence for old work. The absence of the last named virtue in the repairers of the past is one of the reasons why there are so many spoilt old instruments. The best makers are not necessarily, nor even usually, the best repairers. As a matter of fact very few of the leading British violin makers are renowned for their repairs, and the majority of them do not undertake such work at all. I do not think, however, a man can be a good repairer unless he is able to make an instrument, and is thoroughly conversant with the theory of its construction. Repairing is to making what surgery is to anatomy —skill in the one is dependent on a knowledge of the other. There are some scores of repairers of a sort up and down the country, but they are not repairers in the true sense of the word; they are dabblers. An artistic repairer does not merely *mend* the fiddle, he *restores* it—restores it, that is, as near as possible to its original condition, and by the help and with the addition of as *little* new material as possible. He does not, like the vandal Ortega of whom we read, substitute a brand new table for a cracked old one, nor even, indeed, the tiniest splinter, where he can possibly avoid it. All the old pieces that have broken off, if they are not lost, he deftly and cunningly refits in their proper position. It has been said of the repairs of François Gand, of Paris, that they were "masterpieces of ingenuity and delicate workmanship." "The care that he took and the judgment which he exercised in bringing together the various broken parts of an imperfect instrument, that the original appearance might be maintained as closely as possible, cannot be too highly praised. He often accomplished seeming

MISCELLANEA

impossibilities. Splintered cracks were by his ingenuity closed as though no fibre had been severed, while at other times, pieces were so deftly inserted that the most experienced eyes might fail to detect their presence. It was with him a labour of love, and he did not scruple to spend days over work on which others would only spend hours." (Hart.) That is a picture of the genuine restorer and reverent artist! And that is the sort of work every repairer desirous of doing full justice to his art must aim at. The great bane of the fiddle world is the quack repairer, with his "patent" nostrums for this, that, and the other violin ailment. If you value your old instrument, avoid him as you would a pestilence.

There are several clever and conscientious repairers in the country, and the owner of a valuable instrument requiring doctoring up need be under no apprehension in committing his treasure to them for treatment.

* * * * *

The preservation of instruments is a matter of supreme importance, and I do not think I shall be giving superfluous advice when urging upon all owners of valuable violins the necessity of attending to the following points :—

(1) Wipe the instrument carefully with a soft silk handkerchief each time after use.

(2) If the violin is not at all in use, then give it frequent airings, but do not expose it for long to the direct rays of the sun—that would take the colour out of the varnish.

(3) Keep the instrument from extreme tempera-

tures, and never expose it in a damp atmosphere.

(4) Keep it as free as possible from dust. If dust should get into the inside, pour in a handful or two of barley or rice through the sound holes, and shake backwards and forwards till the dust has been released.

(5) Attend to any damage, however slight, without delay : that will prevent further mischief.

(6) If the fiddle should unfortunately fall a victim to the voracious wood borer—the little demon so dreaded by possessors of old instruments—wash the affected parts with hydrogen peroxide (H_2O_2), which may be obtained at any chemist shop. This is perfectly harmless, will not injure the instrument in the least, and is the most effective remedy yet tried.

(7) Last, but not least : give your violin an occasional rest. If the instrument gets a great deal of hard use, the periods of rest must be reasonably frequent and fairly long. If it does not get a respite now and again, it will infallibly get "played out."

* * * * *

A word on the ethics of violin collecting. Some writers hold that it is positively wrong to form collections of old instruments, on the ground that it is selfish, and that it prevents the instruments getting into the hands of players. Others take an opposite view, and regard fiddle maniacs and rational collectors alike as benefactors to the fiddle world. To me this wordy warfare seems to be "Much ado about nothing." The question of the right or wrong of violin collecting is, assuredly, but a small fraction of the very large question of the right of ownership in the abstract. We can well afford to let the smaller matter rest till the larger one has been settled.

PART II

A DICTIONARY OF VIOLIN AND BOW MAKERS

A DICTIONARY OF VIOLIN AND BOW MAKERS

A

ABEL, DAVID, ———. A violin of fairly good workmanship bore a label with this name, without date or place-name. It looked like early nineteenth century work.

ABSAM, THOMAS, Wakefield: 1810–49. I have seen only two instruments of his make, both violins, one on the Stradivari and the other on the Amati model. The workmanship was of average merit. He made chiefly for Pickard, a dealer in Leeds.

ACTON, WILLIAM JOHN, London. He works at 472 Katherine Road, Forest Gate, E. He was born in Woolwich, December 12, 1848, and was educated at Rectory Place Academy, of that place. He was trained by his father, and carried on business at Woolwich till 1898, when he removed to London. He has made up to date 210 violins, 19 violas, 29 violoncellos, 21 contra-basses, and 250 bows. He has also made a large number of replicas of ancient viols and other instruments. The model of his violins approximates closely to that of the grand Strad, the material is excellent, and the workmanship and tone are good. He has latterly specialised in bows, which are excellently made of the finest wood, and well seasoned. His prices for instruments and bows are exceptionally moderate, as prices go to-day. Mr. Acton is considered a very skilful repairer, and being a diligent and conscientious man, he does not lack for work. Facsimile label :—

William John Acton
Maker
Forest-Gate London 1898

ADAMS, CATHUNE, Garmouth. From about 1775 to 1805. He made kits, violins, and violoncellos. The workmanship is fairly good, but the varnish is of poor quality. Tone small, but clear and responsive. Handwritten label.

ADDISON, WILLIAM, London. Period unknown, but probably about 1650–75. It is not certain whether he made violins, but he made viols. Label :—

> WILLIAM ADDISON,
> IN LONG ALLEY,
> OVER AGAINST MOORFIELDS, 1670.

AIRETON, EDMUND, London. From about 1730 to 1807. His best instruments are on the Amati model. The workmanship is good, and the tone of fair quality. The varnish is a spirit one, of a lustreless yellow. It has been surmised that a workman, of the same name, in the employ of Peter Wamsley in 1735, was his father.

AIRTH, WILLIAM, Edinburgh. About 1860 to 1881. He emigrated to Australia in the latter year, where he has remained, only occasionally making violins. Fair workmanship and tone.

ALDRED, ——. A maker of viols about the middle of the sixteenth century. His instruments were very celebrated and much in demand a century later. They were classed with those of Jay, Smith, and Bolles, by Mace in his *Musick's Monument*.

ALLEN, EDWARD HERON–, London. The author of the most popular and reliable work yet published on the art and craft of violin making. The book is entitled: *Violin Making: As it Was and Is*. Without a doubt this work has done great service in creating anew and fostering the love of the " King of instruments " in this country. Mr. Heron-Allen has a practical knowledge of violin making, and has made a few instruments.

ALLEN, SAMUEL, London, contemporary. Chiefly a bow maker. He was for several years in the employ of the Messrs. Hill, and was esteemed by them as a first-class workman. He started business on his account in 1891. He was born in Cornwall in 1858, and was educated for the scholastic profession.

ALLEN, W., Bristol. Nineteenth century. I have not seen any of his work.

ALLWOOD, THOMAS, Barnstaple. Nineteenth century. His work is said to be fairly good.

ANDERSON, HENRY, Edinburgh. He was born in Auchtermuchty in 1839. He has made about 120 violins on the Guarnerius model. He received a diploma and bronze medal at the Glasgow East End Exhibition, 1890, for a case of violins.

ANDERSON, JOHN, Aberdeen. Born 1829, died 1883. He is said to have made about a thousand instruments of every description. If so, the majority of them must have vanished in a mysterious manner, for I have failed to discover one.

ANDERSON, JOHN, Glasgow. He is the son of the preceding John Anderson, and was born at Aberdeen, in 1856. He has made a number of violins on a modified Strad model, and he also makes very good varnish.

ANYON, THOMAS, Manchester. An amateur who makes very beautiful instruments, and for which he is said to obtain prices ranging from thirty to fifty guineas !

ARNOT, DAVID. Born at Crieff, and worked in Glasgow, where he died in 1897. He made a large number of instruments on various models. He had a shop in Stockwell Street, Glasgow, where he carried on extensive repairing business. Handwritten label.

ASKEW, JOHN, Stanhope. Born in 1834, died in 1895. A very clever maker, who, if circumstances had but allowed, would doubtless have produced a large number of instruments of exceptional merit. Mr. Towry Piper had a high opinion of his abilities. In a monograph recently published by Mr. W. Morley Egglestone, entitled : *John Askew the Stanhope Violin Maker*, a full description is given of all the violins by Askew which are known. I have seen only one instrument by this maker ; it was the violin " christened " the *Van Gelderen*, fecit in 1884, and was on the Strad model, with golden amber varnish of a slightly reddish tint, very transparent and lustrous. The workmanship showed the master hand of a born fiddle maker, and the tone was full, responsive, and mellow. He was awarded a bronze medal at the Inventions Exhibition, 1885, and the first prize at the Jubilee Exhibition, Newcastle-on-Tyne, in 1887.

ASKEY, SAMUEL. He worked in London about 1800–40. Originally a tinman, he became a pupil of John Morrison, and worked for some time for George Corsby. The work varies in character, but the tone is usually weak and harsh. No label of his is known.

VIOLIN AND BOW MAKERS 93

ASPINALL, JAMES. He works at Bolderstone. An amateur who produces very commendable work.

ATKINS, JAMES, Cork. He carried on business as music seller for many years in Cork, but has now retired. He is over 80, but still takes an interest in the violin, and it is not long since he laid by his gouge to enjoy a well-earned rest. He has made a number of violins, mostly on the Strad model, which are of good workmanship, and have a full, clear, and responsive tone.

ATKINSON, WILLIAM. He worked for many years at Tottenham, but left there in 1911 for Paglesham, near Rochford, in Essex. He was born at Stepney, October 23, 1851. He is a professional maker, and is recognized as one of the best artists in Great Britain to-day. He received a good early education at Lukeing's Grammar School, Mile End Road, Stepney, and thus laid a solid foundation for his later reading in acoustics and the theory of violin construction. He was married October 6, 1880, to Mary Elizabeth Camper, at Bromley-by-Bow Church, and has two sons, William Camper, and John Benjamin Camper. He made his first violin in 1869, whilst serving his time as a joiner. He has completed up to date about 200 violins, and a corresponding number of violas and violoncellos. He works on two original models; the principal measurements of model No. 1 being :—

Length of body	$13\frac{15}{16}$ inches.
Width across upper bouts	$6\frac{5}{8}$,,
,, ,, middle bouts	$4\frac{3}{4}$,,
,, ,, lower bouts	$8\frac{3}{16}$,,
Depth of ribs at top	$1\frac{3}{23}$,,
,, ,, bottom	$1\frac{1}{4}$,,
Length of sound holes	$3\frac{1}{23}$,,
Distance between sound holes	$1\frac{18}{32}$,,
Elevation, from $\frac{1}{2}$	$\frac{6}{8}$,,

The measurements of model No. 2 are the same, except that it is $\frac{3}{32}''$ narrower across the bouts.

Mr. Atkinson is particularly careful and happy in the selection of his material. He is able to test acoustically his wood, and therefore to reject all that does not come up to the highest standard of excellence. He prefers maple with a figure of medium width, and pine of a " reed " rather under medium width. His outline and model are pure and graceful, and the workmanship is most carefully and delicately finished down to the smallest detail. The scroll is a notable feature of the work : I have never seen it better carved, and rarely quite as good. The width of the back from the scollop down to the first turn opposite the throat is maintained with a gradual and almost imperceptible diminution, just as in the best old Italian work, and certainly in a style which all but the very best of our old English makers failed to reach. The button is nearly semicircular, with gently toned-down edge. The margin is one-fifth wide, and the edges are full, with a very slight elevation above the level of the purfling bed. The purfling, every bit of which Mr. Atkinson makes himself, is one-sixteenth wide, the inner strip having a width which is slightly greater than that of the outer ones combined. The sound holes are of beautiful outline and cleanly cut. The varnish is an oil one, ranging in colour from pale straw to light ruby, is perfectly transparent and elastic, and soft as velvet to the touch. It is laid on in from fifteen to twenty thin coats, and dried in the open air. Few makers are so fastidious as Mr. Atkinson in the matter of varnishing. He removed from Tottenham simply because he believed the air of that place injured his varnish during the drying process. He preferred to sacrifice the prospects of a ready market for his instruments to the less remunerative but vital interests of his art. The Duke of Saxe-Coburg-Gotha was an admirer of Atkinson's violins, and gave proof more than once of the practical interest he took in the welfare of the gifted maker. The tone is remark-

VIOLIN BY ATKINSON.

To face p. 94.

ably clear and responsive : it is powerful, but withal mellow and silvery. Facsimile label :—

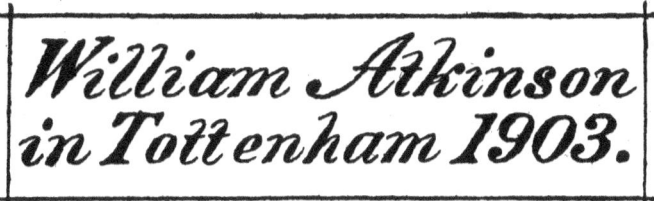

The label is varnished over with the same varnish as that used on the fiddle, to prevent the ink fading. The maker's monogram is also stamped with a cold punch on the back under the button.

B

BAINES, ——, London; about 1780. Nothing is known of him beyond the fact that he worked for Matthew Furber for some time, whose pupil he was.

BAKER, FRANCIS, London. An old viol maker. A bass viol bearing his label has been known.

BAKER, JOHN, Oxford, 1680–1720. He made viols chiefly, but towards the end of his life he is supposed to have turned his attention to violins. No one, however, appears to have seen any of these. Tom Britton had a fine viol of his make in his collection, and a four-stringed viol da gamba was among the exhibits at the South Kensington Special Exhibition, 1872, bearing the following label :—

MADE BY
JOHN BAKER,
IN OXFORD,
ANNO 1688.

BAKER, WILLIAM, Brighton. About 1820-40. He made a number of violins on a model approaching that of the grand Strad, some with grotesque figures instead of the usual scroll. Good wood and workmanship; varnish, golden brown, of good quality. Sound-holes rather weak, inclined to be "knock-kneed." Tone, powerful, but inclined to be metallic and harsh. Label printed in Roman characters:—

>   MADE BY
>   WILLIAM BAKER,
>   GEORGE STREET, BRIGHTON
>   1827.

BALLANTINE, ——, Edinburgh and Glasgow. Nothing known of him except that he worked about 1850.

BANKS, BENJAMIN, Salisbury. He was born July 14, 1727, and died February 18, 1795. He was the second son and the third child of George and Barbarah Banks, of the parish of S. Thomas, Salisbury. In Grove's *Dictionary of Music and Musicians*, Vol. V. p. 306, new edition, it is stated that Banks was not a native of Salisbury, but that " he early migrated there," from London presumably. This can hardly be correct, as it would involve the removal of the parents to London and their return to Salisbury within a short period of time. George and Barbarah Banks were living in Salisbury in 1725 and in 1730. It is not quite certain, of course, where he was born: the old registers of the parish of S. Thomas are lost, and the transcripts in the Diocesan Registry are incomplete. The following are the only entries contained in the transcripts with reference to the Banks family:—

" Baptisms :—

21 March 1722, George, son of George and Barbarah Banks.

8 July 1725, Elizabeth, daughter of George and Barbarah Banks.

15 August 1730, William, son of George and Barbarah Banks.

20 June 1732, Mary, daughter of George and Barbarah Banks."

VIOLIN AND BOW MAKERS 97

There are no transcripts for the periods 1725-1730; 1740-1778. Strange to relate, the burial entries are also missing for the year 1795. Thus were the Fates resolved to cheat the future biographers of Banks of every scrap of information relative to his birth, baptism, and burial! Banks has been styled " the English Amati," a title which he no doubt fully deserves. It ought to be recognised, however, that only in his best work does he soar above Duke, Forster, and one or two others. I have seen some examples of Duke which, in my opinion, were quite equal to the best work of Banks, except as regards varnish. Duke's varnish is mostly thin and lustreless, whereas Banks' varnish is very fine as a rule. Hart remarks that it has " all the characteristics of fine Italian varnish." The work of Banks may be arranged into two classes: (1) the Stainer copies, and (2) the Amati copies. Banks, I believe, when left to his own choice, copied no one but Amati, but his patrons and the trade frequently demanded that he should, in accordance with the taste of the times, supply Stainer copies. No one is responsible for this inference but myself, and perhaps I ought therefore to attempt to justify it. The majority of the instruments made by him for Longman and Broderip, and which bear that firm's stamp on the back, are Stainer copies, and show work which is inferior in finish to that seen in his Amati copies. Similarly, instruments made on the Stainer model for private patrons are lacking in delicate finish, and some have an inferior varnish. It is as though the good man were impatient of his model, and in a hurry to get the instrument out of the way. Patient labour, delicate finish, and luscious varnish were reserved for the model of his own choice. Only when the material happens to be poor or very plain is there any evidence of impatience in the finish of the Amati copies. I have seen a very large number of Banks' instruments, and I cannot recall a single exception to this rule. My inference is to a certain extent justified by the fact that it was long ago recognised that the Amati copies of Banks were his best.

(1) The Stainer copies, as already stated, show comparatively inferior work—inferior, that is, as compared with his best style The model is long, from $14\frac{1}{8}$ to $14\frac{3}{16}$, with a perceptible narrowing of the upper part of the instrument. The arching is somewhat exaggerated, having the ridge accentuated between the sound-holes. One is given the impression that the copyist, having grasped the general idea of the Stainer model, and thinking it sheer waste of time to attempt an extended analysis of it, and to be nice about detail, resolved that it was sufficient indulgence to existing wickedness to reproduce the said feature in any shape. I have not seen one Banks fiddle which can be said to be a faithful Stainer copy, and I do not think there is one in existence. The outline is fairly true, but the curves of the arches are treated with a degree of freedom which removes the work from the category of " copy," in the strict acceptation of the term. These are the so-called copies which have got poor Banks into ill odour with regard to some of his varnishing. His varnish, in some cases, has " killed the grain " of the tables, so Hart informs us, and I dare say he is correct enough, although I do not think there are very many instances where this has occurred. Banks was a great man, and the small faults of a great man are easily seen and usually magnified.

(2) The Amati copies. On the construction of these magnificent copies Banks concentrated his energy, heart and soul. Wood, workmanship, and varnish are almost faultless. The only part of the work to which exception can be taken at all is the scroll, which is sometimes weak, and never quite in the Amati style. It is rather singular that our old makers, even the best of them, should frequently come to grief at the same spot—the scroll. Somehow they fail to respond to the *élan* of the Italian spirit— the great thrust of art-life, which makes for freedom in every bit of carving and painting. The old English scroll is too cramped. There are, of course, some exceptions, but not many. Banks therefore failed where the majority of

 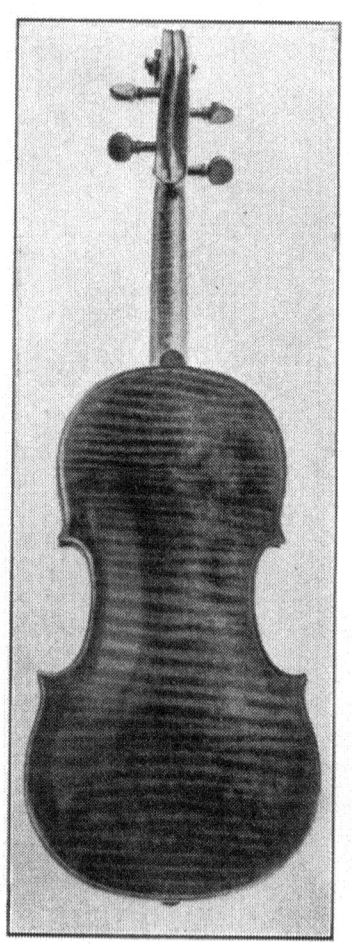

VIOLA BY BANKS.

To face p. 99.

VIOLIN AND BOW MAKERS 99

his brethren failed, both before and after him. It is difficult to account for this failure. Perhaps it is due to the limitations and idiosyncrasies of the individual artists, or to the fact that post-Renaissance Art suffered from the general exhaustion which followed the great Awakening.

But viewing the work as a whole, the Amati copies may be described as faithful and felicitous examples of the imitator's art. Benjamin had sat at Nicolà's feet, and had drank deep of his master's inspiration. It has been said that the noblest function of art, be it the art of painting, sculpture, music, or poetry, is to eliminate what is accidental, trivial, and temporary; and to set before us what is essential, profound, and eternal. How far Nicolà Amati was able to accomplish such a purpose in his art may be a debatable point, but there can be no doubt that what the master accomplished the disciple very successfully attempted.

Nor ought the work of the disciple to be disparaged simply because it is a copy. The Italians were themselves copyists. " The people of Italy," says W. S. Lilly, " are gifted, beyond all other nations, with a sense of form. It was natural that the supreme masters of the arts of design should arise among them. But in other departments of intellectual activity they are mediocre and worse. Great men have been among them. But how few! The race is lacking in veracity, in virility, and therefore in originality. Just as in the present time those who claim to represent its political ideals are mere plagiarists from the French, so in the Renaissance epoch those who claimed to represent its literary and art ideals were mere plagiarists from antiquity." (*Renaissance Types*, p. 31.)

Italian art in general, and that of sculpture and design in particular, owed more to Greek art than we are wont to think. Stringed instruments are not to be excluded from this indictment, for the construction of these is but the application of the principles of design to wood carving.

To despise the work of our old makers because it is more or less an imitation of Italian art, and to extol the art which they copied and dub it "classical," is the usual way with the flippant connoisseur, who does not trouble about the wider issues of history.

The truth is, no work of art is absolutely original, and all nations are copyists by turns. What we borrowed from the Italians in the seventeenth and eighteenth centuries, the Italians themselves borrowed from the Greeks in the fifteenth and sixteenth.

Dr. Johnson said that "No man was ever great by imitation": if that is true, then we must say that Banks was great *in spite of* imitation, for great he most certainly is. His best work, if not original and distinguished by subtle and delicate feeling like the art of the Italian masters, is yet marked by decisiveness of execution, freedom of manner, and exquisiteness of finish. His Amati copies show that he was not only a master of the principles of his art and craft, but also that he was imbued with the knowledge and feeling of form. It is many years since I began to make a careful study of the work of our old violin makers, and it has been my good fortune to come across some very fine examples of Banks' handiwork. I look upon him as summing up in himself the whole tradition of the old British School of violin making. The tradition of that school, if not remarkable for its insight, is sincerely reverent. It has been recorded of Michael Angelo when he was a pupil of Ghirlandaii that "he was wont daily to contemplate reverently the saints and angels whom Fra Angelico seemed to have drawn from heaven." And such is the figure I have drawn in my mind of Benjamin Banks, save that for saints and angels I have substituted violins, violas, and 'cellos. Reverence, I have observed elsewhere, is characteristic of all true art—reverence, that is, for the Idea, in Plato's sense of the term, and not merely for any special form under which the Idea is visualized. The inspired artist loves the form—his model—not so much for what it is as for what it represents. The best work of Banks impresses me with the feeling that the artist had set himself the task of discovering

VIOLINS BY BENJAMIN BANKS.

VIOLIN AND BOW MAKERS

the formulating principle of his master's model, and having discovered it, that he always kept it in mind.

That Banks understood something of the subtle relation between form and sound, and of the modifying effect which the curves of the violin had upon its tone, appears to be pretty evident to me. Whilst he is careful never to depart from the essential features of his model, he nevertheless frequently treats his curves in a manner that suggests either experiment or a reasoned purpose. But he is very cautious: he was seeking knowledge, if haply he might feel after it, and find it. Had he been less cautious and gone further he would have adopted the great Stradivari's model.

I quite recently saw and tried one of the most beautiful of Banks' violins which it has been my fortune to see. The wood was fine, the back being cut on the quarter, with a curl of medium and regular width, slanting at a rather acute angle in the direction of the button. The tone was clear, responsive, and beautifully sweet and mellow.

One of the best toned Banks violoncellos that I have seen was an instrument owned some years ago by a gentleman amateur of Tenby. It was of the smaller pattern, of rather plain wood, and varnished red. It was in perfect condition, and in chamber music it sang mellifluously like a velvet-throated baritone. I took dimensions of this instrument, which I append here :—

Length of body	$28\frac{1}{2}$ inches.
Width across the upper bouts	13 ,,
,, ,, middle ,, .	$10\frac{1}{4}$,,
,, ,, lower ,, .	16 ,,
Depth of ribs at lower bouts .	$4\frac{3}{4}$,,
,, ,, top ,, .	$4\frac{3}{4}$,,
Width of C's	$6\frac{1}{2}$,,
Length of sound-holes .	6 ,,
Distance between sound-holes	$3\frac{5}{8}$,,
Length of stop	26 ,,

Genuine Banks instruments are somewhat rare, considering the large numbers that he undoubtedly must have made. I have not discovered that there are more than about sixty violins, and about twice that number of violas and 'cellos, at present in existence. Of this number a good many are in poor condition, and some have been spoilt by former Goths and Vandals of the art of repairing. I dare say there are some fiddles of his about which have been "touched up" a little and have got Amati labels in them : I know one or two. Some 'cellos that I know are in the possession of wealthy people, who trouble little about their condition, and probably less about their musical merits. More than one poor instrument lies dumb and sad among the folios and quartos of a neglected library, and like

> "The harp that once through Tara's halls
> The soul of music shed,
> Now hangs as mute on Tara's walls
> As if that soul were fled."

Banks stamped his instruments in all sorts of places, below the button, under the finger-board, under the tail-piece and near the button, etc., and he used various labels, such as :—

"Made by Benjamin Banks, Catherine Street, Salisbury, 1770"; "Benjamin Banks, Musical Instrument Maker, In Catherine Street, Salisbury, 1780"; "Benjamin Banks, fecit, Salisbury"; "B. Banks, Sarum."

He was buried in the Churchyard of S. Thomas, Salisbury. His tombstone, which is near the south door, on the right-hand side, bears the following inscription :—

>   RESTORED 1863
>   ANN,
>   WIFE OF MR. BENJAMIN BANKS
>   DIED 14 SEP R
>   1785
>   AGED 57 YEARS
>   MR. BENJAMIN BANKS
>   DEPARTED THIS LIFE
>   18 TH FEB Y 1795
>   AGED 67 YEARS
>   IN MEMORY OF
>   THE MOST EMINENT ENGLISH MAKER
>   OF STRINGED MUSICAL INSTRUMENTS

BANKS, BENJAMIN, Salisbury, London, and Liverpool. He was the second son of Benjamin Banks, senior, and was born September 13, 1754, at Salisbury. He died in Haroll Street, Liverpool, where he last worked, January 22, 1820. He worked with his father for about ten years, but in 1780 he removed to 30 Sherrard Street, Golden Square, London. He did not remain there long, probably because he failed to obtain patronage. Very little of his work is known, and what there is does not reach a high standard of excellence.

BANKS, JAMES and HENRY, Salisbury and Liverpool. They continued their father's business till 1811, when they sold up and went to Liverpool, where they opened a shop in Church Street, and which they removed later to Bold Street. Both were born at Salisbury; James about 1756, and Henry about 1770. The former died on June 15, 1831, and the latter on October 16, 1830. Henry was really a pianoforte tuner, and James the violin maker. James was a very good workman, and ought to have done much better than he did. He followed his father's model, and occasionally succeeded in making a good instrument with a fine varnish. The tone is never good. He is said to have resorted to the deleterious practice of baking the wood, then very much in vogue; if so, that accounts for the inferiority of tone. The brothers left a number of unfinished instruments in the cellar of their shop, most of which were sold to music sellers.

One of their violoncellos, made in 1797, was among the exhibits in the South Kensington Museum, 1872. It was the property of Mr. C. J. Read, of Salisbury. It was said to be a well-finished instrument, with a moderately powerful tone of very good quality. Nothing that I have seen by any one of the sons could be said to possess a tone of any distinction. The father's mantle unfortunately did not fall on the shoulders of the sons.

BARNES, ROBERT, London. He was a pupil of Thomas Smith at the "Harp and Hautboy," in Piccadilly. Afterwards he became a partner with John Norris, with whom he had been a fellow-apprentice at Smith's. Norris and Barnes started business together in 1765. All the instruments which bear their label were probably made by others. Label:—

> MADE BY NORRIS AND BARNES,
> VIOLIN, VIOLONCELLO AND BOW MAKERS
> TO THEIR MAJESTIES,
> COVENTRY STREET, LONDON.

BARR, ROBERT, Belfast. A contemporary maker, mentioned by the Rev. Father Greaven in his booklet on Irish makers. I have not seen any of his work.

BARRETT, JOHN, London. Period about 1714–30. He copied Stainer, and very often exaggerated his arching. He also worked on a modified Stainer outline, which was long, narrow, much grooved, and highly arched. The workmanship is fair, but the tone is small and muffled. As a rule, he used ink-lines instead of purfling. The varnish is yellow and hungry looking, and helps to give a cheap look to the instrument. He is said to have made a better class instrument now and again.

BARTON, GEORGE, London. Period about 1780–1810. Nothing is known of him except that he worked in Elliot Court, Old Bailey, and principally for music sellers.

BARTON, JOSEPH EDWARD, Llanelly, S. Wales. Born at Moulton, in Lincolnshire, October 10, 1846. A very ingenious man who makes all his own tools, and can turn his hand to almost any kind of work. He commenced to make violins in 1869, but did not turn his attention seriously to the craft till a few years ago. He has made a number of violins on an original model, of excellent material, workmanship, and tone. Latterly he has turned his atten-

VIOLIN AND BOW MAKERS 105

tion to the Strad model, and has produced some really high-class work.

BELLINGHAM, T. J., Leeds. An amateur who has made a large number of instruments of excellent workmanship and tone. Accounts have appeared of his work in the press from time to time, in which high tributes have been paid to his ability. I saw some of his work about ten years ago, and thought it very good, but doubtless he has made great progress since then.

BELOE, W. L., Coldstream. Born in 1819, died in 1897. He made a considerable number of instruments on a model somewhat resembling that of Stradivari. The workmanship is fairly good, but the tone is of an indifferent quality.

BENNETT, ——, Cork. Nineteenth century. A short notice of him appeared in one of the Irish papers many years ago, but I know nothing more of him.

BENSON, JAMES, Stanhope. Nineteenth century. He is mentioned in Egglestone's book on John Askew.

BERTRAM, ALEXANDER, Peebleshire. Nineteenth century. He worked at Eddlestone, and made hundreds of fiddles of a very inferior quality.

BERTRAM, WILLIAM, Stobo Castle. He was gamekeeper to Sir James Montgomery, and made a number of violins which it is said he sold to the visitors to the Castle. Honeyman says his work was good.

BETTS, EDWARD, London. He was a nephew of John Betts, and a pupil of Richard Duke. The date of his birth is not known, but the date of his death is 1817. He worked on the Amati model, and produced work which for excellency of workmanship is rarely surpassed. Hart observes that " the workmanship throughout is of the most delicate description; indeed it may be said that neatness is gained at the expense of individuality in many of his works. Each part is faultless in finish, but when viewed as a whole the result is too mechanical, giving as it does the notion of its having been turned out of a mould." The observation is very just, and could not be better put. The one failing of these beautiful (i.e. beautiful to the eye) instruments is their tone, which, as far as my experience goes, does not by a long way reach the same standard of excellence as the workmanship. But it is fair to say that some judges with a much longer experience than I have affirm that the tone of a number of them is of a very bright, sweet, and resonant quality.

BETTS, JOHN, London. Known in his day all the country over as "old Betts the fiddle maker." He was born at Stamford, Lincolnshire, in 1755, died in March 1823, and was buried at St. Giles, Cripplegate. He was a pupil of Richard Duke, and the few instruments there are of his own make show that he had imbibed much of his master's teaching, but he did not continue long to make himself, he chose rather to devote his energies to the building up of a solid business, and to employ others to do the actual making. That he chose wisely goes without saying, for he would not have succeeded as he did financially if he had not left the bench for the counter. He was peculiarly fortunate in his workmen, some of the finest artists of the day having at one time or another worked for him, such as the Panormos, John Carter, his nephew Edward Betts, Bernhard Fendt, Richard Tobin, etc. Into the productions of these fine craftsmen he inserted his own trade label—a species of fiction which did not originate nor, unfortunately, cease with him. There is quite a number of instruments about bearing the label of Betts, which could not have been made by the artists just named : they are of inferior workmanship, and not a few of them have a poor tone. These were possibly the work of apprentices or "improvers." A very clever copy of the famous 'cello known as " King Andreas Amati " was made by (or shall we say *for* ?) John Betts, which was wont to be exhibited by him as " the most exact copy ever made of any of the great Cremonys." Fleming remarks that "this copy is certainly a fine production, which, besides showing paint [sic] in what was apparently the primitive abundance, also shows the wood ; a very great advantage over the original, which is rather ancient now, and dingy-looking " (*Fiddle Fancier's Guide*, p. 42).

Violoncellos with Betts' label are fairly common. There must originally have been a large number of them, considering that there has been a greater depletion in the number of 'cellos than of violins. Betts was one of the first in this country to do extensive business in old Italian instruments, and a large number of fine fiddles found their way here in his time. The story of the " Betts Strad," told by Hart and others, is well known. Writers describe the transaction as " an exceptionally lucky windfall." I am afraid it ought to be described as a smart bit of roguery. If the story is true (and I have never seen it questioned) then Betts must have allowed business considerations to get the better of his moral sense. To pay the unsuspecting owner of a Strad violin the sum of only twenty shillings for what Betts well knew to be worth at least two hundred times as much was a most discreditable thing to do. It was immoral *per se*, it was doubly so if, as was not unlikely the case, the vendor was a needy person. It is deplorable that writers treat this sort of thing as though it were nothing but an exceptionally interesting and clever bit of fiddle dealing. Clever it may be, but more clever than honest. There have been, and there doubtless still are, too many Luigio Tarisios about. If business morality in Britain were generally on a level with the " Betts Strad " transaction, the day would not be far distant when prisons and workhouses would be as numerous as schools and churches. Betts used different kinds of labels, but mostly inserted the following, with the proper date :—

<pre>
        JOHN BETTS, NO. 2 NORTH PIAZZA,
          ROYAL EXCHANGE, LONDINI, FECIT
                 JANUARY 9, 1782.
</pre>

BEVERIDGE, WILLIAM, Aberdeen. Period 1821–1893. He was a native of Craigh, Tough, Aberdeenshire, a man of strong intelligence, a keen student of nature, and an artist of refined tastes. He was for many years curator of the Free Church College Museum in Aberdeen, and made a number of violins during spare time. The workmanship of the one and only example of his art which I have seen was beautiful, and the tone very good. Label :—

W. BEVERIDGE,
FECIT,
TOUGH, 1870.

BLACKBURN, J. H., Colne. Contemporary. An amateur who has made a few instruments, but is mostly engaged in repairing.

BLAIR, JOHN, Edinburgh : 1790–1820. He worked on the Stradivari model and turned out a number of instruments of good workmanship and fair tone. Honeyman is of opinion that he was the teacher of Matthew Hardie, and there is certainly a close resemblance between their work. He used handsome wood as a rule, but his varnish was a spirit one of poor quality. No label, but he usually wrote his name across the table on the inside.

BLAIR, WILLIAM, Crathie : 1793–1884. He made many instruments on various models. The workmanship is generally good, but the tone is harsh and metallic. He baked his wood, and used a hard spirit varnish. He was a noted character, well known in the North as " The Queen's Fiddler."

BLYTH, WILLIAMSON, Edinburgh : 1821–97. A most prolific maker of wretched things shaped somewhat like a violin, but which do not possess any of the usual qualities of that instrument. It is said that he could turn out fairly decent work when he had the inclination, but he rarely got into that mood.

BOLLES, ——, London. A celebrated maker of lutes and viols in the seventeenth century. Mace tells us that he had seen a bass viol of his make which was valued at £100. That was an extraordinary price for an instrument in those days.

BONE, PHILIP J., Luton. He makes mandolines and violins.

BONN, J. EDWIN, Isle of Wight. Born at Fermoy, Ireland, in 1861. He was educated at the Ledbury Grammar School, and was intended for the medical profession, but he abandoned medicine and practised for some time as analytical and consulting chemist. Eventually he entered the violin trade, and is now established at Brading as dealer and maker. He is specially careful in the selection of his material, and the workmanship and tone are good. He uses an amber varnish of his own manufacture. Mr. Bonn has established a wide reputation in the South of England as a reliable dealer, and maker of various specialities for the violin. Facsimile label:—

```
J  EDWIN  BONN.
BRADING, ISLE OF WIGHT. 1898.
```

BOOTH, CHARLES, Burnley.

BOOTH, WILLIAM, Leeds: 1779–1858. He began to make violins in 1809, and continued to make and repair till 1856. He followed the Amati model chiefly, but I have seen one violin of his make which was somewhat after the Long Strad pattern. Fairly good work and tone. Label:—

```
WM. BOOTH,
MAKER,
LEEDS, 1820.
```

BOOTH, WILLIAM, Leeds: 1816–56. Son of the preceding maker, but a much better workman than his father. He died June 1, 1856, and was buried in Burmantofts Cemetery. He made a good number of instruments on a modified Strad model. The varnish is a golden brown colour. Tone rather small but pleasing.

BOOTH, W., Salford. I have not seen any of his work.

BOTHWELL, WILLIAM, Aberdeen: 1870–1885. He made many fiddles of no particular model and of no great merit.

BOUCHER, ——, London: 1764. Nothing known of his work.

BOWLER, ARTHUR, London. He worked ten years ago at 18 Milner Square, Islington, but I know nothing of his present whereabouts. He is a native of Thame, Oxfordshire, and a nephew on his mother's side to the late Georges Chanot. He was principal workman to Mr. J. A. Chanot for some time, but started business on his own account in 1899. He adopts the Stradivari model, and turns out instruments which for finished workmanship and good tone will compare very favourably with the best work produced to-day.

Facsimile label :—

BOYLE, W. F., Enniskerry, Co. Wicklow: Contemporary. A retired Church of England clergyman who has made violins *en amateur* for many years. He was born at Enniskerry in 1860, and served there as Curate for some years after he was ordained. He has a wide knowledge of the violin and its literature, and has the necessary mechanical skill to apply that knowledge to the construction of the instrument. He is specially interested in the varnish problem. He makes beautiful instruments, which have a large and telling tone.

BRECKINBRIDGE, JOHN, Glasgow : 1790–1840. He made several good violins on the Amati model. The wood is of excellent quality and beautifully figured. Varnish pale brown or yellow. The tone is clear and sweet. Label handwritten :—

> JOHN BRECKINBRIDGE
> MAKER,
> PARKHEAD, 1830.

BRIGGS, JOHN WILLIAM, Glasgow. A contemporary professional maker and repairer. He was born at Wakefield in 1855, and was a pupil of William Tarr, of Manchester. He has made a large number of violins, violas, and violoncellos, on various models, but mostly on an original model, which has a nice outline and a moderately pronounced arching. The wood is carefully selected and well seasoned. He has made several facsimile copies of some of the more notable Stradivari and Guarneri violins, the workmanship being faultlessly finished, and the tone very fine indeed. The construction of these beautiful copies must have cost the maker a great deal in time, energy, and patience. Mr. Briggs had the largest exhibit of instruments at the Glasgow Exhibition, and in many respects the best. The wood of the backs and ribs of the instruments shown was exhibited as violin timber at the Paris Exhibition of 1880, and also at Vienna in 1890, where it was awarded a gold medal. The wood of the tables was three hundred years old, and had been obtained from an old church in Warsaw, Poland. Facsimile label :—

James W Briggs,
Glasgow. 1889.

Mr. Briggs, I believe, has acquired sole proprietary rights in Whitelaw's celebrated amber varnish, and has bought the whole of the large stock left at the inventor's death.

BRISCOE, D., Channel Islands. Nineteenth century. His work is said to be very good.

BROAD, J. M., Almondsbury, Glos. A gentleman amateur who has devoted considerable time and thought to the study of violin construction, and especially to the mystery of the old Italian varnish. He has made one or two violins on an original model, more by way of testing certain theories than as a serious attempt at violin making. His sound knowledge of theoretical and practical chemistry has enabled him to make a varnish which for pâte, lustre, and transparency it is not possible to excel. Unfortunately it is not for sale.

BROOKFIELD, EDWARD & SON, Southport : 1872–1898. They made violins and bows, and repaired very extensively. The work of both father and son is said to be very good, but I cannot say, as I have not seen any of it.

BROWN, ——, Huddersfield : about 1870.

BROWN, ALEXANDER, Glasgow : 1855–60. Stradivari model. Good work and tone, it is said, but I cannot say. Handwritten label.

BROWN, ANTHONY, London and Australia : 1850–75. Pupil of John Morrison. He did not make many violins, but he was celebrated for his guitars, of which he made a large number both in this country and in Australia. He worked in Rosamond Street, Clerkenwell.

BROWN, JAMES, Spitalfields : 1755–1834. Started violin making in 1804, under Thomas Kennedy. Ordinary work ; tone fairly good for orchestral purposes.

VIOLIN AND BOW MAKERS

BROWN, JAMES, Norton Folgate : 1786–1860. Son and pupil of the previous James Brown. He made very many bows, and also instruments after his father's death. Average work.

BROWN, JAMES, London : 1813–34. Son and pupil of the preceding. He made only a few instruments.

BROWNE, JOHN, London : 1730–45. He worked at the sign of the "Black Lion" in Cornhill. He copied Stainer and Amati, and turned out a great deal of work of fairly good workmanship, but of poor tone.

BRUCE, ARTHUR, Belfast. A present day maker of considerable ability and skill. A violin made by him on an original model, designed by the Rev. Father Greaven, is of good workmanship, and has a lovely tone.

BRUTON, JAMES, Thornbury, Glos. : 1800–62. He is mentioned in a booklet by Mr. J. Spencer Palmer, of Thonrbury, but I have failed to trace any of his instruments.

BUCKMAN, GEORGE HATTON, Dover. He was born in Snargate Street, Dover, October 23, 1845, and now lives at Kearsney, near Dover. He worked as a professional maker for many years, but has now retired. He was not at any time financially dependent on his profession, so that he was able to devote ample time and abundant care to the construction of his instruments. He has made a large number of violins on the Strad and Joseph models. Some of the Guarneri copies have been made after a fine Joseph which was owned by C. M. Gann, Esq., of Canterbury : these are all made of exceptionally fine wood, and the workmanship is accurate and beautifully finished down to the smallest detail. The Strad copies are of rather full dimensions, the principal measurements being $14\frac{1}{4}$, $6\frac{5}{8}$, and $8\frac{3}{4}$. The height of the ribs in one specimen was $1\frac{1}{4}$, diminishing to $1\frac{3}{16}$, but as a rule it is $1\frac{1}{4}$ throughout. I do not know any modern maker who has copied Joseph Guarnerius with greater skill, and I know of only two or three who have copied him with equal skill. The scroll and the sound-holes are generally the trouble. Somehow our copyists (although they reproduce the outline of the *f*'s correctly enough) fail to produce the same *mental* effect : there is something about the Gothic quaintness of the great master which defies imitation. That something is not the mere type, it is the archetype—the ideal which struggles for expression in matter and form. But Mr. Buckman has come as near the real thing as it is possible, I believe, for a copyist to come. Very many of his Strad copies have the back cut whole, with the curl running at an angle of about forty-five degrees to the longitudinal axis of the instrument, giving a very pretty effect when viewed in certain lights.

Fleming considered that the work of this artist was to be classified with the best that is produced in the British Isles to-day, and with this opinion all must agree who have seen and tried it. Mr. Buckman may not be much known to the public, but that is because he eschews publicity, preferring, like many an artist before him, "To have one fiddle friend in his retreat, whom he may whisper—Solitude is sweet." Label :—

GEO. H. BUCKMAN,
DOVER, *1899.*

BULLBRIDGE, JOSEPH MATHER. I do not know his period or his work, but instruments of his are occasionally advertised for sale in the music papers.

BYROM, GEORGE, Liverpool. He works at 10 Cases Street, opposite the Central Station, as a professional maker and repairer, and has been in the trade twenty-eight years.

VIOLIN AND BOW MAKERS 115

There is another Byrom, a brother, also established somewhere in Liverpool as a professional maker. I regret I know nothing of the work of either. They are said to be clever craftsmen, but whose time is mostly occupied in repairing.

C

CAHUSAC, ——. London: about 1780–1810. Fleming, in an article in "The Bazaar" gives his period as 1780–88, but instruments of his are known dated 1796 and 1799. Little or nothing is known of him personally, except that he was for some little time associated with the sons of Benjamin Banks. There is little doubt in my mind now that the work of Cahusac has been much undervalued. Fleming in the article referred to describes it as "a poor class of work, thinly wooded, with black varnish, somewhat scarce, but of little or no value." This writer is so just and honest a critic that I can but conclude that he had not seen any of the better class instruments made by Cahusac. A violin dated 1796 owned by Mr. R. P. Cardell, of Birkdale, Southport, was made of fine wood, and covered with a dark amber varnish which is perfectly transparent, the workmanship being faultless, and the tone equal, sonorous, and responsive. I have seen three other violins of his make, which were of fine workmanship and tone. Messrs. George Withers and Sons have in their collection a nice example of his work. It is a pity that these old makers should be hastily judged on insufficient evidence. Label printed:—

CAHUSAC
NO. 196
OPPOSITE ST. CLEMENT'S CHURCH,
STRAND
17 LONDON 96

CAIRNS, P., Portobello, Edinburgh. He makes violins on what he calls "the acute angle principle." I saw two of

BRITISH VIOLIN MAKERS

these instruments recently at a music shop in Nicolson Street, Edinburgh. The workmanship was beautiful, but I cannot say what the tone was like.

CAKIN, FRANCIS, Edinburgh.

CALOW, F. W., Nottingham. Son and pupil of the late William Calow. He is established in business at Sussex Street, as a professional maker and repairer. He makes double basses principally, which are on the viol model, with Guarnerian sound-holes. He stamps his name on the back below the button.

CALOW, WILLIAM, Nottingham: 1847–1910. He was born at Tansley, near Matlock, Derbyshire, and was the son of Thomas Calow, who also made a few instruments. He made violins, violas, and a large number of double basses, gaining a considerable reputation for his larger instruments. One double bass which I saw was well made, and had an immense volume of tone of good quality. He used oil varnishes mostly, but he occasionally used a thin spirit varnish for his double basses; colours: orange, and nut-brown. He was considered a first-class repairer. Facsimile label :—

No. 10
Made by
W. Calow
Nottingham
1880

CANNON, JAMES, Dumfries. An amateur who has made several nice instruments on the Strad model. He uses Whitelaw's varnish. Label handwritten.

CARR, JOHN, Falkirk. He was born at Berwick-on-Tweed, in 1839. He had a music shop in Falkirk, where he also had a good connection as a teacher of the violin. He was a pupil of Robert Harvie and James Thompson, and made about seventy instruments.

CARROLL, JAMES & SON, Manchester. I am not sure whether the father is living and working, but father and son were working some years ago in Great Jackson Street, Hulme, and had made up to that time about five hundred instruments of one sort and another. I have seen only two or three violins bearing their label, but I have seen several of their make bearing forged labels of third-rate old Italian makers. Who inserted the spurious labels into these fiddles I cannot say. The workmanship of the instruments I have seen was good, and the tone large and responsive.
Facsimile label :—

James Carroll, Maker,
   Manchester, Anno 1855

CARTER, JOHN, London : 1780–90. He worked mostly for John Betts, and only occasionally on his own account. He was an excellent maker, and helped considerably to swell the fame of Betts. I have seen one violin of his make, on the Amati model, which had a moderately powerful but beautifully sweet and responsive tone. The varnish is usually of a golden brown tint, thinly laid on. Label :—

> J. CARTER,
> VIOLIN, TENOR, AND BASS MAKER,
> WYCH STREET, DRURY LANE,
> LONDON, 1785.

CARTWRIGHT, W. J., Yeadon, Leeds.

CARY, ALPHONSE, London.

CHALLONER, THOMAS, London. Some time in the eighteenth century.

CHANNON, FREDERICK WILLIAM, London. He works at present at 54 Wells Street, Oxford Street, as a professional maker and repairer, but up to about two years ago he lived in Plymouth, where he had been established for many years as a professional maker. He was born at Totnes, in 1862, and apprenticed in early life as a cabinet maker. He made such rapid progress at his trade that at the age of twenty-one he became foreman of one of the largest cabinet shops in Devonport, with about thirty men and apprentices under his charge. At the age of twenty-five he commenced business on his own account, and he was appointed at the same time technical instructor in carving and carpentry to a local institution.

He commenced to make violins in 1887, first as a hobby, and during spare time : in a year or two he resolved to give up all other work and devote the whole of his time and energy to the art of constructing and repairing violins. That he decided wisely is abundantly proved by the very beautiful work he now produces. He is in the foremost rank of present day makers, and it is a pity that so much of his time is taken up with repairs.

Repairing is, of course, of great importance, demanding intelligence and skill, but it is a loss that craftsmen with a

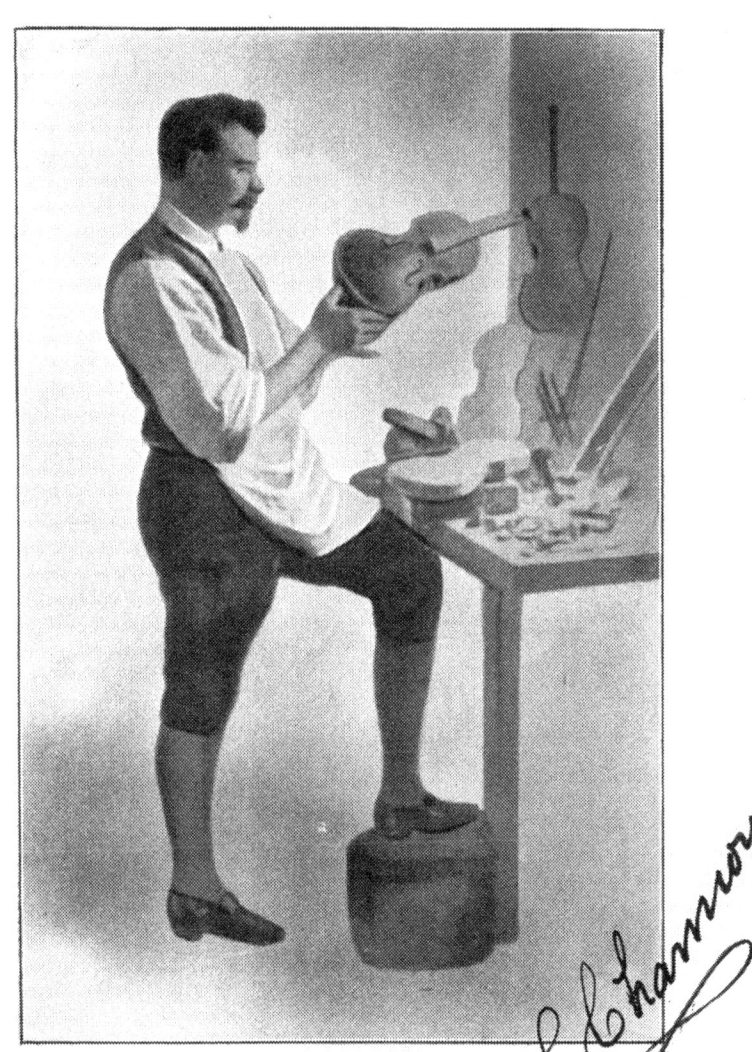

F. W. CHANNON.

VIOLIN AND BOW MAKERS

special gift for designing and making have to devote the best energy of their life to it.

In his earlier work Mr. Channon adhered strictly to the grand Strad model, but latterly he has worked on a model of his own, the principal measurements of which are $13\frac{63}{64}$, $6\frac{36}{64}$, $4\frac{16}{64}$, $8\frac{10}{64}$ (the three last fractions may, of course, be expressed in 32nds.). The sound-holes are 3 inches, and the C's $3\frac{3}{16}$ inch long. The thickness of the back is $\frac{3}{16}$ diminishing to $\frac{1}{8}$, and the table is $\frac{1}{8}$ all over. The outline of this model is simple and graceful, the curves of the C's as they approach the corners being not quite so pronounced as in the Strad model, and the linear difference in the width across the upper and lower bouts is not so great as in the grand Strad. Viewed as a whole the outline is well balanced, and the curves easy and proportionate. The scroll and sound-holes are of Stradivarian character, beautifully designed and placed, and the corners are full without being obtrusive. There is a sense of gentle restraint about the model that is very pleasing to the trained eye. Violin makers, especially beginners, frequently break out into original models, and where the hand and the eye have not been severely trained, there is little control over the curves. To produce a perfect model (using the word *model* here to include outline and arching) due regard must be paid to five cardinal principles: unity, repose, symmetry, purity, moderation. Only he who is able to combine these five principles and to express them in forms can design a perfect violin model. Symmetry and moderation are often lacking in the corners of modern fiddles. There was much solidity and withal moderation and repose in the quaint and quiet corners of old Maggini. When Stradivari waked those corners out of their slumber in his own work, he did all that pure art dare do. Many of his imitators have added two pairs of miniature wings to their instruments, and the result is grotesque.

Mr. Channon has not only succeeded in producing a beautiful model: he also produces a fine tone. After all, the tone is the chief thing, and all the skill and care lavished on the workmanship would be energy wasted if the tone did not come out rightly. Artists who use his instruments say that the tone is rich and mellow, easy to get, and equal on all the strings. The following facsimile is that of the label used by the maker while working in Plymouth; the word "London" being substituted for "Plymouth" in the one now used.

CHANOT, G. A., Manchester. This artist has been long established as a professional maker and repairer in Manchester, and is justly esteemed for his integrity and affability in business and for his ability as a craftsman. The Chanots are Anglo-French, but have been so long settled in this country as to become regarded as almost pure-bred Britons. Their better class work is of a high order (I am speaking of the Chanots generally), and 1 have seen violins made by Georges Chanot ("Old" Chanot, as he was familiarly called) of London, that could with truth be described as modern "classics." I have also seen instruments with the label of one or other of the Chanots in them which were hardly of more than average merit. The disparity is due to the varying ability and experience of the workmen who made them, for they were not all made by the Chanots themselves. All the principal firms of the country employ workmen to make instruments for them, and they put their trade labels in these instruments. This may not be a practice which has much in it to recommend it, but such are the business methods of to-day, and it availeth naught to quarrel with them.

G. A. CHANOT.

To face p. 120.

The Chanots have a lineage reaching back to the middle of the eighteenth century, probably earlier, for there was one of that name, an instrument maker, living and working in Vignon, Provence, towards the end of the seventeenth century, who may not unreasonably be supposed to have some connection with the Chanots of Mirecourt of a generation or two later. François Chanot, who was born at Mirecourt in 1788, was the first to experiment scientifically with the view of learning something of the acoustics of the violin, and he it was that paved the way for the researches of Dr. Felix Savart. Georges Chanot, of Paris, grandfather of the present Chanot of Manchester, and of London, was a maker, expert, and dealer of European repute. His instruments are rising in value annually, and will probably reach a considerable figure in the future. Obviously, the Chanot tradition is of some importance to the student of violin literature, and to neglect it is to leave out one of the most fascinating chapters in the history of violin progress in this country. For, be it remembered, the Chanots have exerted an influence upon other violin makers of their time to an extent which is not, perhaps, realized by the rising generation of professional and amateur makers. To begin with, they were the trainers of quite a number of men who became first-class artists, but of more importance still is the indirect yet wider influence they wielded through their work. For a considerable slice of the second half of last century, Georges Chanot was almost the only really first-class and properly trained violin maker in this country. William Elsworth Hill and George Hart (senior) made few new instruments, and there were only the Withers (father and sons) and some two or three besides. Chanot came to London to work under Maucotel in 1851, full of enthusiasm for his art ; in 1858 he started business on his own account, and it was not long before he was recognized as *facile princeps* of the small band of fiddle makers in this country. For many years before he became a dealer of *some* importance he was a maker of really *great* importance. His new fiddles were bought, played upon, and appreciated. I do not think I am over-estimating his influence when I say it was great. Whether his abilities were of such high order as to stamp him as a genius may very well be questioned, but he was industrious, and it has been well said that : " If you have great talents, industry will improve them ; if you have but moderate abilities, industry will supply their deficiency. Nothing is denied to well-directed labour : nothing is to be obtained without it." (Sir Joshua Rynolds, *Discourse on Art.*)

The revival of violin making in England dates from about the time when Chanot (*père*) had reached his high water mark. In 1882 Mr. Heron-Allen became his pupil, and shortly after gave to the readers of *Amateur Work Illustrated* that brilliant series of articles which has been reproduced in book form under the title of *Violin Making : As it Was and Is.* Various influences gathered into one force at this juncture, and these articles (which embodied the Chanot tradition) acting like a telegraph wire conducted them in the right direction, so that the art was " fanned into a flame out of the embers of its dead self."

This is a most interesting period in the history of violin making in Britain. All real revivals are interesting, whether in art, literature, or religion. We have watched the flowers of winter wither and die, but behold ! out of their mould comes the crop of another spring, flower by flower at first—a laughing primrose or a timid violet—by-and-by a joyous chorus of purple heather : that is what we see in the English violin world in the eighties of last century, and the fiddle fancier looks back admiringly upon it.

A large number of instruments have been turned out by the Manchester firm. Mr. Chanot may not be the actual maker of all of them, because some years ago he employed several skilful craftsmen, but all the work reaches a high standard of excellence. Some of the violins are quite equal to the best work of " Old " Chanot. I tried one last year which had been made about ten years ago, and it had a

GEORGES CHANOT,
("Old" Chanot.)

VIOLIN AND BOW MAKERS

large, clear, and mellow tone, with an unmistakable Italian ring about it. The instrument was on the grand Strad model, varnished golden red.

Another member of the family has a business in London, but I have not seen any of his work. Facsimile label :—

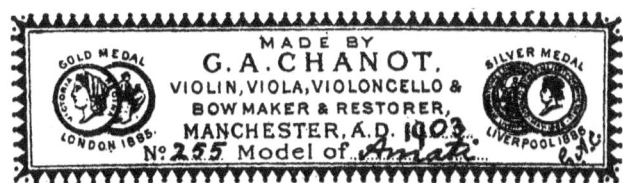

CHRISTIE, JAMES, Dundee. Born at Arbroath in 1857. He has made a good number of violins on the models of Stradivari and Guarneri, considerably modified according to his own ideas. The workmanship is good, and the tone large and bright.

CHRISTIE, JOHN, Kincardine-on-Forth. He died about 1859. He made a large number of instruments on the Amati and some on the Strad models. The workmanship and tone are very good. His work would be excellent if he had used oil varnish.

CLARK, JAMES, London: 1770-95. A pupil of Matthew Furber. He worked in Turmill Street, Clerkenwell. Average work and tone.

COLE, JAMES, Manchester: nineteenth century. He was a pupil of William Tarr, and worked afterwards with George Craske. I have not seen any of his work and cannot say anything about it, but old Tarr did not entertain a very high opinion of his abilities. He used a label in his early work, but for his later work he used a punch stamp.

COLE, THOMAS, London: 1670-90. He made lutes and viols chiefly, and it is not certain that he made any violins. One or two tenors have been seen.

COLLIER AND DAVIES, London : about 1770–80.

COLLIER, SAMUEL, London : 1740–60. He worked at " Corelli's Head," London Bridge. I have seen one violin of his make, on the Stainer model, varnished dark yellow, with a small, husky tone.

COLLIER, THOMAS, London : about 1775. Perhaps the partner of Davies (Collier and Davies), or a son.

COLLINS, WILLIAM HENRY, London. He was born in the parish of Marylebone in 1860, and he works (or did work ten years ago) at 21 Poland Street, W. He has made a good number of violins on the Strad and Guarneri models, and he also repairs a good deal, but I am not aware whether he has adopted violin making and repairing as a profession. The work is beautifully finished throughout, and the tone is of a very good quality. Facsimile label :-

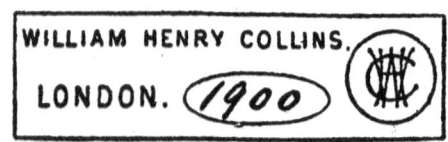

COLVILLE, DAVID, Cupar : 1845–85. He made many instruments on the models of Amati and Stradivari. I saw and tried one of his Amati copies years ago : it was well made, of beautifully figured wood, and had a pure and sweet tone. He was a born artist, and had he led a less chequered career would have produced still better work. He visited New Zealand, Australia, Canada by turns, and never settled down in one place or at one thing long. No label, but written in pencil across the back :—

DAVID COLVILLE,
1857.

COLVIN, GAVIN, Sunderland : 1841–1910. A native of Lerwick, Shetland. He made a number of violins on various models.

CONNOR, ANTHONY, Newcastle. Now living I believe.

CONWAY, WILLIAM, London : 1740-50.

COOPER, HUGH WILLIAM, Glasgow. Born 1848, and as far as I know, is still living. Up to ten years ago he had made fifty violins, or thereabouts—some on the Strad and some on the Joseph model. The later ones were of excellent workmanship and tone. Facsimile label :—

> HUGH W. COOPER,
> Maker,
> 75, DUMAS STREET,
> GLASGOW.

CORSBY, ——, Northampton : 1780. Double-basses principally.

CORSBY, GEORGE, London : 1785-1800. Principally a dealer, but made a few violins on the Amati model, of average merit. Probably a brother of the Corsby of Northampton.

CRAIG, JOHN, Edinburgh. Born at Myreside, Forfarshire, in 1860, and is probably still living and working. He is a joiner by trade, and only makes violins during spare time, but his work is excellent. The model is original and shows that the designer is gifted with the artistic instinct. It is a pity he does not take up the craft professionally. He produces a good tone, and his work will improve with age and good use. Facsimile label :—

> JOHN CRAIG,
> MAKER,
> EDINBURGH.
> A.D.......19.0.0

CRAMOND, CHARLES, Aberdeen : 1800–33. A prolific maker, much of whose work is of considerable merit. He worked on an original model, the outline of which differs only slightly from that of Amati, but which has the arching considerably increased. The wood is usually of good quality, but it is often of a plain figure. The varnish is a spirit one ; colour, yellow to dark brown. The tone is rather small, but clear, sweet, and responsive. He left many of his instruments too thin in wood, and these have not improved with age and use. Label printed :—

> CHAS. CRAMOND,
> MAKER,
> ABERDEEN, 1815.

CRASKE, GEORGE, Bath, Birmingham, Stockport, and elsewhere: about 1791–1889. Craske's father is supposed to have been of foreign extraction, if he was not actually a foreigner. Out of the three thousand odd instruments that he is said to have made, I have seen about a score that I knew for certain to be his work. Doubtless I have seen a good many more which were made by him, but which are now ascribed to somebody else. The material of very many of his instruments is beautiful, and the workmanship fine, but the tone is often disappointing. He was a pupil of " Old " Forster, and he made many instruments for Clementi, and for Dodd, the bow maker. Besides copying Guarnerius—his usual model—he made several clever copies of Amati and Stradivari, from templets and measurements taken from a Strad and an Amati owned by Sir Patrick Blake, of Langlam Hall, Suffolk. Whilst in Birmingham, he is said to have been once engaged by Paganini to do some repairs to his violin.

Craske worked in Salford, amongst other places, for about twenty years, and lived the life of a recluse during the whole of that period, allowing no one to enter his workshop except Mr. George Crompton, his friend, who became his successor in business. He lived retired at Bath for many years before he died, in affluent circumstances. He died in November, 1889, at the advanced age of ninety-eight. He was a man of striking appearance and unique personality. " His head was exactly the same shape and measure as Shakespeare's " —so writes Mr. George Crompton. How he knew I cannot say.

CROSS, NATHANIEL, London: 1700-51. Some suppose that he was a pupil of Stainer, but that is mere conjecture. His instruments, although made on the Stainer model, are sufficient proof, one would think, that he never received a day's training in the great *atelier* at Absam. From 1700 to 1720 (before he entered into partnership with Barak Norman) they are rather plain and tasteless, large and highly arched, with short, blunt corners, and an exaggerated fluting round the edge, forming the purfling bed. From 1720 on the work improves very much, greater attention being paid to accuracy of detail, and both outline and arching being considerably modified, but he never got rid of the acute fluting round the edge. He cut some excellent scrolls. He used a soft, elastic varnish, varying in colour from light yellow to light brown. The tone although frequently small is usually firm, clear, and mellow. He marked his instruments on the back inside with his initials and a ✠ above. After he entered into partnership with Norman the label was:

BARAK NORMAN AND NATHANIEL CROSS,
AT THE BASS VIOL IN ST. PAUL'S CHURCH YARD,
LONDON, FECIT 172—.

CROSTON, J., Leigh, Lancashire. An amateur maker now living.

CROWTHER, JOHN, London: 1750-1810. He worked in Haughton Street, Clare Market, and occasionally for John Kennedy. Stainer and Amati models. Work of average merit.

CUMMING, ANDREW, Portpatrick. Poor work.

CUTHBERT, ——, London: seventeenth century. He was chiefly a maker of viols, and is not supposed to have made many violins. I have never seen any of his work.

CUTHBERT, JAMES, Hownam, N.B. A schoolmaster, now living, who has made a few instruments *en amateur*.

CUTTER, EDWIN, East Compton, near Bristol. Born at Kingsland, Herefordshire, in 1866. He is a wheelwright by trade, but has made a considerable number of violins during spare time. The outline is original, a little bold and squarish in appearance. He uses native sycamore for the back and ribs. The workmanship is very good, and the tone is powerful. With a better model and material he would doubtless produce very good work.

D

DALGARNO, THOMAS, Aberdeen: 1860–70. Workmanship and tone fairly good. He left the majority of his instruments thin in the wood, and the tone will not therefore continue to improve.

DALTON, B., Leeds. I know nothing of him.

DARBEY, GEORGE, Bristol. He lives at Cremona House, Perry Road, where he has a music warehouse, and a large, well-appointed *atelier*. He is one of the best professional makers and repairers in Great Britain at the present time. He was born at Taunton, in 1849, and came to Bristol in early life with his father, who established a cabinet factory there. As soon as he had completed his education, he was put to the bench, and trained as a wood carver and cabinet maker—a splendid foundation for the career he was to adopt later, when left to the exercise of his own free will. He has been established in Bristol as a maker and repairer of

GEORGE DARBEY.

To face p. 128.

VIOLIN AND BOW MAKERS 129

stringed instruments and bows for nearly forty years, and his long, and in many respects unique experience, joined to his extraordinary skill as a craftsman, has won for him a reputation which extends as far as Britain itself, and probably further. Speaking of his skill as a repairer Fleming says: " there is probably no man in this country with a more complete knowledge or a higher reputation in the art of restoring old instruments. Some of his work that I have seen I do not hesitate to place in line with the finest efforts of modern French artists—and that is saying not a little " (*Vide* " The Bazaar, The Exchange and Mart," May 25: 1904).

Judging by what I have seen of Mr. Darbey's work, I thoroughly concur with this verdict. I regret that my acquaintance with this maker's new work is so limited that it does not enable me to form a proper estimate of his abilities and of the qualities of his instruments. I cannot therefore do better than again to quote from Fleming, who says: " Nothing that has passed through my hands for many years approaches this specimen [one of Darbey's violins] in regard to beauty of workmanship or quality of tone. In both respects it is difficult to speak too highly of it. The purity and responsiveness of the tone are altogether remarkable. With the lightest touch it leaves the instrument as freely as with a full stroke, and as that may be called the ideal of tone production no more need be said on that point."

Mr. Darbey has made a few instruments on the models of Amati, Gagliano, and Guarneri, but his favourite model is the grand Strad, and to this he has strictly adhered for many years.

He has made a large number of bows. Of these I have seen not a few, and need only say that I consider them superb. In this branch of his art, Mr. Darbey has succeeded in giving unqualified satisfaction to such players as Sarasate and Wilhelmj. He employs no assistance of any kind: he has no pupils and no workmen. All the work, including the making of the purfling, the fittings for the bows, etc., is made by his own hands, so that instrument and bow alike, from start to finish, are the handiwork of George Darbey.

He uses a beautiful oil varnish of his own make, the colour of which is mostly orange red. Facsimile label :—

George Darbey, Cremona House, Bristol. Anno 1902 (GD)

DAVIDSON, KAY, Huntly: 1860–75. Rather poor work, with a loud, harsh tone.

DAVIDSON, PETER, Forres: 1834–86. Born at Speyside, and went to the United States some years ago, He was only an amateur, but made a number of very fair instruments. He wrote " The Violin : Its Construction Theoretically and Practically Treated," a very interesting but wholly unreliable work. He was an excise officer, and a bookworm.

DAVIDSON, WILLIAM, Edinburgh : 1827–1902. Made a large number of instruments of fairly good workmanship and tone.

DAVIS, RICHARD, London : 1775–1836. He was for some time in the employ of Norris & Barnes, and in 1816, at the death of Norris, he succeeded to the business. He did not make many instruments himself, but employed others to work for him. The few instruments he made are not on any particular model, are indifferently made, and have a rather loud, piercing tone. He carried on a very considerable trade in old instruments. He retired towards the end of his life, leaving the business to William Davis. He died at Bussage in 1836, and was buried in Bisley Churchyard.

DAVIS, WILLIAM, London : about 1790-1850. Cousin to the preceding Richard Davis, and his successor in business. He did not make many instruments, but employed Charles Maucotel and others to work for him. He sold his business in 1846 to Edward Withers, and retired to Bussage.

DAY, JOHN, London : eighteenth century. He copied old Italian instruments closely, and sometimes turned out very good work.

DEARLOVE, MARK, Leeds : 1810-20. He made a few copies of a Stradivari violin which came into his possession.

DEARLOVE, MARK WILLIAM, & CHARLES FRYER, Leeds : 1828-65. Dearlove employed others to work for him, such as Gough, Absam, Fryer, etc. Fryer he eventually took into partnership, and the instruments which have their joint label are fairly well made, on various models, but mostly on that of Stradivari. Label printed :—

> DEARLOVE AND FRYER,
> MUSICAL INSTRUMENT MANUFACTURERS,
> BOAR LANE, LEEDS, 1836.

DEIGHTON, J. R., Newcastle-on-Tyne. Living and working now, I believe, but I am not certain, and I know nothing of his work.

DELANY, JOHN, Dublin : 1795-1810. He followed the Amati model, and was very successful in producing a good tone. I saw one of his violins many years ago in Waterford, which was well made, rather small, and had a clear and sweet tone. The back was of plain wood, cut on the slab. It had rather wide sound-holes, and corners that were a trifle blunt. There is a fine example of his work in the National Museum of Science and Art, Dublin. The Rev. Father Greaven, who knows more about Irish violin makers than anybody else, says that he " was a fine maker and a very erratic genius. He was by trade a cabinet maker, and showed the true artist in wood work." The Republican spirit was strong in Delaney, as in most Irishmen at that time, and he gave expression to it in his label, which ran :—

MADE BY JOHN DELANY,
IN ORDER TO PERPETUATE HIS MEMORY IN FUTURE AGES.
DUBLIN, 1808.
LIBERTY TO ALL THE WORLD, BLACK AND WHITE.

DENNIS, JESSE, London : 1795–1860. Pupil of John Crowther, and for some time workman to Matthew Furber. Very few instruments of his are known, but Mr. P. Pettitt, musical instrument dealer, of Iden, Sussex, reports that he has seen a well-made violoncello of his make.

DEVEREUX, JOHN, Melbourne : nineteenth century. Before he emigrated he worked for some time with B. Simon Fendt.

DEVONEY, FRANK, Blackpool and Canada. He made many instruments before he emigrated, which were on an original model, strongly built but rather roughly made. They were covered with a reddish amber oil varnish of his own make. They have a powerful but rather harsh tone.

DEWARS, WILLIAM, Brechin, N.B., but now of Minneapolis. He is a native of Brechin, and was born in 1878. The instruments he made before he emigrated were very promising.

DICKENSON, EDWARD, London : 1750–90. He worked at the " Harp and Crown," in the Strand. Inferior work on the Stainer model.

DICKESON, JOHN, London and Cambridge : 1750–80. An instrument of his make, on the Amati model, was owned by a Mr. Jenner, of Bath, a few years ago. It had very pretty wood, light brown varnish, and a small, silvery tone. Label :—

JOHN DICKESON,
FECIT IN CAMBRIDGE, 1778.

VIOLIN AND BOW MAKERS 133

DICKIE, WILLIAM, Rotherham. He died about twelve or fifteen years ago. I have not seen any of his instruments, but the late Mr. James Smith, of Ashcroft House, Wentworth, near Rotherham, formerly well-known in musical circles, thought rather highly of them, and said they have a good tone.

DICKSON, GEORGE, Edinburgh. A doctor, a clever amateur, and the maker of a beautiful amber oil varnish. He died about seven years ago, at an advanced age.

DICKSON, JOHN, London: 1725–60. Possibly the same as the John Dickeson noticed above.

DITTON, ——, London: about 1700. Mention is made of a violin by him in the list of musical instruments in the collection of Tom Britton.

DODD, EDWARD, Sheffield and London: 1705–1810. He died in London at the advanced age of 105. He lived in Salisbury Court, Fleet Street, and was buried in St. Bride's Churchyard. He considerably improved the form of violin bows.

DODD, JOHN, London: 1752–1839. He was born in Stirling; he died in Richmond workhouse, and was buried at Kew. He has been styled the English " Tourte," and much of his work justifies the application of that title to him. But a great deal of his work, it must be admitted, is not for a moment to be classed with the work of the great François Tourte. Had he lived a more virtuous life he probably would have made bows of more uniform excellence. Many of his bows were made in haste, and sold for a few shillings, to replenish an empty larder and to quench a great thirst. His frequent bacchanalia brought many troubles on his own head, and much annoyance to those who interested themselves on his behalf. He came nigh unto utter destitution many a time, and had it not been for the kindness of Dr. Sellé and Mr. Richard Platt, of Richmond, he would have prematurely ended his days on the roadside. He ended them in the workhouse as it was.

He was a pupil of his father, the Edward Dodd previously noticed, and he improved so much upon the work of his father, and upon the work of everybody else in England in those days, that his bows have maintained an undiminished reputation down to the present time. His method of cutting his bows was primitive, and it has not been adopted by any great bow maker since his time. He cut the bow in a curve out of a block, and thus dispensed with the usual plan of cutting it straight and bending by heat. In his case, a roundabout way became a shorter cut. I have seen a fair number of Dodd bows, and I am convinced that all I have seen were cut in this manner.

Dodd's name was stamped on all sorts of bows—some of them wretched enough—in the middle of last century, and his fame has suffered much in consequence. But his work has suffered more than his fame, for there are hundreds of mongrel " Dodds " about, some with genuine heels, others with genuine heads, and not a few patched up in divers ways. The owner of a genuine Dodd bow, of anything like full length, made in his best style, and in good preservation, has a treasure he can well be proud of.

DODD, EDWARD & THOMAS, London : 1830–43. Pupils of Bernhard Fendt. Thomas died at an early age, and Edward was accidentally drowned, in 1843.

DODD, THOMAS, London : 1786–1823. He was a son of Edward Dodd, of Sheffield, previously noticed. He did not make many instruments himself, but employed very clever workmen to do so for him. He was first of all a bow maker in Blue Bell Alley, Mint Street, Southwark, and became a violin maker and dealer in 1798, opening a shop in New Street, Covent Garden, which he removed in 1809 to St. Martin's Lane. Later on he added another sail to his craft, and became a harp and pianoforte maker. The instruments which have his label are mostly the work of

John Lott and Bernhard Fendt. These were excellent enough workmen in themselves, but the spirit of Dodd brooded over them whilst fashioning these magnificent instruments. Dodd was an enthusiastic connoisseur, with a mind steeped in Italian lore, and he brought his knowledge to bear upon the work at every turn. It is impossible to say how much of the work beyond the varnishing was actually his own, probably very little. With two such clever men to carry out his instructions, there was no occasion for him to handle the gouge and chisel. When the instruments were completed "in the white," Dodd overhauled them carefully and then varnished them himself. His varnish is excellent. It is quite equal to that of Benjamin Banks, and he applied it more skilfully than Banks was sometimes wont to do. It ranges in colour from golden amber to deep golden red, and it is rich and transparent. He kept its composition as a great secret, and was careful to let no one see him make or apply it. The ingredients were, however, only the ordinary and well-known gums and resins, mixed in better proportions and more methodically than was customary then. Most of the varnishes of the early part of the nineteenth century were hard, inelastic, and lustreless enough, and Dodd's oil varnish showed to great advantage by contrast with them.

Instruments bearing Dodd's labels are of various models: Stradivari, Guarneri, Amati, Bergonzi, Stainer, etc., but are of uniform excellence as regards finish and tone. He used two kinds of labels:—

(1).

T. DODD,
VIOLIN, VIOLONCELLO, AND BOW MAKER,
NEW STREET, COVENT GARDEN.

(2).

DODD, MAKER,
92, ST. MARTIN'S LANE.

Perfect copies of Stradivari, Amati, Stainer, &c. Note.—The only possessor of the recipe for preparing the original Cremona oil varnish.

DODDS, EDWARD, Edinburgh : 1817 till about 1890. He worked at 1 Charlotte Place, as a professional maker and repairer, and made about three hundred instruments. I have not been fortunate enough to see one instrument of his make, but I was assured by the late Dr. Dickson that they are of excellent workmanship and tone.

DOLLARD, ——, Dublin. Mentioned by Father Greaven as a contemporary and follower of Thomas Perry.

DORANT, WILLIAM, London : 1800–20. He worked at 63 Winfield Street, Brick Lane, Spitalfields. Average work.

DUFF, WILLIAM, Dunkeld : 1810–82. A gamekeeper on the Athole estate, and an amateur fiddle maker. Rather poor work and varnish, but the tone is sometimes of fair quality.

DUGHLEY, JOHN, Leicester : 1850–70. Poor work.

DUKE, RICHARD, London : 1750–80. There are no reliable biographical particulars of this great artist. I have searched numerous records, registers, and transcripts for the dates of his birth, marriage, and death, but could discover nothing that I was quite sure referred to him. A Richard Duke, son of Richard and Catherine Duke was baptized in the parish of S. Giles, Cripplegate, on June 10, 1709, and the entry may, or may not, refer to him. The name of Duke I found to be common enough in the registers and diocesan transcripts of old London parishes appertaining to the eighteenth century, and it was quite hopeless in the absence of some definite clue to look for the information I wanted.

Duke adopted the Stainer and Amati models, and one or two writers say that he made a few violins on the Strad model, but these are so few in number that they may be considered a negligible quantity. It has been said that

VIOLIN BY DUKE.

To face p. 137.

VIOLIN AND BOW MAKERS 137

" imitation is the sincerest form of flattery " ; if that is so, then Duke is the most sincerely flattered of all the old English makers. His fame in the eighteenth century was greater even than the fame of Banks. The reason for this is not far to seek : he made the best copies of Stainer that were ever produced in this country, and as Stainer was the ruling idol, naturally the instruments which most nearly approached his model would have the preference. In this way Duke won his laurels. The Duke cult was at the heyday of its popularity when Banks and Forster were turning out their best Amati copies. For some reason or another Richard was strongly prepossessed in favour of the German model, and he did not copy the Italian model as often nor as felicitously as he might have done. For example, the soundholes of his Amati copies differ very little from those of his Stainer copies. Not that he put inferior work into his Amati copies, as Banks was doing when copying Stainer ; on the other hand, his workmanship is always fine, whatever he did or whomsoever he copied, but he had drunk more deeply of the German than of the Italian spirit. In the opinion of connoisseurs to-day the Amati copies may be the more valuable, but there is not the slightest doubt in my mind that Duke and his patrons did not share in the same view. His patrons were mostly rich and well-to-do people. Many Duke violins are in the possession of county people at the present time : I know several. Fleming expresses the opunion that genuine Duke instruments are extremely rare. I am of the opinion that there exists a larger number of genuine Duke fiddles than there does of Banks and Forster ("Old") fiddles put together ; but they are not to be found in dealers' shops, they are fossilizing in dust heaps in the garrets of country mansions. There were hundreds of fine amateur players among the gentlefolk of those days, when the facilities for attending music halls, opera houses, etc, were so few and far between. Vivid sidelights are thrown on the manners and customs of society by the gossipy diary of old Samuel

Pepys: these are concerned with a century earlier, it is true, but the habits of the people had not materially changed in the middle of the eighteenth century. Pepys enters in his Diary under November 21, 1660: "At night to my violin (the first time that I have played on it since I came to this house) in my dining-room, and afterwards to my lute there, and I took much pleasure to have the neighbours come forth into the yard to hear me."

It will be admitted, I think, with regard to the workmanship of Duke, that it evinces consummate ability and skill. The finest examples of this artist are not a whit inferior to those of Banks, except as regards model and varnish, and in one particular, at least, they are superior, viz., in the carving of the scroll, but this remark applies to only the very finest of them. Duke was a busy man and did not always have the time at his command to make his best. Banks and Forster worked more at leisure, and the former was helping to create a taste for better things—a task which generally has a modifying effect on the relation between demand and supply. I do not understand why it is thought that Duke's Stainer copies are not quite so good as his Amati copies. I submit that they are *as* good intrinsically, and *better* copies. Duke was too thoroughly imbued with Stainer ideas to allow room in his mind for anything else. There is no perceptible difference in the tone, be the work German or Italian in character. It is a responsive, silvery, mellow tone in either case.

Duke's varnish is elastic, tender, and transparent, but it lacks "fire." If I were asked to give an imaginary pen-picture of the man, I should describe him as thick-set, broad-browed, keen-eyed, and dignified-looking, and as one who had a very correct but somewhat cold taste in matters artistic. That is the sort of man I see in my mind's eye hard at work fashioning these chaste, sober, broad-chested tenors.

Fine specimens of Duke's work rarely come into the market; when they do, they fetch a fair price. Violins in good condition sell at anything between £25 and £35. Needless to say, the market is flooded with counterfeit "Dukes." With the exception of the great Stradivari I do not think anybody has been counterfeited so often; certainly not in this country.

As far as is known, Duke had only three pupils, his son Richard, John Betts, and Edward Betts. He often branded his instruments under the button "Duke, London."

Labels :—

(1).   RICHARD DUKE,
        LONDINI, FECIT 1760.

(2).   RICHARD DUKE,
        MAKER,
        HOLBORN, LONDON,
        ANNO 1768.

Both of these were usually hand-written, but No. 2 was sometimes printed. The following was always printed :—

(3).   RICHARD DUKE.
        MAKER,
        NEAR OPPOSITE GREAT TURNSTILE,
        HOLBORN, LONDON,
        1769.

DUKE, RICHARD, London: about 1770–85. Son and pupil of the preceding. The few instruments of his make which remain show that he was greatly inferior to his father as a craftsman. He branded his violins similarly to his father, and usually left them unlabelled.

DUNCAN, ——, Aberdeen: about 1760.

DUNCAN, GEORGE, Glasgow: 1855–92. He was born in 1855, and left this country for America in 1892.

There appears to be little doubt that he has made some magnificent instruments, on the models of Stradivari and Guarneri, and varnished with a beautiful oil varnish of a golden red or orange red tint. He was awarded a gold medal for a case of violins at the London Exhibition of Inventions and Music in 1885. The tone of his instruments is large, rich, and beautifully clear and responsive. He had made about forty violins before he left this country, all of them of the highest standard of excellence.

DYKER, GEORGE, Drumduan, Forres, N.B. An amateur now living who has made several beautiful violins on the Strad model. He uses excellent wood, and the workmanship is faultless. The artist hand is seen in every detail of the work, and the tone is fine. I have never seen better work by an amateur. Scotland is peculiarly fortunate in possessing a large number of talented craftsmen who employ their spare hours in " moulding ribs, carving heads, and shaping fiddles."

DYKES, GEORGE LANGTON, London, contemporary. He is a son of the well-known violin collector and expert, Mr. Harry Dykes, of 61 New Bond Street, and was born in Leeds, October 11, 1884. After receiving a sound education, which included a working knowledge of French and German, he became a pupil in violin making of the late Paul Bailly, of Mirecourt and Paris, and was early initiated into the mysteries of the craft. His rare gifts enabled him in a short time to master the science and art of fiddle construction, and although he is still a comparatively young man, it is doubtful whether any one in this country, even among his seniors, possesses a profounder knowledge of the subject in all its branches than he does. Apart from a regular apprenticeship, served under a master, he has had the immense additional advantage of the sound expert knowledge and long experience of his father to draw upon. His opportunities, moreover, have been almost unique, for

G. L. DYKES.

To face p. 140.

VIOLIN AND BOW MAKERS

some of the finest instruments in existence have passed through the hands of the Messrs. Dykes and Sons, whose establishment is of world-wide reputation.

Mr. Dykes made his first violin in his early teens, and he had completed quite a considerable number of instruments by the time he had attained his majority. The workmanship, as was naturally to be expected, is of a high order, and the tone of a very fine quality. Latterly, he has turned his attention to antique instruments of the viol tribe, being specially interested in the viol d'amour, which instrument he thinks is likely to be revived in the near future, both for orchestral and chamber purposes. Most of his time, however, is taken up with the business of the establishment, more especially in superintending the important work carried out in the repairing and making department.

Mr. Dykes is a born artist ; he lives, moves, and has his being in an atmosphere of art, and he venerates art for its own sake. Fine art, Ruskin tells us, " is that in which the hand, the head, and the heart of man go together " : if so, I know of no one who can lay better claim to-day to the title of High-Priest of Fine Art than this enthusiastic devotee of the fiddle cult.

E

EADIE, J., Glasgow : nineteenth century. I have not seen any of his instruments, but the late Dr. Dickson, of Edinburgh, had seen a number of them, and said they were very well made and had a good tone.

EGLINGTON, —— ; about 1800.

ELLIOT, WILLIAM, Hawick : contemporary. He was born at Kirton, in the parish of Cavers, about four miles from Hawick, in 1862. After receiving a sound elementary education—as most Scottish children do—he was apprenticed to the joinery trade. His forbears, as far back as their history goes, were all connected with the joinery, carpentry, or wood-carving trades, so that heredity may be said to count for much of the penchant which Elliot showed early in life for chisel, gouge, and calipers. He made his first violin in 1885, and since then he has been steadily making, having completed up to date just over a hundred instruments. A great deal of his time is taken up with repairs, and he is consequently unable to make as rapidly as he would like to. The greater number of his violins are on the Strad and Joseph models, but latterly he has been making on an adapted model of his own. All his work reaches a high standard of excellence, and his later instruments are exceedingly fine. The work, both inside and outside, is finished with a degree of precision and delicacy which it is not possible to surpass. He is remarkably successful in producing a fine tone. It has all the characteristics of the old Italian tone, saving only the mellowness which comes with age and judicious use. The work of this artist is bound to come to the front. Fascimile label:—

ERVINE, ROBERT, Belfast: contemporary. One of the small band of present day makers who is doing all it can to maintain worthily the fine traditions of Ireland for art and craft work. I have not seen any of his work, but I have it on the best authority possible—that of the Rev. Father Greaven—that it reaches a high standard of excellence. Father Greaven in a letter to me describes it thus: "Ervine submitted one of his latest violins to me for my inspection, and I have it now by me. It was made for Mr. Crymble's firm, Musical Instrument and Music Dealers, of Wellington Place, Belfast. It is a beautifully constructed instrument; the workmanship both inside and outside being faultless. The model is that of the Betts' Strad, and may be described as being more graceful than massive. The scroll is of moderate proportions, and is beautifully cut. The instrument is covered with a transparent, warm light-brown varnish. The tone is sweet and penetrating, with just a suspicion of newness which will naturally mellow down with age and use. The violin is a most creditable and artistic piece of work."

Mr. Ervine has made a large number of instruments, and also repairs extensively. Facsimile label :—

Made by Robert Ervine in Belfast 1914. No. 103

EVANS, RICHARD, Anglesey and London : 1730–65. While he was in Wales he made several *crythau* (plural of *crŵth*) and a few violins. He removed to London about 1750, and made only violins thereafter. *Vide* also Appendix B.

EWAN, DAVID, Cowdenbeath. Born in 1838. He has made a large number of instruments of good average merit on the Strad model.

EYLES, CHARLES, Bedford : contemporary. He was born in London in the early fifties. He received a good education, at the completion of which he was articled to a pianoforte maker. Later, he studied art in London and Paris, and he exhibited pictures for several years at the Royal Academy and other important exhibitions. He took up the study of violins as a hobby about the year 1886, and has made a hundred instruments up to the present time, several of which are owned by well-known players. The outline is that of Stradivari or Guarneri, but nothing more than the outline is copied, the maker being of the opinion "that no copyist can ever excel or even equal the original," and that it is better therefore he should allow his inventiveness and imagination to work unfettered. I have seen only one of his instruments, and do not therefore know his work well enough to be able to give a description of it in general. The violin I saw and tried was beautifully made, and had a wonderfully bright, sweet, and pleasing tone. It appears from press notices and the opinions of several eminent artists that Mr. Eyles has made quite a number of violins which have an extraordinarily clear and mellow tone for new instruments. He is particularly careful in the choice of his wood, and he patiently covers the instruments with thin coats of tender, elastic, and transparent oil varnish.

EYLING, THOMAS, Gloucester: 1800–20. Fairly good work on the Amati model. Tone small but pleasing.

F

FENDT, BERNHARD, London: 1756–1832. He was born at Innsbruck, in the Tyrol, died in Aylesbury Street, Clerkenwell, and was buried in Clerkenwell Churchyard. An exceedingly clever craftsman who entered the employ of Thomas Dodd, q.v.

FENDT, BERNARD SIMON, London: 1800–52. He was a pupil of his father, and learnt his trade in the workshop of John Betts. He worked with Farn for some time, and later became a partner of George Purdy. Other biographical particulars are given in the various books on the subject; it suffices to say here that he was as clever and ingenious a workman as ever handled gouge and calipers in this country, and, in my opinion, as unscrupulous as he was clever. He made scores of counterfeited "Strads" and "Josephs." Hart says that he made some hundreds of copies of Guarneri

VIOLIN AND BOW MAKERS 145

alone. These were not all "fakes," it is true, but very many of them were, and they have been sold time and again as the genuine work of the masters whose forged labels they carry.

All the Fendts were counterfeiters, more or less—generally more, not less—and in so far as they departed from the paths of "righteous dealing," they deserve nothing but the execration of posterity and the contempt of the historian, their cleverness notwithstanding. Cleverness does not atone for fraud. I have seen it stated somewhere that the Fendts were the creatures of circumstances, and could not very well help themselves: a species of apology which, doubtless, every utterer of counterfeit coin in our own day could advance with equal plausibility. Fiddle-makers, like everybody else, are all creatures of circumstances—for who is complete master of his environment?—but they are not all forgers all the same. The clever forgeries of the Fendts, more especially those of Bernard Simon and of Jacob, have deceived hundreds of fiddle fanciers from time to time: they have deceived even experienced experts. For example, to name one instance out of a large number of cases which I could cite, the very clever counterfeit " Strad " owned by the late James Smith, Esq., of Ashcroft House, Wentworth, and which was the work of Jacob Fendt, had been certified by two experts to be genuine—so the owner informed me in a letter under date of May 7, 1904! When I review in my mind the work of the Fendts, I cannot but wail with Scott:

> "Oh what a tangled web we weave
> When first we practise to deceive!"

FENDT, FRANCIS, London and Liverpool. Fourth son of Bernhard Fendt.

FENDT, JACOB, London: 1815-49. Third son of Bernhard Fendt, and in some respects the best maker of the family. What I have said above of the work of Bernhard Simon applies equally to the work of this maker. It is matter of profound regret that enthusiasm for the instruments of these artists is held in check by the knowledge that " they ever dissemble and often deceive."

FENDT, MARTIN, London. Son of Bernhard Fendt. He worked for Betts.

FENDT, WILLIAM, London: 1833-1852. Son of Bernard Simon, and a very clever workman. His violas and double basses were celebrated.

FENWICK, ——, Leith. His instruments are occasionally advertised for sale, but I have never seen one.

FERGUSON, DONALD, Huntly, Aberdeenshire. Work of average merit.

FERGUSON, WILLIAM, Edinburgh: 1790-1820. Fairly good work and tone.

FERRIER, WILLIAM, Dundee: contemporary. Fairly good work.

FINDLAY, JAMES, Padanaram: 1815-96. He was born at a farm near Brechin, in Forfarshire. He made about five hundred instruments, mostly on the Guarneri model. His wood as a rule is plain, and the varnish a spirit one, thinly laid on, but the tone is frequently very good.

FINGLAND, S., —— : contemporary, apparently.

FIRTH, G., Leeds: 1830-40. Ordinary work.

FLECK, WILLIAM, High Wycombe: 1852-1914. A doctor of medicine, and a very clever amateur violin maker and player. He was born at Ballymena, Co. Antrim, Ireland, and died at High Wycombe early in 1914, where he had been in practice for thirty years, and where he had filled important positions, such as town councillor, Justice of the Peace, etc. He made a number of instruments, including violins, violas, and one violoncello, on the Stradivari and Guarneri models, all of very beautiful workmanship. Dr. Fleck was a keen connoisseur, and a man of wide reading and very refined artistic tastes.

FLECK, ETHEL, High Wycombe: contemporary. She was the wife of the Dr. Fleck previously mentioned, and not only assisted him with the varnishing of his instruments, but has made several violins herself, all the work from the fashioning of the rough blocks to the last finishing touches being her own unaided effort. She continues to make, and to take a deep interest in the violin, and in other branches of art. She follows the Stradivari model, and the workmanship is beautifully and delicately finished.

FLEMING, J., —— : nineteenth century.

FORD, JACOB, London: 1780–95. He worked on a model which very closely resembles that of Stainer. He evidently had Stainer in his mind, but he had also seen and handled Amati copies, or perhaps he had seen genuine " Amatis," and had been somewhat influenced by them, so that he had become unsettled in his ideals. The workmanship is excellent, and the wood very carefully chosen. The varnish is an oil one, of light or deep amber colour. His margins are wider than is usual in Stainer copies, and the edges are nicely rounded and solid looking. The tone is not a large one, but is of a very good quality. Altogether Ford was a superior maker, and the few examples of his art which remain to-day should be more highly valued than they are. Label :—

JACOB FORD,
MAKER,
LONDON, 1792.

FORSTER, JOHN, Brampton : 1688–1781. The first member of this celebrated family to make fiddles. Messrs.

Sandys and Forster in their *History of the Violin* give a somewhat lengthy account of various Forsters, Foresters, or Fosters who were anciently connected with the northern counties, but whether these were ancestors of John Forster they are not prepared to say. It is not very material whether they were or not. This first Forster to come across the path of the violin historian made only an occasional instrument, on the Stainer model, of rather rough and unfinished workmanship.

FORSTER, SIMON ANDREW, London : 1801–70. He was a son of William Forster (1764–1824), born May 13, 1801, and died February 2, 1870. He worked at Frith Street, and also at Macclesfield Street, Soho. He is more famous as the collaborator with William Sandys of the work referred to above than as a violin maker. All his work that I have seen reflects little or no credit upon the great name of Forster. He was a pupil of his father, of his brother, and of Samuel Gilkes. He worked sometimes on the Stradivari and sometimes on the Stainer model, but always arched his instruments in a grotesque manner. I am not sure that he did not sometimes bake his wood, as the tone is often of a wretched character.

Label :—

> S. A. FORSTER,
> VIOLIN, TENOR, AND VIOLONCELLO MAKER,
> NO. — LONDON.

FORSTER, WILLIAM, Brampton : 1714–1801. He was a son of John Forster, and, like his father, made and repaired an occasional fiddle. The workmanship is a little better than his father's, but the tone is about the same. His instruments are unpurfled, and spirit varnished.

FORSTER, WILLIAM, Brampton and London : 1739–1808. He is known as " Old Forster," and is the greatest maker of the family, and one of the greatest of all the old British makers. Haweis says he was " the greatest maker

VIOLIN AND BOW MAKERS 149

in all England " (*Old Violins*, p. 126), but I cannot concur with his opinion. He was born in 1739, baptized on May 5 of that year, and died on the 14th December, 1808. He may be described as the British counterpart of the great French maker, Vuillaume, since like him he was characterised by a degree of shrewdness, versatility, and worldly wisdom above his compeers. When French players wanted a Stradivari or a Guarneri fiddle, Vuillaume met their demands and sold them those new-old instruments which set the Seine on fire : similarly Forster, when the British public wanted Stainer copies, or Amati copies, immediately supplied them with their requirements : he was always equal to the occasion and never disappointed his customers. Where the analogy fails is that Forster, in addition to his versatility, possessed that other and sometimes inconvenient gift called conscience. Forster never "faked," and never attempted to pass his new instruments as "Old Masters."

Had Forster lived among more discerning people, that would demand Stradivari copies, his work would rank to-day beside that of Vuillaume. He was a "Jack of all trades," and master of more than one. By turns a spinning-wheel maker, gun-stock maker, cattle driver, publisher, fiddler— he could manage to eke out a living at any one of them. As a violin maker he rose from being a humble Cumberland repairer to the rank of instrument maker to the Court. He *ought* to have been England's greatest maker, and would have been but for this many-sidedness, and the indiscrimination of his countrymen. His artistic work at Brampton was confined to the repairing of old instruments, and the making of a fiddle now and again on the Stainer model. In 1759 he came to London, and after meeting with some reverses, entered the shop of one Beck, of Tower Hill, where he remained for about two years making fiddles. In 1762 he set up on his own account at Duke's Court, whence he removed to St. Martin's Lane. From this place he again removed to 348 Strand, where he remained for the rest of his days.

He followed three models: Stainer, A. & H. Amati, and Nicolas Amati.

He appears to have followed Stainer exclusively from 1762 to 1772, but at the latter date he put aside that model, never to take it up again. From 1760 to 1790 the influence of Banks was felt far and near, and British players were awaking to the superior merits of the Amati model. Forster was still a young man of only thirty-three, and had the better and longer half of his life before him. When he turned his back on the German he was in possession of his full strength and able to swim fast with the flowing tide. It was not so with Duke, who had less than a third of his life to live when the star of Nicolas Amati appeared on the horizon. Now was Forster's chance.

> "There is a tide in the affairs of men,
> Which, taken at the flood, leads on to fortune."

Forster might have reached the broad sea of artistic fame had he not paused by the way. He dallied with the model of A. and H. Amati, and gave up much time to musical enterprise of one kind and another, which, although profitable enough both to him and to the public, kept him from looking steadily on. If Forster had been a man of one ideal, and had kept that ideal steadily in view, posterity would have rewarded him by conferring upon him the title which has been given to Banks. As matters stand, he must rest content with perhaps a third place on the list—at least that is my opinion. His Stainer copies are very good, but do not compare for finished workmanship and tone with the instruments of Duke. The Amati copies are on an altogether higher level. When copying A. and H. Amati he was at his very best, and the result shows what he was capable of when at his best. But the tone of these copies is rather small and glassy. One beautiful specimen I have seen and tried: it was made of fine wood, with maple of narrow, regular, and well-defined curl, very pretty to look

VIOLONCELLO BY "OLD" FORSTER.

at, and varnished with dark, golden-amber oil varnish of excellent quality. Its principal dimensions were —

Length of body	$13\frac{13}{16}$ inches.
Width across upper bouts	$6\frac{11}{32}$,,
,, ,, middle ,,	$4\frac{5}{16}$,,
,, ,, lower ,,	$7\frac{27}{32}$,,
Width of C's	$3\frac{3}{16}$,,
Length of f's	$2\frac{7}{8}$,,
Depth of lower ribs	$1\frac{1}{4}$,,
,, upper ,,	$1\frac{3}{16}$,,

His Nicolas Amati copies are very faithful, but I do not think they could be palmed off as "originals." The violoncellos are finer than the smaller instruments. Here delicacy of detail is not so necessary, and solidity and rugged grandeur show to better advantage. His larger work is of moderately full proportions, not usually so large as the larger-sized violoncellos of Banks. But he varied his model a great deal, sometimes widening the waist, sometimes flattening the upper bouts, narrowing the width all over, lengthening the body, or even modifying the arching. The departure from the lines of N. Amati is occasionally so considerable as to almost constitute a different model.

The tone of the violoncellos is excellent, and was greatly appreciated in England before the finer Italian instruments had been brought here. It will yet be appreciated, and to a far greater extent, when we think it worth our while to coax the old veterans out of the sullen silence into which they have been obliged to retire. There are not many fraudulent "Forsters" about: I have not seen any, but have heard of one or two. Of the number of "Old Forster" instruments still in existence it is difficult to form an estimate: one thing is certain, they are becoming fewer every year. Quite a number of them found their way to America during the last quarter of the nineteenth century. The average price for the violoncellos from 1890 to 1900 was £23, but it is higher now, and will be very much higher a few years hence.

Those varnished dark amber were preferred a hundred years ago, but the red ones are more in favour to-day. The amber ones which I have seen were not so well stocked with wood as the red ones. Probably the greater thickness of the latter placed them at a slight disadvantage when new, which is the very reason why they are the better sort to-day. He is said to have used fossil amber for the basis of his varnish on his later instruments, in the solution of which he was assisted by the chemist, Delaporte. There is a close resemblance between the said varnish and that made some time back by the Messrs. Caffyn, of London. Forster made only four double basses, three of which were for the private band of King George III. Labels :—

(1).

WILLIAM FORSTER,
VIOLIN MAKER,
IN ST. MARTIN'S LANE, LONDON, 17—.

(2).

WILLIAM FORSTER,
VIOLIN, VIOLONCELLO, TENOR, AND BOW MAKER.

N.B. The above instruments are made in the best manner, and finished with the original varnish; and a copy of every capital instrument in England may be had.

FORSTER, WILLIAM, London : 1764–1824. " Young Forster " was a son of the great Forster. He was born January 7, 1764, and died July 24, 1824. He maintained to some extent the traditions and reputation of his father, but failed, or did not try, to maintain the same standard of excellence throughout. His work varies more in quality than does that of any maker, past or present, that I am acquainted with : some of it is no better than factory work, and some is fully as good as the best of his father's.

Haweis says there was an erratic vein in the Forster family, which in the great Forster took the shape of " amazing versatility," but in the younger members of the family

VIOLIN AND BOW MAKERS

degenerated into " speculative eccentricity." Be that as it may, it is certain " Young Forster " was capable of great things, and it is equally certain that he made but indifferent use of his capability.

One of the finest instruments by this maker that I have seen is a violin owned by Charles Bartlett, Esq., of Woodhill, Portishead, near Bristol. It is made of beautiful wood, on the N. Amati model, and covered with a brownish red varnish of excellent pâte ; and of perfect transparency and lustre. It has a clear, sweet, and responsive tone.

The following is a facsimile of the label in Mr. Bartlett's violin :—

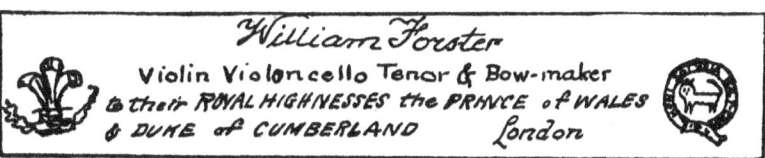

FORSTER, WILLIAM, London : 1788–1824. He was the eldest son of the previous Forster, and his work (the little there is of it) has much the same characteristics. He was a pupil of his father, and of his grandfather.

FRANKLAND, ——, London : 1780–90. He was probably a pupil of one of the Forsters, and he worked for " Young Forster " for some time. Ordinary work.

FRYER, CHARLES, London and Leeds : 1820–40. He was for some time partner with W. M. Dearlove, of Leeds. Very little of his work appears to be known.

FURBER, DAVID, London. Period unknown, but probably about 1760–80. He was a pupil of John Johnson, and made many instruments of pretty much the same characteristics, on the Stainer model. He was the first fiddle maker of the rather long line of Furbers.

FURBER, HENRY JOHN, London: about 1825–68. He was a son and pupil of John Furber. He made a large number of instruments, on different models, but mostly on that of Stradivari. Hart says that he was an excellent workman, but I cannot say that I like his instruments very much: perhaps it has not been my fortune to see the best of them.

FURBER, JAMES, London. Eldest son of Matthew Furber, senior. I doubt whether he was an actual maker, and not merely a dealer. I have never seen any instruments which were supposed to be his work, and I do not know of any one who has.

FURBER, JOHN, London: about 1810–45. He was the third son of Matthew Furber, senior, and a pupil of his father and of John Betts. He made a large number of instruments on the grand Amati model, and a few copies of the " Betts " Stradivari, when that famous masterpiece was in the possession of Betts. His work is excellent in every respect. I have seen a great deal of his best copies, and I must say that I considered some of them superb examples of the copyist's art. A specially fine specimen had the wood of the back of broad " flame," with the curl slanting very slightly towards the lower end of the instrument. The varnish was golden red, mellow, tender, and not too thickly laid on. The tone was particularly fine. Some of his Amati copies are a little too much grooved near the edge, but they are very fine nevertheless. His violins, when in fine condition, realize as much as £25 to-day, and will sell at a higher figure at no distant date. Furber worked for John Betts at the Royal Exchange, and many of the fine instruments which have the label of Betts were his work. His own label ran:—

JOHN FURBER, MAKER,
13 ST. JOHN'S ROW, TOP OF BRICK LANE,
OLD ST., SAINT LUKE, 1839.

FURBER, MATTHEW, London: 1730–90. Son and pupil of David Furber. Very little of his work is known. He died in 1770, and was buried in Clerkenwell Churchyard.

FURBER, MATTHEW, London: 1780–1831. Son and pupil of the preceding, He made a large number of instruments, some of which are very good. His violins are frequently advertised in catalogues of old instruments.

FURBER, WILLIAM, London: about 1820-40. 1 have seen only one violin with his label, which was very well made, but had a rather harsh tone.

FURLOUGH, HENRY, Bath: 1800–20. Very fair work, on the Amati model.

FURNOW, WALTER, Cheltenham: about 1800. Stainer model, with a much exaggerated arch.

G

GARDEN, JAMES, Edinburgh: nineteenth century. An amateur who made a few violins.

GARDENER, ——, Stokescroft. Violins of his make have been advertised in the papers, but I know nothing of him or his work.

GASKIN, G. H., ——.

GASKING, G. K., Shortlands: contemporary. Possibly there is an error here, and " Gaskin " and " Gasking " may be one and the same individual. I know nothing of their, or his, work.

GAY, WILFRED, Bristol: contemporary. A clever amateur who lives at 37 Brynland Avenue, and a pupil of Mr. Henry Lye, the veteran violin maker of Camerton. He has made several excellent instruments.

GIBBS, JAMES, London : 1800–45. It is not certain that he made any instruments on his own account, but he worked for J. Morrison, G. Corsby, and S. Gilkes.

GILBERT, JEFFERY JAMES, Peterborough : contemporary. He was born at New Romney, August 16, 1850, and is a son of Jeffery and Eleanor Langley Gilbert. He is a lineal descendant of an old Kentish family, one of the most notable members of which, in recent times, was Sir Jeffery Gilbert, " The accomplished exchequer baron." He was educated at Crockley Green Grammar School. Mr. Gilbert is a professional maker, and belongs to the very élite of the craft, the workmanship, varnish, and tone of his instruments giving him a place among the few who occupy the innermost circle of present day makers.

Although of a musical and artistic turn of mind, he had reached manhood before he had entertained any thoughts of becoming a violin maker. The thought that he could construct an instrument had no sooner entered his mind, however, than he found himself fast in the grip of the " fiddle disease." The purely mechanical part of the work never gave him any trouble, but he soon recognized that it required something more than an expert use of carving tools to fashion a great violin. Fortunately for him, he made the acquaintance about this time of several eminent connoisseurs and experts, notably that of the late Charles Reade, the late George Hart, Dr. John Day, and Mr. George Withers, all of whom took an interest in him and gave him useful advice from time to time. Charles Reade was specially kind, and not only imparted to him valuable knowledge, but kept in touch with him down to the time of his death.

Mr. Gilbert has made, up to date, about three hundred instruments, including violins, violas, violoncellos, and " viola-altas." He is not a rapid worker, and has not made more than about eight instruments in any single year, but the amount of patient attention he devotes to each instrument is extraordinary indeed. " Every instrument that is

 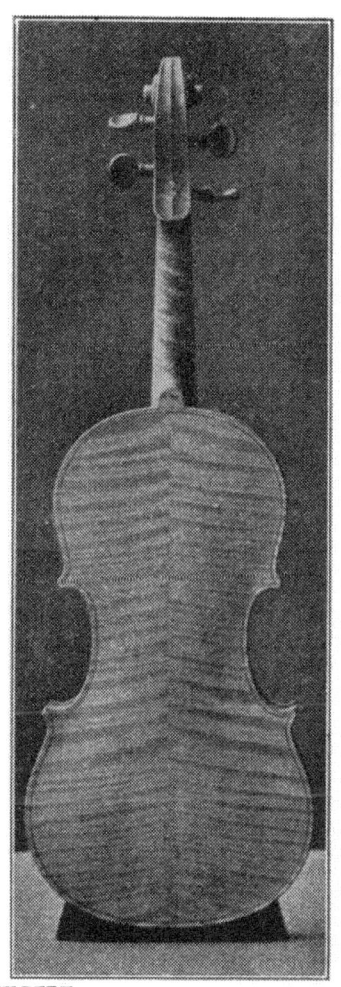

VIOLIN BY GILBERT.

To face p. 156.

worthy the name," he remarked to me, " has individuality and a temper all its own, and must be studied as you would a child, if you would form a thing of beauty, that will sing with the voice of melody."

He works on original models, the principal measurements of which are :—

Violin.

(a)

Length of body	. . . .	14 inches.
Width across upper bouts	. .	$6\frac{1}{2}$,,
,, ,, middle ,,	. .	$4\frac{3}{8}$,,
,, ,, lower ,,	. .	8 ,,
Depth of lower ribs	. . .	$1\frac{1}{4}$,,
,, ,, top ,,	. .	$1\frac{3}{16}$,,
Length of f's	. . . .	$3\frac{1}{16}$,,

(b)

Length of body	. . . .	14 ,,
Width across upper bouts	. .	$6\frac{5}{8}$,,
,, ,, middle ,,	. .	$4\frac{1}{2}$,,
,, ,, lower ,,	. .	$8\frac{1}{8}$,,
Ribs and f's same as (a)		

Viola.

Length of body	. . . .	16 ,
Width across upper bouts	. .	$7\frac{5}{8}$,,
,, ,, middle ,,	. .	$5\frac{1}{8}$,
,, ,, lower ,,	. .	9 ,,
Depth of lower ribs	. . .	$1\frac{1}{2}$,,
,, upper ,,	. .	$1\frac{3}{8}$,

Viola-Alta.

Length of body	. . . .	17 ,
Width across upper bouts	. .	$8\frac{1}{8}$,
,, ,, middle ,,	. .	$5\frac{5}{8}$,
,, ,, lower ,,	. .	$9\frac{1}{2}$,,

Depth of ribs $\frac{1}{16}$ inch more all over than in those of viola.
Length of sound-holes for viola and viola-alta is $3\frac{5}{8}$ inch.

Violoncello.

Length of body	29¾ inches.
Width across upper bouts	13¾ ,,
,, ,, middle ,,	9¾ ,,
,, ,, lower ,,	17½ ,,
Depth of ribs	4 9/16 ,,
Length of *f*'s	5 11/16 ,,

The outline of each of these models is very pure. The scroll is a masterly bit of carving, and is in the best Italian style. The width from boss-edge to boss-edge is 1 9/16 inch, and the depth of the peg-box at the deepest part is 1⅝ inch, diminishing to 1 1/16 inch at the throat. The scollop is nicely rounded and projects only just enough to give piquancy to its outer line. The curves of the volute are most delicately scooped at the base, and the fluting at the back of the box gives the correct balance in lines of subdued boldness. The button is nearly semicircular, strong, and in keeping with the contour of the instrument. The edges are fairly full, being neither too rounded nor yet in relief, but turned in a manner that gives " definity " to the outline of the fiddle. The sound-holes are Stradivarian in character, and are cut with extreme delicacy, even the little notches coming in for an artistic " touch."

The varnish on Mr. Gilbert's later instruments is of the finest quality: it is brilliant, elastic, and transparent, the colours ranging from light amber to a very deep and rich red. It is, of course, an oil varnish, but " not linseed, nor any other heavy oil, which destroys all that is good in colour,"—so Mr. Gilbert informs me.

The tone is of a beautiful quality: it is large, clear, rich, and responsive.

Mr. Gilbert's instruments have gained the following awards :—International Exhibition, Crystal Palace, 1884, Silver Medal, being the highest award ; International Inventions Exhibition, London, 1885, Silver Medal ; International Exhibition, Edinburgh, 1890, Gold Medal.

Facsimile label :—

Jeffery J. Gilbert. Peterborough Fecit. Anno MDCCCXCIX.

GILCHRIST, JAMES, Glasgow : 1832–94. An amateur maker who was by trade a philosophical instrument maker. He made eighty-six instruments of every description, of very good workmanship and very fair tone.

GILKES, SAMUEL, London : 1787–1827. He was a native of Morton Pinkney, Northamptonshire. His work is greatly appreciated by the best judges. There is not a great deal of it, but what there is justifies the opinion that if Gilkes had lived a few years longer he would be accounted to-day one of England's greatest violin makers. He died a comparatively young man, just as he was beginning to give the world the fruit of ripened talent. The Amati and Stradivari copies he made from about 1820 to the time of his death are excellent in every way. He was a pupil of Charles Harris, to whom he was also related, and he worked for a few years with William Forster. Label :—

GILKES,
FROM FORSTER'S,
VIOLIN AND VIOLONCELLO MAKER,
34 JAMES STERET, BUCKINGHAM GATE,
WESTMINSTER.

GILKES, WILLIAM, London : 1811–75. He was a pupil of his father, whom he succeeded in business. He made many double-basses and other instruments, which are of about average merit.

GIRVAN, THOMAS, Edinburgh : nineteenth century. Average work.

GLENDAY, JAMES, Padanaram : nineteenth century.

GLENISTER, WILLIAM, London : contemporary. He was born at Chenies, Bucks, in 1850, and lives at 23 Beak Street, Regent Street, W. Although only an amateur, he has made a large number of violins, violas, and violoncellos, which he advertises for sale in the music papers. He has made violins on the models of N. Amati, Guarneri, and Stradivari, but latterly makes on the Strad model exclusively. Mr. Towry Piper in reviewing his work in the issue of " The Strad " for June 1915, says that " so far as tone is concerned these instruments [i.e. Glenister's] will bear comparison with any new fiddles I have tested in recent years, one of the white examples, made in 1914, being quite remarkable for the beauty and quality of its tone." I examined about twenty of Mr. Glenister's instruments at his shop quite recently, and must say that I consider both workmanship and tone to be excellent. Facsimile label :—

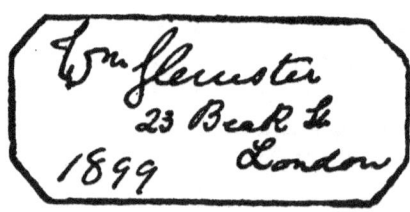

GLENNIE, WILLIAM, Aberdeen : contemporary. He works with Mr. John Marshall (q.v.), whose business he has practically managed for the last few years. He is an excellent craftsman.

GLOAG, JOHN, Galston : contemporary. An amateur who has made a number of good violins.

GOODMAN, JAMES, Brentford : nineteenth century.

GORDON, ——, Stoneyford, Ireland : nineteenth century. The Rev. Father Greaven mentions him in the

VIOLIN AND BOW MAKERS 161

following brief statement : " well-known about the North are violins by the philanthropist Gordon, of Stoneyford. They possess a good strong English tone, though the workmanship is rough."

GORDON, ——, about 1830-40. Dr. Richard Humphreys, of 6 Cressington Park, Liverpool, has a violin of his make, dated 1838, with his name stamped on the back under the button, and the date written in ink inside. He says it is a well-made instrument.

GORRIE, J., —— : nineteenth century. Instruments of his make have been advertised in catalogues of old violins.

GOTHARD, F., Huddersfield : nineteenth century.

GOUGH, JOHN, Leeds : about 1820. He worked for Mark William Dearlove.

GOUGH, JOHN, Thornbury, Glos. : 1803 till about 1870. He is mentioned in a booklet by Mr. J. Spencer Palmer, of Thornbury, who says that he had the reputation of being a fine maker. The Messrs. Hill have a copy of his label. I have made a careful but fruitless search in Bristol and its neighbourhood for information respecting him. Mr. C. Benson, of Cardiff, has a fine example of his work.

GOUGH, WALTER, Leeds : about 1820-40. Related, perhaps, to John Gough, of Leeds. Indifferent work.

GOULDING, ——, London : about 1800. Fairly good work.

GRAY, JOHN, Fochabers, N.B. : 1860-75. He did not make many instruments.

GREGSON, ROBERT, —— : contemporary. Ten years ago he worked in Blackburn as a professional maker and repairer, but I do not know his present whereabouts, nor have I seen any of his more recent work. I have heard that his later work is very good.

GRIME, HAROLD, Accrington : contemporary.

GUITON, R., Cork : contemporary. An excellent amateur who has made several beautiful violins on the models of Stradivari and Guarneri. The quality of his workmanship and the tone of his instruments are of so fine a description that it is a pity he does not devote the whole of his time to the craft.

GWYTHER, HENRY, Gloucester : 1830–50. Rather rough work, but tone very fair.

H

HALL, WILLIAM H., Oldham : contemporary. He has made a number of beautiful instruments on the models of Amati, Guarneri, and Stradivari. The tone of the only violin of his make which I have tried was not large, but it was bright, responsive, and sweet.

HAMBLETON, JOSEPH, Salford : about 1850. Fair work.

HAMILTON, WILLIAM, Uddingston : contemporary. A consulting engineer by profession, who makes violins *en amateur*, and who has produced some excellent copies of Gasparo da Salò.

HAMILTON, W. T. R., Edinburgh : contemporary.

HANDLEY, HENRY, Worcester. I do not know whether he is alive, but he was carrying on business a few years since as a professional maker and repairer. He has made a large number of instruments on the Guarneri model. Those I have seen were carefully made, and had a good tone.

HARBOUR, ——, London : 1780–90. He lived in Duke Street, Lincoln's Inn, and later in Southampton Buildings, Holborn. Very ordinary work.

VIOLIN AND BOW MAKERS 163

HARDIE, ALEXANDER, Maxwelltown : 1797–1855. He did not make very many violins, but the few there are left show that he was a skilled workman.

HARDIE, ALEXANDER, Galashiels : 1811–90. He made violins on his father's (the Hardie previously mentioned) model, which is a sort of cross between the models of Stainer and Amati. Fair work.

HARDIE, JAMES, Edinburgh : 1800–56. This Hardie was not related to any of the other makers of the same name. Amati and Strad models considerably modified. Very good work.

HARDIE, JAMES & SON, Edinburgh : contemporary. Mr. Hardie, senior, was born at Aquhedley, in the parish of Ellon, Aberdeenshire, January 1, 1836, and is probably the oldest professional maker and repairer now living and working in the country. He is a son of William and Mary Hardie, and is one of thirteen children. His mother died only a few years since, at the advanced age of 103. Hardie comes of a good stock, and is himself hale and hearty, although bordering on eighty. I saw him in his workshop at 99 Nicolson Street only a short time ago, when he was busy at work over a difficult and delicate bit of repair. He must have been a powerful man in his day. He is tall, well-built, and in spite of his years, stands erect, and looks good for another ten or fifteen years' work. He is a shrewd man, genial and kind-hearted, with a fund of anecdote and quaint humour ready at his command. He looks at you over his spectacles as you enter his shop with a half-enquiring, half-doubtful smile, and a twinkle in his eye : the smile broadens and the twinkle becomes a flash as some waggish remark of yours evokes a smart repartee. You pull out of your case a fine fiddle, and instantly the humour is metamorphosed into eagerness, and the face is lit up with excited admiration. Such is James Hardie. There are not many fiddle makers of his stamp left. He belongs to a past generation, and his old-time ideas, his trustfulness, and his kindliness sometimes place him rather out of joint with the age.

Hardie had the advantage of a first-class education, and was probably intended for the scholastic profession, since he went through a course of training at the Normal College, Edinburgh. But his grandfather's workshop at Dunkeld had greater attractions than Normal College, and fiddle heads were prettier than algebraic symbols. He played at fiddle making at the age of nine : he made a complete instrument at the age of fifteen. Vacations found him, not at his books, but behind the bench at old Peter Hardie's workshop, with sleeves tucked up, " shooting " joints. Before he was twenty-one he had made a number of violins, and a few violoncellos. In 1862 he was married to Elsie Milne Davidson, and he shortly afterwards went to Edinburgh, where he started business as a professional maker and repairer. Here he has been for upwards of half-a-century, wedded to art and toiling for a livelihood. The lot of the professional maker is not an easy one in modern times, and it happens but rarely that his lines are fallen in pleasant places. There have been periods of his life when Hardie had to struggle hard for bare existence, and the burden he had to carry was not a light one—there were thirteen children to feed, clothe, and educate. But he worked hard and struggled on. For many years he produced two new instruments every week, and there were repairs in addition. It had to be done, for otherwise the wolf would be at the door. Naturally these fiddles were not of a very high order, many of them were, as he expressed it, "rattled up in haste, and sold for a few shillings, to keep the pot boiling." But there came better days and better work. From about the year 1880 to 1900 Hardie produced on the average only about a dozen new instruments per year, and the quality of the work reaches a much higher standard. There are fiddles of his make which for excellence of material, workmanhip, and tone are unsurpassed. This is saying much, I know, but not too much. I have a violin of his make now before me, completed in 1895, on the Maggini model, which for grandeur and purity of tone is rarely equalled and never

VIOLIN AND BOW MAKERS

excelled. Mr. Honeyman in his *Scottish Violin Makers* remarks that "Hardie's best work will bear comparison with that of any living Scottish maker," and further that Hardie "has the rare power of producing violins which have a large and telling tone," and that "the mantle of Matthew Hardie has fallen upon his shoulders," and I thoroughly agree with him. According to the strictest account Hardie has made in all well over two thousand instruments, including violins, violas, 'cellos, and basses. About two hundred of these are of the best material and in his best style. The models are Stradivari, Guarneri, and Maggini. He has a decided preference for the Maggini model, and as far as my experience of his work goes, nearly all his best instruments are on that model. These are double purfled, and in some instances ornamented on the back as well.

One or two of his sons have assisted him from time to time with certain minor parts of the work, but not one of them is actually a maker. Mr. William Hardie made one violin some years ago, but he never took the tools in hand again. The varnish is of his own make, and has fossil amber for its basis: it is of two colours, golden amber, and golden red.

He has exhibited instruments on several occasions. At the Edinburgh International Exhibition, 1886, he gained a bronze medal; at the Glasgow Exhibition, 1886-7, an honourable mention; and at the International Exhibition, Edinburgh, 1890, a gold medal. Facsimile label:—

HARDIE, MATTHEW, Edinburgh : 1755–1826. He was born in Edinburgh in the year 1755, he died in St. Cuthbert's Poorhouse, August 30, 1826, and was buried in Greyfriars' Churchyard. His remains were laid to rest in the portion of the churchyard allotted to paupers. I visited this celebrated churchyard a year ago, and the exact spot of Matthew Hardie's grave was pointed out to me by one of the keepers : it is in one of the corners of the first enclosed block in the portion of ground known as the Covenanters' Prison. There is not a stone nor a brick to mark it. "Modern Athens," that is justly proud of its famous sons, and that has erected a hundred-and-one monuments to their memory, cannot afford to put up a plain head-stone over the remains of Scotland's greatest violin maker ! The neglect need not concern us very much, for it may be that if the shade of old Matthew were consulted on the matter it would exclaim with Cato : "I had rather it should be asked why I had not a statue than why I had one." That would be quite in keeping with the manner of the old humorist when he tabernacled in the flesh.

Matthew Hardie has been named the "Scottish Stradivari," and not without justice. His work is excellent, and deserves much more attention than has been given it by English connoisseurs and writers. It has been said that he copied the Stradivari model exclusively, but that is wrong, he copied Amati too. I have both seen and handled numerous genuine examples of his Amati copies. It is quite possible that he had abandoned Amati during the last few years of his life, for I do not remember seeing any copies of this model that were made after about 1810. Except as regards varnish the Amati copies will compare very favourably with the work of Benjamin Banks. His tone is larger than that of Banks, but what it gains in quantity it sometimes loses in quality.

He must have been a prolific maker, and his fame had spread far in his own day. His instruments found their way to the south of England, to South Wales, and even to the west of Ireland early in last century. A beautiful violin on the Amati model was for over fifty years in the possession of the Barham family, at Trecwn, in far away Pembrokeshire. I saw this fiddle many years ago, and have a vivid recollection of its beautiful workmanship and fine tone. In my time I have seen about thirty violins of this maker, the majority of which were, so far as my memory serves me, on the grand Amati model. I do not think his Stradivari copies show better work, but they are of course more valuable to-day by reason of their greater volume and finer quality of tone.

Matthew Hardie made no attempt at creating an original model, as far as I am aware : he endeavoured to copy Amati and Stradivari as faithfully as possible, but he sometimes bordered on originality in spite of himself. His strong personality refused to be altogether tied down to curves and figures. Look, *e.g.*, at the sound-holes of the Amati copies, and the scrolls of the Strad copies. The quaintness of the one and the sauciness of the other are evidence of a mind that did as it listed. It has been said that Hardie made many cheap instruments, into which he put poor wood, and which he did not purfle, in his early days. It is quite possible, though I have never seen a poor instrument of his make. Most great makers have turned out indifferent work at one period or another of their life. Art is very much the creature of circumstances. There are artists living to-day who are capable of great things, did circumstances but allow them to procure the best material and devote time to the fashioning of their fiddle idols. Like Michael Angelo, who saw his " David " in the rough block of marble, they see " Strads " in the unhewn timber, but have not the means to buy the tree. Hardie must have been sometimes badly off for timber, if it be true that he used to work up odd pieces of wood, old, weather-beaten, half-decayed paling slabs, and such like material.

It is true that much of his maple is of plain figure, but it is not necessarily inferior wood on that account. Some old

Italian fiddles with a grand tone have backs that are almost figureless.

In his best instruments the workmanship is very fine. The scrolls, as I have remarked, although copies, have the stamp of genius upon them. The buttons are usually longer and more oval than those of Amati and Stradivari. The sound-holes in the Strad copies are just a fraction short, but are of good outline and clean-cut. The margins are moderately full, but the edges might be slightly stronger than they are. The modern taste has improved upon that of the old makers in respect to the strength of the edges.

Hardie's varnish is a spirit one, thinly laid on, varying in colour from pale amber to yellow-brown or yellow-red.

He was a great artist, and a great enthusiast. His enthusiasm was of the contagious sort : quite a coterie of cultured men gathered around him, who became in time infected with the fiddle fever. Among them were Peter Hardie, of Dunkeld, his cousin, and a student at the Edinburgh University; David Stirrat, John Blair, George M'George, Alexander Yoole, a solicitor, and others. Matthew Hardie was himself an educated man, and his society was sought by these men as much on account of his cultured humour as on account of his ability as an artist. Many a congenial hour did these men of like passions pass together in the little *atelier* in Low Calton. What a pity a Sir Joshua was not there to delineate on canvas with his sympathetic brush those faces radiant with the joy of the fiddle, or a Boswell with his faithful pen to draw for posterity word-pictures of those unique personalities !

Labels :—

(1).

MADE BY
MATT. HARDIE & SON, EDINBURGH,
1797

(2).

MADE BY
MATTHEW HARDIE, EDINBURGH,
1810.

(3).
**MATTHEW HARDIE,
EDINBURGH,
1809.**

The last two figures of the date are handwritten.

HARDIE, PETER, Dunkeld : 1775–1863. He was a son of Dr. Hardie, an army surgeon, and was probably born abroad. He died in November 1863, and was buried in Dowally Churchyard, Perthshire. He was known in the north as " Highland Hardie," and was a man of powerful physique and striking appearance. His model was a cross between that of Stainer and of Amati. The tone of his instruments is usually good.

HARDIE, THOMAS, Edinburgh : 1800–58. A son of the great Matthew Hardie. He followed the model of his father, but resorted to the deleterious method of baking his wood, and his instruments, although beautifully made, have a very poor tone.

HARE, JOHN, London : about 1700. Work resembles that of Urquhart.

HARE, JOSEPH, London : 1700–40. He made a good number of instruments on the Stainer model. The work is good, and the varnish of excellent quality.

HARKHAM, ——, London : about 1760–90.

HARRIS, CHARLES, London and Adderbury : 1770 till about 1830, but there is no certainty. While in London he worked in Cannon Street Road, Ratcliffe Highway. He is one of our fine old makers, but there is comparatively little of his work left, that is to say, of work bearing his own label. He foolishly sold his birthright for a mess of pottage, in other words, he sold his instruments unlabelled

to the trade, and thus deprived himself of the credit which he
ought to have got for excellent work. He made instruments
chiefly on the Amati and Stradivari models. His 'cellos
were highly prized and eagerly bought during his lifetime,
and are very much valued to-day. I have recently seen
some half-a-dozen of his violins, all Strad copies, the workmanship of which I considered excellent and the tone very
fine. Charles Close, Esq., of Leeds, owns a magnificent
viola of his make, and Mr. R. Waters, of Penarth a fine
violoncello.

Labels :—

(1).

> CHARLES HARRIS,
> FECIT IN CANNON STREET,
> LONDON, 1791.

(2).

> MADE BY
> CHARLES HARRIS,
> ADDERBURY, OXON.,
> 1826.

HARRIS, CHARLES, London : 1795 to about 1840.
Son and pupil of the above. He worked for John Hart for
some time. Very good work, but it bears no comparison
to that of his father.

HARRIS, GRIFFITH, Swansea : 1810–40. I have
seen only one violin of his make, which was fairly well made.

HARRIS, JOHN EDWARD, Gateshead-on-Tyne : contemporary. He was born at Wednesbury, near Birmingham,
in 1862, and commenced violin making in 1894. He is at
present established in the music business at 37 and 41 Nile
Street, Gateshead-on-Tyne, and is a professional maker,
repairer, and manufacturer of amber oil varnish. He has
made about forty instruments up to date, on various models.
I have seen only one violin of his make, which was on the

To face p. 171.

VIOLIN AND BOW MAKERS

Strad model, of handsome wood, well made and beautifully finished. Those who are better acquainted with his work say he is a very careful maker, and that his instruments are well liked.

HARROD, ROBERT, London and Oxford: about 1810–30. High model, dark varnish, workmanship good. I recently saw a viola of his make, which was evidently copied from one of Duke's violas; it was made in St. Peter's Churchyard, Oxon, 1812. It had a very fair tone.

HART, JOHN THOMAS, London: 1805–74. A pupil of Samuel Gilkes. He did not make many instruments, but attained great reputation as repairer and connoisseur. He brought together many remarkable collections of Italian instruments, such as the Goding, the Plowden, and a large part of the Gillot, etc. I have never seen an instrument bearing his label, and cannot say what his work was like. Label:—

JOHN HART,
MAKER,
14 PRINCES STREET, LEICESTER SQUARE,
LONDON, 18—

HART, GEORGE & SON, London: contemporary. Mr. George Hart, who is established at 28 Wardour Street, as a violin maker, bow maker, repairer, dealer, and expert, is a son of the late George Hart, the well-known expert, and author of various works on the violin, and was born near Warwick on January 4, 1860. He was educated at Grove House School, Highgate, at which the Rev. Mr. Tough was then headmaster (who was a pupil of the great Dr. Chalmers, of Disruption fame) and after completing the usual course here he was sent to Paris to finish his studies. On June 17, 1882, he was married to Miss Katherine Jepson de Betham, daughter of John de Betham, Esq. He has three children— two daughters and a son, named Katherine, Irene, and Frank.

Mr. Hart is not, of course, an actual maker, but he employs a large number of skilful and experienced English and French workmen, and the firm turns out a very considerable number of instruments annually. These instruments, naturally, like all work produced by these large firms, are of various kinds and qualities, but the better class instruments reach a high standard of excellence, and will bear comparison with the finest work of some of the more famous workshops of the Continent. The personal supervision and genius of Mr. Hart is evident in every department of the work, especially in the choice of material for the more expensive class of instrument.

The Messrs. Hart make a special feature of their facsimile copies of old Italian masterpieces. Some years ago I had one of these " new-old " violins down for inspection : it was an exact copy of the famous " D'Egville " Joseph, and so close an imitation that it was almost impossible to distinguish it from the original. The skill and patience which had produced this facsimile were not of the ordinary kind. The tone of the fiddle was remarkably clear, rich, and resonant, for a new instrument. The following is a facsimile of the label put into it :

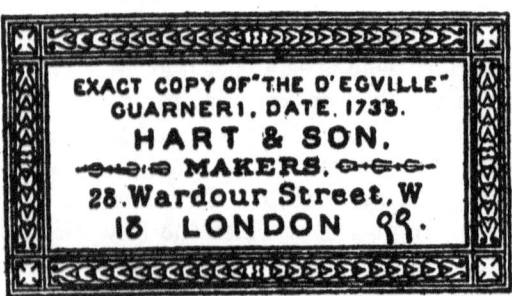

Messrs. Hart have made a special feature also in recent years of case making. Many of the violin cases they have made are extraordinarily elaborate and costly, and are beautifully designed and finished. Some are of satin wood, inlaid with silver filigree work, others are richly carved and silver mounted. The makers themselves have spent as much as £70 or £80 on a single case, exclusive of the time and labour devoted to the making of it.

Quite recently they also commenced to specialize in bows, and their work in this department is now recognized as being of exceptional merit.

It is pretty generally known that Mr. George Hart is a connoisseur and expert of undoubted ability. His opportunities, of course, have been great. Nearly all the famous instruments of the world have passed through his hands, such as the " Dolphin," " Betts," " Emperor," and " Paganini " Stradivaris ; the " Leduc," " Vieuxtemps " Guarneris, etc. His present collection of instruments is a very large one, containing several fine specimens of the work of the old masters. In addition to the knowledge he has gained from personal connoisseurship extending over a period of nearly forty years, he reaped the benefit in early life of his father's vast knowledge and experience. The late George Hart was without a doubt one of the greatest authorities on the violin in all Europe. His works : " The Violin : Its Famous Makers and their Imitators," and " The Violin and its Music," will remain classics for all time. Facsimile label :—

HARVEY, ERNEST, Penarth, Cardiff : contemporary. An amateur who has made several instruments on the Stradivari and Guarneri models, of very good workmanship and tone.

HARVIE, ROBERT, —— : nineteenth century.

HAWKES, ——, Coventry : eighteenth century.

HAYNES & CO., London : contemporary. Chiefly dealers.

HAYNES, JACOB, London : c. 1750. He made fairly good copies of Stainer.

HEAPS, ALFRED WALTER, Sydney N.S.W. : 1854 to about 1906. He was a son of John Knowles Heaps, of Leeds, and was apprenticed to Handel Pickard, of Leeds, in 1869, with whom he remained till 1874. In 1876 he obtained an appointment in Sydney as manager of the musical department of a wholesale house. He soon relinquished this post, and devoted the rest of his life to violin making and repairing. His work is said to be very fine.

HEAPS, JOHN KNOWLES, Leeds : nineteenth century. He made very good instruments.

HEARNSHAW, FRANCIS, Nottingham : contemporary. I have not seen his work.

HEATON, WILLIAM, Gomersal, near Leeds : 1827 to about 1906. He made a large number of instruments on the Amati, Guarneri, and Stradivari models, some of which reached a high standard of excellence. Mr. Arthur Broadley thought very highly of his violoncellos, and gave him a great deal of work from time to time. A 'cello built specially to his order was said to be a very fine instrument, with a large and telling tone. Facsimile label :—

```
WILLIAM HEATON,
       MAKER,
HILL TOP, GOMERSAL.
           Nr. Leeds.
```

VIOLIN AND BOW MAKERS 175

HEESOM, EDWARD, London: 1745–55. Stainer model; indifferent work.

HENDERSON, DAVID, Aberdeen: nineteenth century. Very poor work.

HESKETH, THOMAS EARLE, Manchester: contemporary. He was born in Manchester, August 14, 1866, and was apprenticed to Mr. G. A. Chanot in 1885, for five years. In 1891 he commenced business on his own account as a professional maker and repairer, and he worked for many years in Lower Mosley Street. I believe he is still working in Manchester, but am not certain of his whereabouts. He is one of the best of our modern makers, and his instruments are in great demand and highly appreciated by orchestral and other professional players. He has made a large number of instruments on the following models: Amati, Stainer, Ruggeri, Maggini, Guarneri, and Stradivari, the greater number being on the two last models.

He also works on an original model, the principal measurements of which are:—

Length of body	14 inches.
Width across upper bouts . . .	$6\frac{3}{4}$,,
,, ,, middle ,, . . .	$4\frac{19}{32}$,,
,, ,, lower ,, . . .	$8\frac{5}{32}$,,
Length of C's	$3\frac{5}{32}$,,
,, ,, f's	$3\frac{3}{32}$,,
Distance between f's at upper turns .	$1\frac{5}{8}$,,
Depth of ribs $1\frac{1}{4}$ inch diminishing to .	$1\frac{7}{32}$,,

He has made several magnificent violas on a model closely approximating to that of A. and H. Amati, one was to the order of Mr. Rawdon Biggs, of Halle's, the Brodsky, and other quartettes, and is considered by its owner a superb instrument. Its principal dimensions are:—

Length	.	.	.	.	.	$16\frac{5}{8}$ inches.
Width, top	.	.	.	.	.	$7\frac{7}{8}$,,
,, centre	.	.	.	.	.	$5\frac{1}{4}$,,
,, bottom	.	.	.	.	.	$9\frac{3}{4}$,,
Depth of ribs $1\frac{8}{16}$ diminishing to	.	.	$1\frac{7}{16}$,,

He has made excellent violas on the Strad model, $15\frac{3}{4}$ in., and a few on the Ruggeri model, $16\frac{1}{4}$ in., and on one the Maggini model, $15\frac{7}{8}$ in.

The violas of this maker are much valued for their excellent qualities, the tone having the depth and richness of colour which distinguish the best tenors of the old masters, and being wonderfully free from the nasality which too often characterises modern work. His wood, workmanship, and varnish are faultless. He has a considerable store of wood which was once the property of Craske, who is said to have bought it at Forster's sale. Much of the maple is of rather plain figure, but its tonal properties are of the best. A Vuillaume-Strad model violin which I once tried had a beautiful tone. It had a back cut on the quarter, made of wood with a fairly wide and very well marked curl. The varnish was a tender and elastic oil one, of rich, dark golden amber, which lit up the "flame" of the wood so that it appeared like watered silk seen through a sheet of stained glass. The fiddle was the work of an artist. Facsimile label :—

Thomas Earle Hesketh Manchester Fecit 1900 (EH)

HIGSON, DANIEL, Ashton-on-Ribble : 1849 to about 1906. He made many instruments on an original model.

HILL, HENRY LOCKEY, London : 1774–1835. He was a son of Lockey Hill, a grandson of Joseph Hill, and

the father of William Ebsworth Hill. He was a pupil of
his father, and worked for some time with John Betts. Later
he became partner with his father and brothers, and contributed largely by his excellent work to make the name of
Hill one of the greatest in the history of violin making in this
country. The workmanship and tone are generally magnificent—sufficiently so in a number of his best instruments
to furnish the forger with an excuse for extracting the
maker's label (if there was one) and substituting another
bearing a more honoured name. I have seen several
Lockey Hill violoncellos with an Italian " passport." A
renowned 'cello player uses one at the present time, with a
" Stradivari " label. It is of the same measurements as the
Strad 'cello sent by Friedrich Wilhelm II of Prussia to John
Betts in 1810, to be sold in this country, and is in all respects,
except as regards the varnish and purfling, a perfect copy
of that celebrated instrument. The varnish, although of
excellent quality, is not to be compared with that of Stradivari, and the purfling, which is carefully inlaid, is not in
the manner of the master. Any one carefully examining
the mitring at the corners will perceive the difference.
Careful comparison will reveal the similarity of this specimen with the known Lockey Hill violoncellos. Some years
ago I saw a violin by this maker, made on the N. Amati
model, with a slab back of beautiful figure, which had
a moderately powerful and very sweet tone. The
colour of its varnish resembled the brownish-purple tint of
the bark of birch in autumn. Hill frequently used a light-coloured varnish, which is perfectly transparent and elastic.
I have seen only one of his violas, which was on a modified
Amati model, with a widened waist, and not over-pronounced
arching. The tone of this instrument was large and sonorous on the lower strings, but not quite so full and clear on
the upper strings. The scroll was in the best Italian style,
and the sound-holes well designed and carefully cut. Altogether the work of Lockey Hill is very fine, and it is a pity
there is not more of it.

HILL, JOHN, London: c. 1794. Nothing known of him except that he apparently worked in Red Lion Street, Holborn.

HILL, JOSEPH, London: 1715–1784. He worked at "Ye Harp and Hautboy," in Piccadilly, under Peter Wamsley, where he was a fellow-apprentice with Benjamin Banks: he worked also in various other places, and was assisted by his sons William, Joseph, Lockey, and Benjamin. Haweis says that he "was proud to trace his descent from the Mr. Hill mentioned in Pepys' Diary as being employed to alter his lute and viall" (*Old Violins*, p. 137). It is rather curious that I cannot discover in my copy of this celebrated Diary any reference at all to any "Mr. Hill" as having been employed by Pepys to repair his instruments. The "Mr. Hill" referred to so frequently by Pepys was a merchant, and not a musical instrument maker. I have read the Diary very carefully, and have marked all the references to the "Mr. Hill" in question, but have not happened on the information given by Haweis. I should much like to have the particular entry where Haweis got his "facts" from pointed out. Albeit it is not very important whether Joseph Hill was descended from the "Mr. Hill" mentioned in the Diary or not, his fame rests not on his descent but on his fiddles. That he was a very capable craftsman does not admit of doubt. I have quite recently seen three instruments of his make—one 'cello and two violins—which were of beautiful workmanship and tone. One of the violins, on the Amati model, is now with me, and is made of excellent wood and varnished pale amber. It is rather on the small side, its length being $13\frac{13}{16}$, but it has a round, clear and beautifully sweet tone. It would be difficult to find a fiddle with a tone more suitable for drawing-room purposes.

Joseph Hill's violoncellos and double basses have been long admired for their excellent tone.

WILLIAM EBSWORTH HILL.

To face p. 179.

HILL, WILLIAM, London: 1740-80. Son of the above Joseph Hill. His work is said to be very good, but I have not seen any instruments which could with certainty be ascribed to him, and cannot therefore say what they are like.

HILL, W. E., & SONS, London: contemporary. The period of Willim Ebsworth Hill is 1817–95; the present members of the firm are: William Henry, born June 3, 1857; Arthur Frederick, born January 25, 1860; Alfred Ebsworth, born February, 1862; and Walter Edgar, born November 4, 1871. The name of William Ebsworth Hill is almost as well known in the violin world as that of the great Stradivari himself. There is nothing extraordinary about this, for next in importance to the greatest maker is the greatest restorer, and it will be readily admitted, I think, that William Ebsworth was the greatest restorer this country has ever produced, and one of the greatest in all Europe. He was a pupil of his elder brother, Joseph, and he worked for a time with Charles Harris, at Oxford, whom he left in 1838, returning in that year to London and settling down, first in Southwark, then in Wardour Street, and finally in New Bond Street. I cannot discover that he made very many new instruments, but such work as he did make was of a high order of merit. Miss Stainer in her *Dictionary of Violin Makers* says that " he exhibited some very beautiful violins of carefully finished work and an excellent viola of large pattern, with full round tone, in London, in 1862, obtaining special commendation and a prize medal." But if he was not a prolific maker, he was the most indefatigably industrious restorer of old instruments that has ever been known, and his skill, patience, and trustworthiness in this branch of the art deserve to be, and will be, ever held in the greatest esteem by all lovers of the " King of instruments." Violin repairing in his hands became violin restoration, and he raised what had hitherto been regarded in this country as a humble craft to the dignity of fine art.

I have already said something of violin restoration in the

Introduction, but I really only touched the fringe of the subject. It is a topic on which another volume might be written, and it might be written not only with advantage but with a touch of the "human" about it, by making William Ebsworth Hill the pivot on which the information turned. In addition to possessing a vast knowledge of violins, and unsurpassed skill in their restoration, he had an interesting personality. The Rev. H. R. Haweis, who knew him intimately, has given us a vivid pen picture of the old craftsman under the appropriate heading of " A Vignette of W. E. Hill " in his *Old Violins* (pp. 133–145). I have not the slightest doubt that the picture he draws is a faithful one, and that Hill was very different from ordinary mortals—that he was, in fact, cast in a mould by himself, and strangely unique. The description given by Beatrice Harraden of Paul Stilling is in many respects applicable to him. " Paul," she says, " was one of those strange beings born aloof, and with no mental approach to a normal condition of thought or circumstance. He had a rare gift, the passion of which had absorbed him from his earliest years. He knew the whole subtle secret of violin-making ; and they said at Mirecourt, where he was sent to have his training, that he was a born fiddle-maker of unerring instinct. His birth in the nineteenth century was an injustice to him. He should have been born in the seventeenth century and taken his place at the luthier's bench side by side with Stradivari or Guarneri. But his spirit held undoubted communion with them ; and life, which had denied him many privileges, had conceded to him the joy of knowing that he was indeed their fellow-craftsman and belonged by birthright to their order " (*Interplay*, p. 21).

The distinguishing trait of his personality seems to have been his extraordinary intuition—" unerring instinct " is the right term for it. He knew the work of the masters, and knew it with the infallibility of direct vision. He remarked once to Haweis that there were days when he could not tell. But they were not many, and the fact that

VIOLIN AND BOW MAKERS

there were any such days at all is proof that his knowledge was intuitional rather than intellective, for had it been of the demonstrative—the two and two make four—order, he would always have been able to tell, or, at least, to pretend to tell. And had it been of the intellective order he would have differed little or nothing, perhaps, from the crowd of fiddle experts who rely more on the mathematics of their trade than on its psychology.

Hill had all the qualifications of a great restorer : he had a perfect knowledge of violin construction, skill, patience, ingenuity, reverence, and the " artistic sense." It is not necessary to dwell at length on each of these qualifications, but I would point out as an instance of his profound reverence for the work of the masters the fact that he appreciated the absence of precision in an old instrument, and never attempted to rectify it, as an ordinary repairer would certainly do, for the sake of appearances. Some of the old makers, it seems certain, built their instruments without a mould, with the result that the curves are not always true, and the halves of the instrument (on either side of the longitudinal axis) not in exact contra-facsimile. This absence of precision in old art and craft work often imparts a pleasing tone to the general effect, but it requires the artistic sense to appreciate it. Hill both appreciated and reverenced it.

His reverence is further shown by his very sparing use of fresh material in his restorations. No artist ever deplored more deeply the necessary renewal of parts which could not be re-set. He restored faithfully because he preserved faithfully. And this is the essence of all true restoration of art work. Imitation of old work may be tolerably faithful, but it is *not* old work, and it cannot be referred to as such ; it is like the lifeless body, the spirit has taken its flight, and has left but the vague semblance of what it once was. And if haply any life-like spirit *is* infused into the reproduction, it is not the spirit of the old, but the spirit of a new life ; and bears the impress of the mind, not of the ancient artist, but of the modern.

There are two virtues which a restorer must possess—they are the background of reverence, as it were—these are self-control and self-denial. A writer on Christian Art observes that "not only political but aesthetical regeneration is inseparably dependent on self-denial and self-control." This is literally true of the art of restoring violins. There are hundreds of old instruments in existence which have been repaired, or rather *im*paired, by bunglers who could not resist the temptation of "trying on" some of their "patents," or of discarding an old rib or two, or even the table, and substituting brand new work of more "scientific" construction. It can with truth be said of these old wrecks as Ruskin said of Fra Giocondo's loggia that they "have been daubed and damned by the modern restorer."

I had not the privilege of knowing the great William Ebsworth in the flesh, but I know him in the spirit, and I know him in his works. There is no name in fiddle lore for which I feel a profounder respect, and there is nothing in fiddle craft that I admire more than his beautiful restorations.

The Messrs. Hill—*i.e.* the present firm—are makers, repairers, experts, and authors of several works on celebrated violin makers and violins. Naturally, they have a great reputation. To say that they are worthily maintaining the reputation of their father is at once to say too much and too little. It is saying too much because no individual, or combination of individuals, can, in my opinion, ever equal the wonderful work which William Ebsworth Hill accomplished as a restorer of classical instruments. That work, whether viewed from the point of view of quantity or quality, stands unrivalled. Nor can any individual, or combination of individuals, ever again have the same opportunity of learning the mind of the great Italian masters as he had. The opportunity he enjoyed has visited the world only two or three times. It came once when Tarisio trudged the dusty roads of Italy: it came again when the pedlar sold his ill-gotten ware to the luthiers of Paris: it

VIOLIN AND BOW MAKERS 183

came the way of William Ebsworth when the husky veterans needed doctoring. Whoever says the same opportunity *is* now, or will come again, knows little of history, and is more sanguine than wise.

It is saying too little because the sons are more business-like than their father. By all accounts the father was as notable an example as might be found anywhere of the man who " took no thought for the morrow." He was not a spendthrift, nor a waster, nor an epicure, but merely an artist who was so absorbed in his work that he had not room in his mind for pounds, shillings, and pence.

The present establishment is thoroughly up-to-date in its business methods, and is, without a doubt, the most successful first-class violin concern in all the world to-day. The advertisement at the end of their volume *Antonio Stradivari* is a fair indication of the nature and extent of the business carried on by the enterprising sons of the king of British violin restorers. It runs : " Messrs. William E. Hill & Sons come of a family who for generations have been engaged in the making of violins and kindred instruments. Carrying on the traditions they have inherited, they have devoted their attention to the improvement and perfection in this country of their art in its various departments ; with the result that they have now at their service a highly trained and skilled staff, while at the same time they have organized and brought up their works at Hanwell to such a degree of completeness and efficiency as enables them effectively to meet the demands which have been so long pressing upon them, and to deal promptly with all calls which may henceforth be made upon them. In their endeavours to revive a craft in the exercise of which England once held a position of repute and distinction, Messrs. W. E. Hill & Sons have been aided by one salient advantage. They have had through their hands nearly all the most famous violins of the world ; and they have not failed to avail themselves of their unique opportunities of studying, with a view to reproduction, the characteristics and details of these instruments. They can therefore offer copies of the most celebrated Stradivaris, such as the 'Messie,' the 'Tuscan,' the 'Betts,' the 'Alard,' the 'Rode,' the 'Viotti,' etc. The price of these instruments is £35." There is nothing of the ordinary trade " puff " about this, and the business is exactly such as it is described. Haweis concludes his account of the present establishment by saying that it is " when considered in all its branches, the largest individual violin-dealing industry in the world."

The firm also make fine bows, cases, and all fiddle accessories " on a scale hitherto unattempted in this country." Their bows have a great reputation, and are used by many distinguished players. They are violin and bow makers by royal appointment to H.M. the King, H.M. the King of Italy, H.M. the King of Portugal, H.M. the Ex-Queen Regent of Spain, H.M. Queen Maria Pia of Portugal. They have won the following awards for exhibits of instruments and bows :—Prize Medal, London, 1862 ; Sole Gold Medal, Society of Arts, 1885 ; Gold Medal, Inventions Exhibition, London, 1885 ; Gold Medal, Paris Universal Exhibition, 1889 ; Diplôme d'Honneur, Brussels International Exhibition, 1897.

They have one of the largest and finest collections of stringed instruments in the world, the collection embracing some of the best of our old British fiddles. I was very courteously allowed to inspect the collection a short while ago, and was greatly impressed by the wonderful wealth of art it displayed. The Messrs. Hill are the authors of several important works, a list of which will be found in the Appendix.

HILTON, THOMAS JAMES, Gorleston : contemporary. A professional maker, repairer, and player. He was born in 1868, and commenced violin making about twenty years ago, since when he has completed forty-seven violins, some on the Strad, and some on the Bergonzi model. A great deal of his time is taken up with repairs, and he

VIOLIN AND BOW MAKERS 185

makes only three or four new instruments in the year. The work is carefully finished, and the tone is excellent.

HIRCUT, ——, London : c. 1600.

HOLLARD, GEORGE, Compton-Dundon : 1812–94. Made a few fiddles, and did a little rustic repairing. He played the fiddle at the local parish church for many years, and was a " character " in his way.

HOLLOWAY, JOHN, London : 1775–95. He worked at 31 Gerard Street, Soho. Indifferent work.

HOPKINS, ——, Worcester : nineteenth century. Fairly good work, but he artificially seasoned his wood.

HORRIDGE, WALTER PERCIVAL, Stamford : contemporary. Born in York, March 2, 1875. An amateur who makes lovely violins on the Strad model. He is a professional wood carver, and his skill in the use of keen edged tools is manifest in the beautiful workmanship of his instruments. He is a pupil of Mr. A. L. Scholes, of Rushden.

HOSBORN, THOMAS ALFRED, London : c. 1630. A maker of lutes and viols.

HOSKINS, JAMES, Camerton, Somerset : early nineteenth century. Average work, of no particular model. There is a fairly well made 'cello of his still in use in the little village of Camerton.

HOWARD, H. H., ——. I have seen his name as a violin maker somewhere, but cannot trace it.

HOXBY, THOMAS, York : nineteenth century.

HUDSON, GEORGE, Skegness : contemporary. A son of Richard Hudson, well-known in parts of Lancashire as " Dick o' New-laith," a famous country fiddler. He has made over a hundred instruments, on various models, of good and careful workmanship.

HUME, A., Peterborough: contemporary. A professional maker and player. I have not seen any of his work.

HUME, CHARLES DAVID, Hawthorne, Melbourne: contemporary. A native of Liverpool, who emigrated to Australia about twenty years ago, and who is said to be a very good maker. He obtained a Diploma of Merit for a case of violins at the Bendigo Exhibition in 1903.

HUME, RICHARD, Edinburgh: c. 1530. A famous viol and lute maker.

HUMPHREYS, RICHARD, Carnarvon: c. 1760. A repairer of *crythau* (plural of *crwth*) and the maker of rustic fiddles.

HURLEY, ARTHUR, Tondu, Glamorgan: contemporary. Has made a few violins on an original model.

I

INGRAM, DAVID, Edinburgh: 1800–10. Average work.

INGRAM, HENRY, Durham: c. 1820. Very few of his instruments have been seen.

INGRAM, WALTER, Bristol: c. 1830. Very neat work, but baked wood, and poor tone.

IRESON, FRANK HERBERT, Bishop Auckland: contemporary. An amateur who has made a number of nice violins on the model of Walter H. Mayson.

VIOLIN AND BOW MAKERS 187

J

JAMES, STEPHEN, Bristol : c. 1800. Average work.

JAMIESON, THOMAS, Aberdeen : 1830-45. Fair work and tone.

JAY, HENRY, London : c. 1640-60. A maker of viols. His work was considered excellent. Mace's references to it are well known.

JAY, HENRY, London : 1746-68. A maker of kits chiefly. His work was very neat, and the varnish of good quality. The tone of one of these kits which I tried some years ago was clear and sweet. He is said to have got £5 for a kit—a remarkable figure, equivalent to about £10 to-day. He made violoncellos for Longman & Broderip. Label :—

> MADE BY HENRY JAY,
> INSTRUMENT MAKER,
> IN LONG ACRE, LONDON, 1750.

JAY, THOMAS, London : c. 1690-1720. He made a number of instruments of superior workmanship, which had a rather small but pleasing tone.

JENKINS, THOMAS, Haverfordwest : 1819-90. He made a number of instruments on various models, of good workmanship and tone. He played the 'cello regularly for many years in S. Martin's church, and he possessed a clear alto voice of wonderful compass.

JOHNSON, JOHN, London : 1750-60. Fair workmanship. The tone although not large is clear and penetrating. A very high-arched violin, with thin, dry, yellow varnish had the following label :—

> MADE BY JOHN JOHNSON,
> CHEAPSIDE,
> 17 LONDON 55.

JOHNSTON, JAMES, Pollokshields: nineteenth century. Alexander Murdoch, in a little work entitled: " The Fiddle in Scotland," has the following note on his work: " An amateur who has turned out some of the best specimens of recent violin making in Scotland. Mr. Johnston has a fine taste for, and a genuine admiration of, the fiddle, as well as a superior practical genius for its construction. He is the possessor of a very valuable Strad violin."

JONES, ——, Barnstaple: contemporary.

JONES, DAVID, Merthyr Tydfil, Glamorgan: 1760–1840. A most ingenious man who made clocks, mechanical toys, artificial teeth, and fiddles, and other curious things. A full account of him and his numerous inventions appeared in the " Merthyr Express " some years ago.

JONES, JOHN, Port Dinorwic, N. Wales: 1833–1906. An amateur who made a few fiddles of no particular model. The workmanship was rough, but the tone was not so bad. He played the 'cello for many years at the parish church of Llanfairisgaer.

K

KELMAN, JAMES, Aberchirder, N.B.: nineteenth century. Commonplace work and tone.

KENDAL, GEORGE, ——: contemporary.

KENDLE, PHILLIP, Hereford: c. 1820. Average work.

KENNEDY, ALEXANDER, London: 1695–1785. Very fair work on the Stainer model.

KENNEDY, JOHN, London: 1730–1816. A nephew of Alexander Kennedy. Indifferent work.

VIOLIN AND BOW MAKERS 189

KENNEDY, THOMAS, London : 1784–1870. He was a prolific maker, and it is said that he made at least two thousand instruments of all sizes. The workmanship is good, but the tone is not of equal merit, being often harsh and metallic. A violin with a birch back and yellow varnish had the following label :—

> THOS. KENNEDY,
> LONDINI, 1860.

KIRKWOOD, ROBERT, Edinburgh : nineteenth century. A goldsmith, and a clever amateur who made a number of lovely violins.

KNAPTON, ——, London : c. 1830.

KNIGHT, ALFRED, Worcester : 1800–10. Ordinary work.

L

LANCASTER, ARTHUR CATTON, Colne, Lancashire : contemporary. He was born at Bishop Auckland in 1869, and works now at 5 Smith Street, Colne, as a professional maker and repairer. He has made a number of violins, a few 'cellos, and one double bass, on the Stradivari and Guarneri models. The workmanship is beautiful, and the tone bright, sweet, and responsive. A violin made to the memory of the late W. Hartley, band master to the ill-fated *Titanic,* was made of very fine wood, carefully finished in every detail, and covered with oil varnish of excellent quality. It had a large and telling tone. Hartley and Lancaster at one time played first violins in the Colne Orchestra, and Lancaster played the violin at his friend's funeral. The work of this maker is bound to come to the front.

LAUGHER, WILLIAM, Redditch : 1830 to about 1906. A manufacturer of steel and plated pins by trade, who made a number of violins as a hobby.

LEWIS, EDWARD, London : 1695–1730. A magnificent old maker, whose work is, unfortunately, very rare. I have seen only three violins of his make, one of which was on a model approximating to that of Maggini, the wood, workmanship, and tone being very fine indeed. The varnish was an oil one, of a rich golden-red colour, perfectly transparent, and elastic. No label of his is known.

LIGHT, EDWARD, London : 1780–1805. A lute and harp maker chiefly; he made very few violins.

LINDSAY, ——, Newcastle-on-Tyne : contemporary.

LINDSAY, DAVID, Edzell, N.B. : contemporary. An amateur who has made about forty violins of good workmanship, on the models of Stradivari and Guarneri.

LINDSAY, MICHAEL, H., Stockton-on-Tees : 1837 to about 1906. He was a professional maker and repairer, and made a large number of instruments, chiefly violins, on the Strad model. He used excellent wood, and a very fine amber oil varnish of his own make. The work is carefully finished all over, and the scroll especially is well carved in the best Italian style. The tone is not very powerful, but is of a very pleasing quality. Lindsay had a paralytic seizure in 1902, which put a period to his making, and during the few remaining years of his life he was unable to do anything beyond a little repairing. He won a medal for an exhibit of violins at the Liverpool Exhibition some years ago. He was a real artist, and his instruments will improve with age and careful use. Facsimile label :—

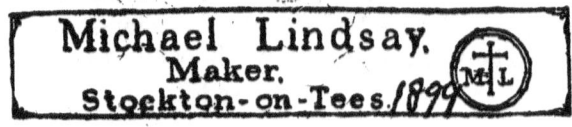

VIOLIN AND BOW MAKERS 191

LISTER, JOHN, Leeds : 1720–30. Very ordinary work on the Stainer model.

LOGAN, JOHN, Biggar, N.B. : contemporary. An excellent amateur maker and repairer. He has made a considerable number—between fifty and sixty I think—of violins on the Joseph, Strad, and Maggini models. His work is beautifully finished, and it is a pity he is not able to devote his whole time to the craft. Label :—

MADE BY
JOHN LOGAN,
ABINGTON, N.B., 1895.

LOMAX, JACOB, Bolton : contemporary. He worked at 11 Durham Street, where he also carried on the business of pawnbroking, but I have an idea that he has left Bolton and that I saw him in London recently.

LONGMAN & BRODERIP, London : 1750–73. They were dealers, and not actual makers. They bought all sorts of instruments, into which they put their trade label.

LONGSON, ——, London.

LOTT, GEORGE FREDERICK, London : 1800–68. He was the eldest son of John Frederick Lott. A very clever workman, and a very clever imitator—too clever, indeed. He worked for many years with Davies, of Coventry Street.

LOTT, JOHN FREDERICK, London : c. 1800–1871. He was the second son of John Frederick Lott, senior, and was born in London about the year 1800. He is the hero of Charles Reade's " Jack of all Trades : A Matter-of-fact Romance." He was an exceedingly clever craftsman, and a man, as Hart says, of " strangely varied talents." There is no doubt about it, and among the variety of talent he displayed was one for brilliant forgery. Some of his skilful counterfeits have deceived the ablest judges. I can only reiterate what I have said before that all the talent and skill a craftsman of this sort has will not atone for a life of fraud.

LOTT, JOHN FREDERICK, London : c. 1795–1853. He was born in Germany in 1775, and it is supposed that he came to London about 1795. He died there in 1853, and was buried in the Churchyard of St. Giles-in-the-Fields. He was a cabinet maker at first, but under the influence of Fendt he before long discarded that trade for the more congenial one of violin making. In 1798 he obtained work with Dodd, for whom he made those violoncellos and double basses which helped to swell the fame and fortune of the Englishman. The work of Lott, more especially his basses, was of the highest order, and it is the unanimous verdict of experts that it will bear comparison with the best Italian work. Hart sums up his merits briefly by saying that " he was certainly the king of the English double-bass makers."

LUTON, GEORGE, Leicester, c. 1840. Fairly good work.

LYE, HENRY, Camerton, Somerset : contemporary. He was born at Camerton in 1832, and has lived there all his life. He was for fifty-six years employed as carpenter on the Camerton Court Estate, and during these long years he devoted all his spare time to the construction of violins. An article on " Camerton Court and its History," which appeared in *The Bristol Times and Mirror* for June 6, 1914, contained the following reference to Lye : " Camerton Court, a mansion built and occupied by Mr. John Jarrett, and after his death by the Misses Jarrett . . . Miss A. M. Jarrett found great pleasure in wood carving, while Miss Emily Jarrett, who was more musically inclined, was an accomplished organist and violinist. Several violins and violas were made and supplied to her by Mr. Henry Lye. . . . This remarkable old gentleman, although over eighty-two years of age, can still see to read without glasses. His work at the Court ended about three years ago, but he is still busy at his favourite hobby, and has a number of his violins waiting for purchasers." Mr. Lye is now in his eighty-fourth year, but (thanks to splendid health, a steady nerve, and keen sight) is still able to wield the gouge. He has made a large number of violins, and a considerable number of violas and violoncellos. The instruments are solidly built, the workmanship of uniform excellence, and the tone large, bright, and responsive.

M

MACGREGOR, ——, Glasgow: nineteenth century. Said to have been a good maker.

M'GILL, JAMES CAMPBELL, Arran: nineteenth century. Fairly good work.

M'INTOSH, JAMES, Blairgowrie: 1801–73. Good work. He used spirit varnish, but it is put on so thin that the tone is not materially injured. A Mr. Case, of 14 Park Avenue, Handsworth, Birmingham, owns the finest specimen of his work that I have seen. It has a back cut on the slab, with a rather thick neck and sound holes that are rather straight and stiff: the model approximates to that of Amati. There is a character about the work which is rather striking, and the tone of this fiddle is certainly good. He made about two hundred and fifty instruments, including violins, violas, and violoncellos.

MACINTOSH, JOHN, Galston, N.B.: contemporary. An artist and antiquary who makes violins *en amateur*.

M'INTOSH, WILLIAM, Dundee: contemporary. Very good work.

MACKINTOSH, ——, Dublin.

M'GEE, ——, Belfast: nineteenth century.

M'GEORGE, GEORGE, Edinburgh: 1796–1820. A pupil and follower of Matthew Hardie who made excellent instruments. He used a spirit varnish which is of a slightly better quality than that of Hardie. There does not appear to be much of his work left.

M'KENZIE, MALCOLM, Dumbarton, N.B.: 1828 to about 1904. Made many instruments, of average merit.

M'LAY, WILLIAM, Kincardine-on-Forth: 1815 to about 1890. Very poor work.

M'NEILL, JOHN, Edinburgh: contemporary.

M'NEILL, ——, Dublin: early nineteenth century.

M'NICOLL, ALEXANDER, Padanaram: nineteenth century. Indifferent work.

M'SWAN, JOHN, Partick: contemporary. An amateur who has made a number of violins of about average merit.

MAGHIE, JOHN FISHER, Dalston: contemporary. Said to be a good maker, but I cannot say, as I have not seen his work.

MALLAS, ALEXANDER, Leith: 1826–91. Mr. Honeyman says his violins are well made, with a good tone.

MANN, JOHN ALEXANDER, Glasgow: 1810–89. It appears from the numerous letters that I have received in reference to my remarks upon this maker's work that I have very much under-estimated the ability of Mann and the merits of his instruments. It may be that I have, and that the following remarks which I cull from " The Fiddle in Scotland," by Alexander G. Murdoch, give a more just estimate of his work :—" Mr. Mann settled in Glasgow as a musical instrument maker and machinist. This would be about the year 1845, at which date his direct professional connection with fiddle making and repairing first began. In this fine field Mr. Mann found excellent scope for the exercise of his superior genius and taste. A mind of so much vigour and wealth of invention would not long remain a mere copyist in the make and repair of violins. Impelled by sincere artistic instincts, he made a long, patient, and careful study of the delicate construction and complex acoustics of the instrument, and his previous knowledge of chemistry—which had been a study of his youth—had made him perfectly acquainted with all the gums and solvents used in the manufacture of violin varnish. In this way Mr. Mann soon became a deft worker, . . . and as years increased, his fame spread, till latterly he has come to be recognised as one of the most distinguished of our present-day fiddle makers. Widely known as a maker, he is equally celebrated as a repairer of valuable old violins. In this respect he has had an unsurpassed experience. In the course of his professional career, some of the finest and most valuable of our old historic violins have from time to time been submitted to his judgment and inspection, or left in his skilful hands for repair." Mann was a personal friend of J. B. Vuillaume, whom he used to visit regularly at Paris once a year. The fact is, if I must give expression to my honest conviction, these visits were more than friendly visits, and had for their primary object business of a definite nature. I believe many of the instruments bearing Mann's labels were supplied him " in the white " by Vuillaume, Charles Jacquot, or some other Parisian makers whom he used to meet at Vuillaume's table. Some of Mann's work has a very striking resemblance to some of Vuillaume's. Albeit, I have not the slightest doubt that Mann was singularly gifted, and that he has made many violins of the highest merit.

MANN, T. H., Cardiff and Bedford : contemporary. A very gifted civil engineer who has made about thirty instruments, of very beautiful workmanship and good tone. He has given much time and thought to the theory of the construction of stringed instruments, and is a keen art critic.

MANUEL, EVAN, Merthyr Tydfil : early nineteenth century. He made many fiddles and a few Welsh harps. I have seen only one violin of his make, which was on the Stainer model, high-arched, rather well made, but with a tone inclined to be harsh and shrill.

MARLAND, JOHN & SEPTIMUS, Hurst : nineteenth century. Very fair work.

MARNIE, JOHN, Padanaram : nineteenth century. Poor work.

MARSHALL, JOHN, London : 1750–60. Fairly good work on the Stainer model.

MARSHALL, JOHN, Aberdeen : contemporary. He was born in the parish of Methlick, Aberdeenshire, in 1844, and has been established in Aberdeen nearly half-a-century as a professional maker and repairer. He has made upwards of three hundred instruments, including violins, violas, and violoncellos, of excellent workmanship and tone. He has followed the Amati, Guarneri, Stradivari, and Gagliano models. For many years now he has worked on the model of a beautiful Alessandro Gagliano which he had through his hands for repair, and of which he took careful measurements. I examined quite a number of these at his workshop in Woolman Street, about a year ago, and thought them solidly constructed and well finished instruments. Mr. Marshall is highly respected throughout the north of Scotland as a skilful repairer and conscientious man, and the practical evidence of this respect is the abundance of work which he always has in hand. For the past nine years he has been assisted by Mr. William Glennie, a maker and repairer of undoubted ability. Facsimile label :—

Marshall died on March 16, 1919.

MARTIN, ——, London. Little or nothing is known of him.

MARTIN, HENRY, Nottingham : c. 1800. Fairly good work, which would be better but for the exaggerated arching.

MAYSON, STANSFIELD, Manchester : contemporary. Son, pupil, and successor of Walter H. Mayson. He has made about twenty instruments on his father's model, which are of good workmanship and tone. It is too soon to predict whether he will attain the excellence of his father, but he has undoubted abilities.

MAYSON, WALTER HENRY, Manchester : 1835-1904. He was born at Cheetwood, near Manchester, on November 8, 1835, and was the fourth son of Mark and Elizabeth Mayson. His father was a descendant of an ancient Cumberland family, and in the days of his prosperity owned considerable property in Keswick. His mother's maiden name was Green, and she was a daughter of William Green, the painter, whose work was so highly esteemed by Professor Wilson (" Christopher North "), Hartley, Coleridge, and William Wordsworth, the poet,

Mayson was educated at the celebrated school of Thomas Whalley, where he early gained distinction at English composition, his essays being often selected by the headmaster for public reading before the school. At the age of seventeen he was apprenticed to a firm of merchants in Manchester, with whom he served five years. During this time he devoted his spare hours to the pursuit of music and literature, and he contributed verses and occasional essays to the periodicals and local press. He made his first fiddle in 1873, and very shortly afterwards he resolved to give up his post (he was now in a good position with a large firm of merchants) and to devote his life to the art and craft of violin making. From this time to the end of his life he steadily made at the rate of about two instruments per month. The total number he made reached the high figure of eight hundred and eleven, all entirely made by himself, with the exception of the last instrument, which was only half finished when the hand of death was laid upon him. Of these, twenty-seven were violas, twenty-one violoncellos, and the rest violins. As far as I can gather from Mayson's correspondence, and from my own observation, about one-fourth of the total number of instruments made by him are of his better class, the rest being of a lower—some of them of a much lower—grade of excellence. It is very unfortunate that this fine artist was during the greater part of his life entirely at the mercy of circumstances—circumstances over which he could possibly have no control, and for which he was not at all responsible. I am morally certain of one thing, that Mayson never turned out a poor instrument from his hands by choice or by neglect. But he was poor, and at times very poor, so that he was often obliged to put inferior material into his instruments, and often inferior (or less finished) work too, and thus to sacrifice to the need of the moment much of his fame with posterity. It is when we contemplate the cruel lot of a genius like Mayson that the truth is borne in upon us that poverty is a crime.

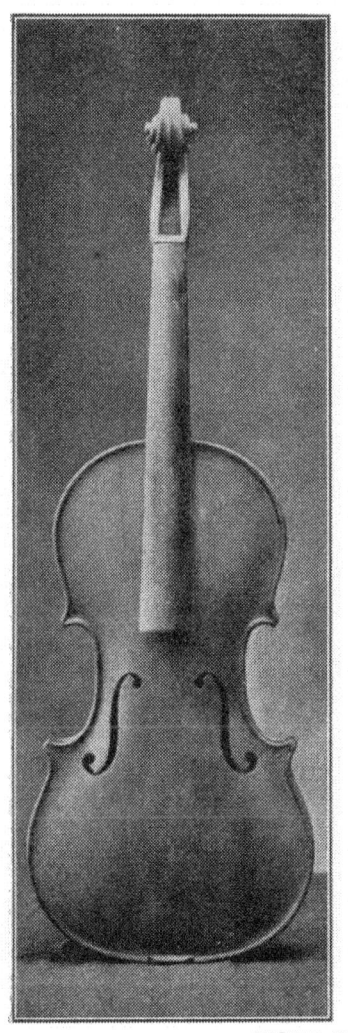 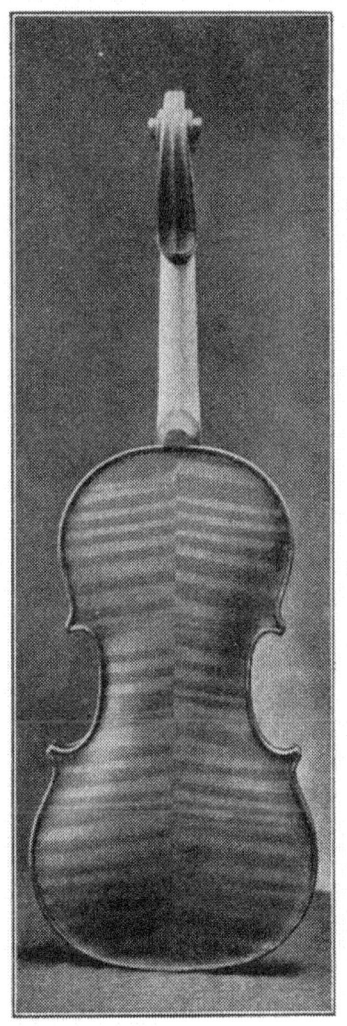

VIOLIN BY MAYSON.

To face p. 198.

VIOLIN AND BOW MAKERS

But Mayson's best work is magnificent. It will bear comparison with the finest work produced in modern times by any maker in this or any other country. In his earlier days he made a number of instruments on the models of Stradivari and Guarneri, but his strong mind refused to bend for long to the mind of another artist, even though he were a Stradivari, and he struck out on original lines. The principal measurements of his original model for violins are :—

Length of body	$14\frac{5}{16}$ inches.
Width across upper bouts . . .	$6\frac{7}{8}$,,
,, ,, middle ,, . . .	$4\frac{1}{2}$,,
,, ,, lower ,, . . .	$8\frac{1}{2}$,,
Depth of ribs at lower bouts . .	$1\frac{1}{4}$,,
,, ,, upper ,, . . .	$1\frac{1}{8}$,,
Length of sound-holes	3 ,,
Distance between ƒ's at upper turn .	$1\frac{5}{8}$,,

The arching is slightly more pronounced than it is in instruments of the grand Strad pattern.

Mayson made about a dozen instruments with carved backs, that is, with landscapes, flowers, or figures carved thereon in bas-relief. The relief is only one-fortieth of an inch, and the effect is wonderful in so slight a cutting. Fine as these are, however, as works of art, I do not think they represent the finest success of Mayson for tone, probably the inequality of thicknessing due to the carving affected the tone detrimentally—it certainly could not improve it.

Mayson worked at various places, first at " The Polygon," Lower Broughton, next in Burton Arcade, Deansgate, Manchester, where he remained for some time, and made many instruments; he removed thence to Croft House, Newby Bridge, at the foot of Windermere, where he remained for six years, and made much of his best work. From Newby Bridge he went back to Manchester, opening a shop at 62 Oxford Street: here he worked for several years.

In 1899 he opened a workshop at 256 High Holborn, London, but this venture turned out a disastrous failure, and he was obliged once more to turn his face towards Manchester. Broken in fortune and bruised in spirit the poor artist's health gradually gave way, and a paralytic seizure at the close of the year 1904 completed a work already commenced by adversity. He died in his seventieth year. Facsimile label:—

Walter H. Mayson, Manchester, Fecit "Panope". 1903

Each instrument was named, and the label was worded accordingly. Mayson was awarded medals at Cork, in 1883; Inventions, London, 1885; and Melbourne, in 1888. Many tributes were paid to his genius in his lifetime by men who knew his work well, and the press was lavish in its praise of the old craftsman when he had laid by for ever his gouge and calipers.

Mayson published several works, including "Colazzi," "The Heir of Dalton," "The Stolen Fiddle," "Violin Making," etc., and he left a number of others in manuscript.

MEARES, RICHARD, London: 1660–80. A maker of lutes and viols.

MEARES, RICHARD, London: 1675–90. Son of the preceding. He made a few violins, but left the trade soon after the death of his father.

MEEK, JAMES, Carlisle: contemporary. He was born at Cleator, Cumberland, in 1862, and has been working as a professional maker and repairer at 15 Tait Street, Carlisle, for twenty years. He has made fifty-three instruments up to date, nearly all violins, some on the A. and H. Amati model, but the majority on the Strad and Guarneri models. Most of his time is taken up with repairs, and he can make only two or three violins in the course of a year. His work is beautifully finished, and his material selected with scrupulous care. A violin of his make on the A. and H. Amati model which I saw and tried some years ago was one of the most delicately and exquisitely finished objects I have ever handled. The wood of its back was of narrow but definite and perfectly regular curl, and the instrument was covered with a golden amber varnish of wonderful "fire." The tone was not large, but it was sweet and responsive. Mr. Meek has a high reputation as a repairer of all kinds of stringed instruments. Facsimile label:—

James Meek.
Carlisle. 1914.

MEIKLE, ROBERT, Lesmahagow: 1817–97. Ordinary work.

MEGGISON, ALFRED: Manchester: c. 1800. Workmanship very fair, but high arching.

MENTIPLY, ANDREW ADAM, Ladybank, Fife: contemporary. An amateur maker and repairer of considerable ability and skill. He has made a large number of violins, some on the Strad model, but the majority on an original model, which is of rather large dimensions, with somewhat peculiar sound-holes. The tone is very good.

MENZIES, JOHN, Falkirk: 1820–31. His work is said to be fairly good.

MEREDITH, L., London: c. 1720–50. Mr. W. M. Groundwater, of Salford, Manchester, had a fiddle through his hands in 1910 labelled: "L. Meredith, St. Paul's Churchyard, London, 1734," which he described as being rather large and somewhat on the lines of Maggini, with deep ribs, and covered with brown varnish, rather thick in pâte. The tone was fairly good.

MERLIN, JOSEPH, London: 1765–80. Stainer model, fairly good work, but rather poor tone. The varnish is mostly dirty yellow or brown of an inferior quality. His mechanical pegs for violins and 'cellos were in demand at one time. Label:—

> JOSEPHUS MERLIN CREMONAE EMULUS,
> NO. 104, LONDINI, 1779, IMPROVED.
> 69 QUEEN ANN STREET EAST, PORTLAND CHAPEL,

MIER, ——, London: c. 1780.

MILLER, ——, London: c. 1750. Little or nothing is known of him.

MILLER, or MILLAR, Belfast: contemporary apparently. The Rev. Father Greaven gives his name in his list.

MILLER, ALEXANDER, St. Andrews: 1813–77. A pupil of Thomas Hardie. The work is very good, but the tone often disappointing. At his death Miller left a large stock of excellent wood, which was bought by Mr. John Logan, of Biggar.

MILLER, JOHN, Dundee: contemporary. His work is said to be very good.

MILNE, PATRICK G., Aberdeen: contemporary. He was born at Aberdeen in 1873, and works there now at 16 Guild Street as a professional maker and repairer. He is one of the best of present day Scottish makers. He has

VIOLIN AND BOW MAKERS 203

made a few violins on the Guarneri model, but nearly all his later work is on the grand Strad pattern. He is very particular about the material he uses, and only puts wood into his instruments which thoroughly satisfies him as to its proper seasoning and acoustical qualities. All the work is executed by Mr. Milne personally, and every detail is scrupulously attended to and beautifully finished. The varnish is an oil one, the colour varying from light orange to dark red: it is of excellent quality and perfectly transparent. He has made about fifty violins and a few violas and violoncellos. His instruments are well liked by professional players. Much of his time is taken up with repairs. Facsimile label :—

MINER, D. BROWN, Dunfermline : contemporary.

MITCHELL, GEORGE, Edzell : 1823–97. Average merit.

MITCHELL, JOHN, Dunfermline : contemporary.

MITCHELL, ——, Captain, Toronto, Canada : contemporary. Very glowing accounts of his work have appeared in the Canadian press.

MOFFATT, W. J., ——. His violins are occasionally advertised in catalogues of old instruments, but I cannot say when or where he worked.

MOLYNEUX, ——, Dublin : c. 1800. A very fine violin of his make is in the Dublin Museum, which is quite Italian in character. Father Greaven thinks he was a foreigner who had settled down in Dublin in early life.

MONK, JOHN KING, Lewisham, and Blackheath : contemporary. He was born in 1846, and is a descendant in the direct line of General Monk, of Commonwealth fame. He has carried on business for many years as a professional maker and repairer, and is considered a clever and conscientious craftsman. He has made a large number of violins on a model which closely approximates to that of the grand Strad. He uses excellent material, and a lustrous oil varnish of fine quality, ranging in colour from pale amber to deep golden red. He is of an inventive turn of mind, and has introduced and put on the market, I believe, some " patent improvements," such as the " triple bar system," the " Maggini bass bar," etc. All lovers of classical methods, and adherents to the old traditions, look with suspicion upon these innovations, and not without very good reasons. Mr. Monk, however, makes instruments of the orthodox type, and his best work is excellent in every way. Facsimile label :—

MORGAN, JAMES, Edinburgh : 1839 to about 1906. A cabinet maker who made a number of excellent violins and other stringed instruments during spare time.

MORGAN, WILLIAM, Dunnottar Castle, Stonehaven : contemporary. He was born in 1844, and has been keeper of the celebrated castle of Dunnottar for many years, and a professional violin maker for the last ten or dozen years. He has fitted up a workshop in a part of the romantic old ruins of the castle by the sea, and there, to the wild music of the waves, he muses and carves and fashions his fiddles. Morgan is a " character " of an old-world type, with a mind steeped in ancient lore, and a memory packed with reminiscences and quaint anecdote. The old ruins are to him a palace, and fiddle making a golden dream. He has made about a hundred violins, some of which are on the Stradivari and Guarneri models, but the majority on that of Alessandro Gagliano, with the arch slightly reduced. The workmanship is characterised by masculine strength and a kind of pleasing ruggedness rather than by delicacy and *finesse*. The remarkable thing about his work is the fine tone he obtains. All his instruments that I have tried have a large, brilliant, and sonorous tone. There is no mistaking its quality—it is such as we always associate with the name " Italian." When time and use have had their mellowing effect upon it, nothing better will be desired—nothing better will be possible.

Facsimile label:

MOORE, ANTHONY JOHN, Sunderland: contemporary. An artist by profession, who has taken up violin making as a hobby. I have not seen any of his recent work, but some of his instruments are said to have a beautiful tone.

MORRIS, J., BATH: nineteenth century. I know nothing of him or his work. A violin of his make was sold at Messrs. Puttick & Simpson's sale on June 8, 1906, which was well made and had a good tone.

MORRISON, ARCHIBALD, Glasgow: 1820-95. He worked in Great Hamilton Street, where he had a music shop, and where he made a large number of fiddles of all sorts. His shop was a rendezvous of fiddle enthusiasts and players, who were known about Glasgow as "Morrison's Band."

MORRISON, JAMES, Dunfermline: nineteenth century.

MORRISON, JOHN, London: 1760-1827. He worked mostly for the trade.

MORTIMER, JOHN WILLIAM, Cardiff: contemporary. Born at Gomersal, near Leeds, in 1857. He is a pupil of William Heaton, Gomersal, and he received some instruction also from W. J. Cartwright, of Yeadon. He has been established in Cardiff for about fifteen years as a professional maker, repairer, and double bass player. Mr. Mortimer is unique amongst violin makers: he has seven sons, all professional players, each of whom plays upon an instrument of his father's make. This surely constitutes a record, and it is worthy of remark that every member of this wonderful family is a musician and an artist of undoubted ability. Mr. Mortimer has made a considerable number of instruments, including violins, violas, 'cellos, and double basses. His larger instruments are noted for their full, sonorous, and responsive tone. One double bass which I have seen was made of exceptionally fine and beautifully figured wood: it had an immense tone of excellent quality. His smaller instruments, which are on an original model, are very carefully constructed, and have a large and telling tone. The violas are made in two sizes, the larger one being $16\frac{1}{2}$ inches long, with widths of 8, $5\frac{1}{4}$, and 10 inches. He has used various varnishes, such as Whitelaw's,

Briggs', and on some of his larger instruments an amber varnish of his own make.

Having been trained originally as a cabinet maker and wood carver he is very skilful in the use of keen-edged tools, and his repairs show the practised hand of the qualified craftsman. Being the only properly trained repairer within a radius of thirty or forty miles, and living as he does in a populous centre and in a very musical city, nearly all his time is taken up with repairs. He is an intelligent and conscientious man, an ardent musician, an excellent bassist, and a painstaking and capable craftsman.

MURDOCH, ALEXANDER, Aberdeen : 1815–91. Said to have made a large number of instruments.

MURPHY, BARTHOLOMEW, Cork : 1780–1830.

MURPHY, JOHN, Cork : c. 1820–50. Possibly a son of the preceding.

MURPHY, DENNIS, Dublin : c. 1830.

MURRAY, DAVID, Gorebridge : contemporary. An amateur of considerable ability, who has made several beautiful violins.

MURRAY, JAMES, Dumfries : contemporary.

MURRAY, JOHN BROWN, Clarebrand : contemporary. An amateur who has made several good violins.

MUST, FREDERICK, Shrewsbury : c. 1800. Amati model with a much exaggerated arch.

MYERS, CHARLES, Hereford : c. 1820. I have seen his name in a catalogue of old instruments.

MYLES, FRANCIS, Cardiff : c. 1840. Rather poor work.

N

NAYLOR, ISAAC, Headingly, Leeds : 1775–90. A pupil of Richard Duke, many of whose characteristics he reproduced in his work.

NEWCOMBE, GEORGE, Leicester : nineteenth century.

NEWTON, ISAAC, London : 1775–1825. He made mostly for the trade, particularly for Betts. Fairly good work.

NICHOLAS, EDWARD, Bristol : c. 1800. I have seen his name in a catalogue of old instruments..

NICOL, THOMAS, Glasterlaw : 1840 to about 1910. He made about seventy or eighty violins on the models of Stradivari and Guarneri. Careful work.

NICOLSON, JAMES, Stirling : 1770–90. His name appeared in a Scottish catalogue some years ago.

NISBET, WILLIAM, Lint Mill, Prestonkirk : 1828–1902. An extraordinarily versatile man, of whom the Rev. G. Marjoribanks, Vicar of Stenton, wrote as follows in the *Haddington Courier* : " It is not too much to say that in whatever direction Nisbet has turned his energies he has always excelled . . . he is a man possessed not only of rare technical skill, but of such accurate and extensive information, gathered mainly from personal observation and study in the fields of natural history and science, whether as photographer, wood-carver, carpenter, basket maker, violin maker, the productions of his genius and labour have been equally appreciated, etc." He made a hundred and twenty violins, some on the Maggini and some on the Amati model. The workmanship is excellent, and the tone very good. He was awarded two bronze medals for an exhibit of instruments at the Edinburgh International Exhibition in 1886.

NOBLE, HUGH, Dundee : contemporary. An amateur.

NOLTON, CHRISTOPHER, Bristol : c. 1810. His name has appeared in catalogues.

NORBORN, JOHN, London : c. 1720.

NORDEN, RICHARD, Crewe : 1830–50. Average ability.

NORMAN, BARAK, London : 1688–1740. He was a pupil of Thomas Urquhart, and worked first in Bishopsgate and afterwards in St. Paul's Churchyard He worked on the Maggini model, which he however modified in some respects. No violins of his are known. He is supposed to have been the second violoncello maker in this country. His instruments are of very full proportions, and the work is, as a rule, beautifully finished. The varnish is usually dark brown or dark amber, and is of excellent quality. The tone is powerful and sonorous. He became partner to Nathaniel Cross about the year 1715, and both worked at the sign of the " Bass-Viol."

NORRIS, JOHN, London : 1739–1818. A pupil of Thomas Smith, and for some time partner with Barnes.

O

OLDHAM, THOMAS, Tewkesbury : c. 1820.

OLIVER, JAMES, Reading : 1810–40. He used baked wood.

O'MAHONY, JAMES, Mitchelstown, Ireland : contemporary. A contractor and builder by trade who has made about sixty violins during spare time. His work is nicely finished and his instruments have a good tone.

OMOND, JAMES, Kirbuster, Stromness : 1833 to about 1907. He was originally a schoolmaster, but had to give up that profession through a break-down in health. He picked up watchmaking and repairing, and a few years later violin making and repairing, and to the latter craft he adhered to the end of his days, eventually becoming a professional maker of some importance. He made in all about three hundred instruments, including violins, violas, and violoncellos. He worked on the Stradivari and Guarneri models, but these models in a number of his instruments were considerably modified. Some of his Joseph " copies " could hardly be described as copies at all. The work is very carefully finished throughout, and the tone is moderately powerful and of a good quality. He would have obtained a larger tone if he had given his plates a greater taper. His fiddles are overstocked with wood. It is a wise provision to leave plenty of wood in a new instrument, but a great error to leave too much—almost as great as leaving too little. Omond obtained four diplomas of merit and bronze medals at various Exhibitions.

ORCHARD, JOSEPH, Worcester : 1840–50. His name has appeared in old catalogues.

ORTON, PHILLIP, Hereford : 1845–60. Ordinary work of no particular model.

OSBORNE, HENRY, Sherborne, Dorset : c. 1860. Poor work.

OSMOND, WILLIAM, Evesham : 1810–35. He made a few fairly good instruments, and a good number, apparently, that can only be described as rough, amateurish work.

VIOLIN AND BOW MAKERS

OTTLEY, JACOB, Bristol: c. 1800. I have seen his name in catalogues of old instruments more than once. One instrument advertised was described as having a large and fine tone.

OUTRAM, FREDERICK, —— : early nineteenth century, apparently. I saw a violin with his name written in ink on the wood, a few years back, which was a well-made instrument with a good tone.

OWEN, JOHN WILLIAM, Leeds: contemporary. He was born in Leeds, May 28, 1852, and is the only son of William and Hannah Owen. His mother, whose maiden name was Rimmer, was a professional designer of fancy work, and was considered to be without a rival in the northern counties in that department of art and craft. Owen received early education at an elementary school in his native town, but it was discontinued at a stage which made it necessary for him to supplement it by attendance at technical classes in the evenings later on in life. He was apprenticed to the engineering profession, but his health giving way he was obliged to relinquish that profession and to seek lighter work. During a long illness he had attempted violin making as a means of whiling away the idle hours, and succeeding beyond his expectation he resolved to adopt the craft as a profession as soon as health permitted. He acquired a theoretical knowledge of violin construction from books, and a practical knowledge from expert workmen, and from an extended visit to one of the larger workshops in France.

He commenced as a professional violin maker and repairer in 1884, and since then he has completed about two hundred instruments, including violins, violas, and violoncellos, and his list of repairs (of which he keeps a strict record) is an extraordinary one, standing at just over five thousand instruments.

He works on the Stradivari and Guarneri models, also on

an original one, the principal measurements of which are :—

Length of body	$14\frac{1}{8}$ inches.
Width across upper bouts	$6\frac{5}{8}$,,
,, ,, middle ,,	$4\frac{3}{8}$,,
,, ,, lower ,,	$8\frac{1}{4}$,,
Length of C's	3 ,,
,, ,, f's	3 ,,
Depth of ribs $1\frac{1}{4}$ inch diminishing to	$1\frac{5}{32}$,,

The outline of this model is very pure, and every individual part is in perfect keeping with the whole. The margins are full and the edges strong, slightly raised, and beautifully rounded. The scroll is an exquisite piece of carving, and in the best Italian style. Every detail of the work, both inside and outside, is finished with scrupulous care. The mitres of the ribs were geometrically true in all the instruments examined by me, having facets of nearly a millimetre in width—a mode of finishing this little detail which I considered to be more suitable to the model than the "knife-edge" facet. The sound-holes were clean cut, but there was nothing mechanical about them, as there is, *e.g.*, about many of the better class modern French work, in which the sound-holes appear as though they had been cut or punched out with one blow with an f-shaped tool.

Mr. Owen is particularly successful in obtaining a fine tone. A violin of his make which I have, and which has been in regular use for the last fifteen years, has developed a very responsive, broad, and brilliant tone, and it is a tone which is improving steadily every year.

His violoncellos are specially liked. The late Mr. Van Biene, Mr. Arthur Broadley, Mr. David Dixon, and other well-known 'cellists have written in the highest terms of their merits. Mr. Owen is an enthusiast in and for his art. To an outsider he would doubtless appear as one that has no room in his soul for anything save fiddles. He lives in his workshop all the year round, and every day of the year,

 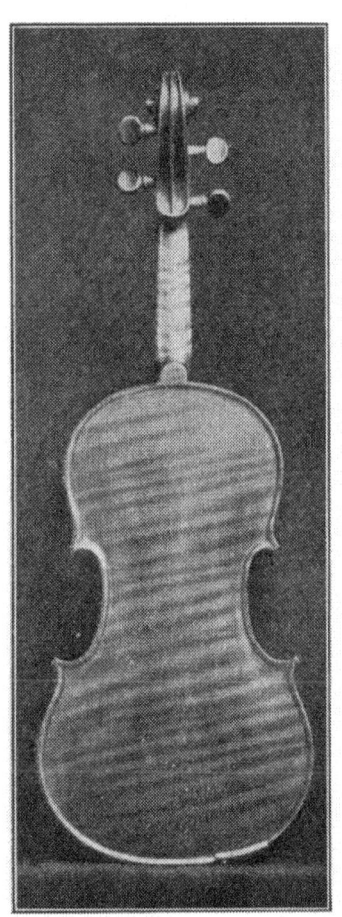

VIOLIN BY OWEN.

VIOLIN AND BOW MAKERS

except Sundays, when he seeks a little relaxation in the form of long walks during the day and some music in the evening. He is not an enthusiast of the kind Matthew Arnold had in his mind when he wrote that " unfortunately few people who feel a passion think of learning anything from it " : Mr. Owen has learnt a great deal—he has learnt that there is much in life worth living for, and that in art, especially, the good, the true, and the beautiful are worth possessing for their own sake. There can be little doubt that his instruments will be much valued in time to come.

Facsimile label :—

The date is not on the label, but is inscribed on the bare wood after the maker's autograph.

OXLEY, JOSEPH, Cambridge : c. 1800. His name appears in an old list (1884) of instruments for sale.

P

PAMPHILON, EDWARD, London : 1670-90. A fine old maker in many respects, and if he had worked on a better model his work would rank higher than it does. His model is a sort of cross between the Brescian and Tyrolese types, the outline, scroll, double purfling, being Brescian, but the arching distinctly Tyrolese, and often an exaggeration of even that pattern. He used an oil varnish of good quality, ranging in colour from pale amber to light brown. The tone of his instruments is not large, but it is clear, sweet, and responsive.

PANORMO, EDWARD, London : nineteenth century. He was a son or grandson (it is not certain which) of Vincenzo Panormo. He worked in London and in Ireland.

PANORMO, GEORGE, London : nineteenth century.

PANORMO, GEORGE LEWIS, London : c. 1810-40. He was the second son of Vincenzo Panormo, and worked in Oxford Street, and afterwards in High Street, St. Giles-in-the-Fields. He was an excellent bow maker, but did not reach the same high standard in violin making as his father.

PANORMO, JOSEPH, London : c. 1800-30. He was the eldest son of Vincenzo Panormo, and worked in New Compton Street, and later in King Street, Soho. He was an excellent craftsman, and his violoncellos had a high reputation at one time. Very few of his instruments are left, or (which would be nearer the mark) very few of them are now known as his work.

PARKER, DANIEL, London : 1700-45. The information which is usually given about this maker is misleading, and most writers content themselves with repeating early errors in almost the same words. Hart, Haweis, and Miss Stainer, give his period as 1740-85, and Fleming as 1715-85. As a matter of fact there are undoubtedly genuine examples of his work still in existence bearing the dates 1700, 1708, 1712, 1719, 1726, and 1732. The earliest which I have actually seen and tried is dated 1712, a specimen which has been pronounced genuine by the Messrs. Hill, and the Messrs. Hart, and which I also think genuine, all except the scroll. Mr. Richard Hilton, of Derby House, Matlock Bridge, is (or was, ten years ago) the owner of this interesting

 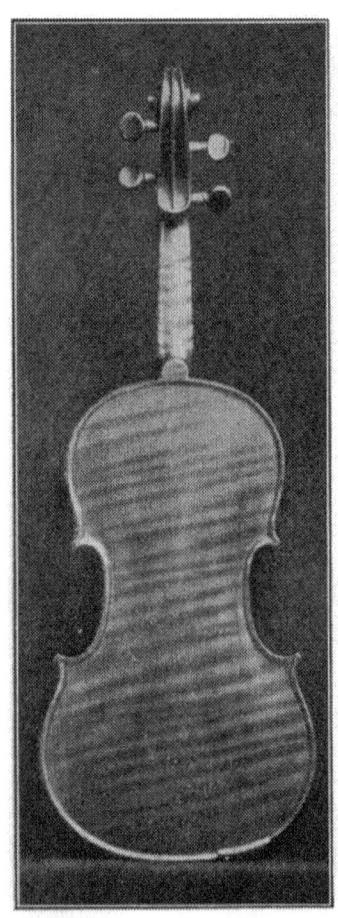

VIOLA BY PARKER.

To face p. 215.

VIOLIN AND BOW MAKERS

and early example of Parker's art. I have in my possession a very beautiful violin of his make, on the Strad model, and in his best style, bearing a label dated 1719. This is genuine in all its parts, and is of excellent workmanship and tone. What is considered to be the finest Parker violin in existence is owned by Clarkson Close, Esq., The Poplars, Newton Park, Leeds. This is on the "Long Strad" model, with rich golden red oil varnish, of fine pâte and lustre. This instrument is considered by the Messrs. Hill to belong to the year 1700, or thereabouts. It is not dated, and it is impossible to be certain when it was made, but I certainly think it resembles the instruments made in 1726 and 1732 much more than it does the instruments made in 1712 and 1719.

It has been surmised that Parker was a pupil of Pamphilon, or of Urquhart, or of both, but on what grounds I quite fail to understand, as there is not the remotest similarity between his work and the work of either of these makers. It is not necessary to suppose that he was a pupil of anybody, for he was a born artist, and endowed by nature with a special aptitude for the use of fine-edged tools.

His work is thoroughly British in character: it is solid, chaste, and very "correct"—*i.e.* correct in the sense in which the word is used when it is applied to the poetry of the classical school. I do not think the work of any of our old makers reflects so clearly the spirit of the eighteenth century as does that of Daniel Parker. I may be rather fanciful, but I look upon him as the Pope of old British fiddle makers, that is to say, what Alexander Pope was to the rest of the poets, that was Daniel Parker to the rest of the old fiddle makers. Pope is not our greatest poet, nor is Parker our greatest luthier. There is not one of our old makers whose work has interested me more, and I have been at pains to seek out his instruments and to carefully examine them when I have come across them. Art, to my mind, reveals the spirit of an age quite as fully and clearly as literature does. Who that is familiar with the works of Hogarth will deny that they tell us quite as much about the state of society in the eighteenth century as the writings of Johnson, Addison, Steele, Lamb, Swift, etc., do ? An old fiddle is certainly not expected to tell as much as an old picture or an old book does, but it tells a lot to the man who knows how to interpret its language. Old William Ebsworth Hill used to say that he could tell from the internal organism of the fiddle the kind of tool that had been used in fashioning it. And the connoisseur imagines that he can see in the contour, curves, and style of a fiddle the reflection of the face of the age in which it was constructed : that is, if the instrument is a good example of the work of a typical artist.

I see in Parker's work that " correctness " which I see in the poetry of the " classical " school. There is about it the same sense of solidity, sanity, and mathematical exactness that is observable in the writings of Pope and his numerous satellites and imitators. We know nothing about the man except what is recorded in his work, but that is enough to inform us that he was an artist of great ability, with tastes (moulded and regulated in the manner of the age) that were strictly chaste and coldly "correct."

He copied Stainer, N. Amati, and Stradivari, but his Strad copies are far and away his best work. The tone is always fine, and in some instances almost equal to the tone of Bank's best Amati copies. The plates of the violins are well stocked with wood, and with due care the instruments may be expected to last in first-class condition another hundred years at least. Comparatively few of his instruments have his own label in them : he made principally for the trade, and it is not improbable that he sometimes sold his fiddles " in the white." It does not matter whose labels these fine old instruments carry, they are easily recognized by the expert who has made a study of the work of the old English School.

PATERSON, JAMES, Edinburgh : 1834-98. A cabinet maker by trade, who made a number of violins on the Guarneri model, and a few on the " Count Cessol "

VIOLIN BY PARKER.

VIOLIN AND BOW MAKERS

Strad model. He obtained a bronze medal for a case of violins at the Edinburgh Exhibition, 1890.

PATRICK, WILLIAM, St. Andrews : contemporary.

PAYNE, R., South Shields : contemporary.

PEARCE, GEORGE, London : 1820-56. He worked for S. A. Forster.

PEARCE, JAMES & THOMAS, London : 1780-1810. They were brothers, and had their workshop in Peter Street, Saffron Hill. Indifferent work.

PEARCE, WILLIAM, London : nineteenth century. Average ability, but he managed to obtain a bronze medal at the International Exhibition, London, 1885.

PEMBERTON, EDWARD, London : c. 1660. Little or nothing is really known of him. The legend of the " Earl of Leicester " violin has been laid to rest, and it would be of no interest to revive it again.

PERRY, JAMES, Kilkenny : c. 1780-1800. He was a cousin of Thomas Perry, of Dublin, and a protégé of the Ormonde family, of Kilkenny Castle,—so Father Greaven informs us. He made a large number of instruments, of rather rough workmanship, but of excellent tone.

PERRY, JOSEPH, Dublin : c. 1800. Probably another cousin of Thomas Perry. He is said to have made a large number of instruments of excellent workmanship and tone. The Rev. Father Greaven says that some of his violins are almost on a level with the work of Benjamin Banks. This is saying a very great lot, and it deepens my regret that I have not seen any of his work.

PERRY, THOMAS, Dublin : c. 1757-1818. A new light is thrown on the life and work of this celebrated old maker in an interesting article published in the "Museum Bulletin" of the National Museum of Science and Art, Dublin, for July, 1911, by one of the Assistant Keepers, Mr. A. McGoogan. The article is the result of a very painstaking research, and the violin world is greatly indebted to Mr. McGoogan for this timely and valuable contribution to the literature of the leading instrument. I reproduce here a large portion of the article for the benefit of those who take more than a passing interest in the history of British violin makers: that will be more satisfactory and more honest than if I were to paraphrase or condense it and claim any credit for myself. Mr. McGoogan writes: "It is a pity that research, which has done so much towards illuminating the history of the Irish harpsichord and pianoforte makers of the eighteenth century, has done so little to place the life-story of Thomas Perry, the great violin maker of the same period, on a firm foundation. At present there is nothing better to rely upon than the unscientific records of tradition. Even the country of Perry's origin is not known for certain. Guesswork has assigned his birth to the year 1767, but circumstances show that he must have been born at least ten years earlier. It is said that, like Molyneux, his Dublin predecessor in the art of violin making, he was of Huguenot descent. It is also stated that he was related to Claude Pierray, a noted violin maker who flourished in Paris. . . . Allied with the tradition that associates him with Claude Pierray of Paris is another of a contradictory order which would have us believe that Thomas Perry was originally a pupil of Duke, the London maker. The only foundation for this assertion lies in the fact that Perry's earlier violins, the instruments he made before coming to Ireland, are distinctly of the contemporary English type. According to the traditional account (which is unassociated with any particular date), Thomas Perry, on first coming to Dublin, set up in business in a house near Christ Churchyard, in a locality long since altered beyond recognition. Be that as it may, the first definite trace of Perry in Ireland at a

VIOLIN BY PERRY.

VIOLIN AND BOW MAKERS 219

specific address occurs in 1787, when his name is recorded in *Wilson's Dublin Directory* as a musical instrument maker, of No. 6 Anglesea Street. Year after year his residence is given at that address until 1803, when he removed to No. 4 in the same street, and there remained until the period of his death.

" Tradition accounts for the great difference between the fiddles made in England by Thomas Perry and those afterwards made by him in Ireland by the plausible assertion that his Dublin-made instruments were modelled on a rare old Italian violin lent him by the Duke of Leinster. There can be little doubt that he followed here the Amati model, but, even if we accept the Leinster story it does not account for his knowledge of that mysterious, rich, golden amber varnish he employed, and to which much (but of course not all) of the fine quality of his violins was due. Accustomed to receive a good price for his instruments, sometimes as much as £20, he was particularly careful in the selection and seasoning of the wood. For the belly of his violins he usually chose a delicately-grained Swiss pine wood, making the back and sides of maple. Although he now ranks as one of the best of the later eighteenth century instrument makers, his reputation is wholly posthumous, and of comparatively recent date. Connoisseurs have awakened to his merits, and his violins, already valuable, are found to command a steadily-increasing price, more particularly as comparatively few of them appear to be extant. The National Museum is in possession of five notable examples of his work; a quartet, formerly the property of Sir Francis Cruise, and a double bass viol, whose value may be estimated when it is said that no other Perry instrument of that class can now be traced.

" It has been occasionally stated that the firm of Thomas Perry was altered during his lifetime to Perry & Wilkinson, that Perry took into partnership a quondam apprentice of his named William Wilkinson, who had married his daughter Elizabeth. This is not the case, the firm remained ' Thomas

Perry' till his death, which took place, as a transcript of his will in the Public Record Office shows, in 1818, and not in 1830, as is frequently stated. From the period of his death until at least 1831 (according to the evidence of *Wilson's Dublin Directory*) the business was carried on at No. 4 Anglesea Street, under the name of 'Perry & Wilkinson.' From 1831 to 1834 the same Directory gives only the name of William Wilkinson in connexion with that establishment. But, on referring to *Pettigrew and Dalton's Dublin Directory* for the next few years, we find that from 1834 till 1838 the firm was known again (if indeed any change had previously taken place) as 'Perry & Wilkinson.' In 1839 the business disappears altogether from Anglesea Street, but in that, and the following year, we find a William Wilkinson, musical instrument maker, trading at No. 5 Essex Quay, and residing at No. 5 Rosanna Place, Portobello. Tradition, however, says this was not Thomas Perry's son-in-law. Connoisseurs have frequently noted the bewildering inequality in Perry's violins without ever divining the reason. The whole thing is due to a lack of historical knowledge and to a bunching together of violins made by Thomas Perry before 1818 with violins by Wilkinson, trading as 'Perry & Wilkinson,' after that date. There can be little doubt that after Perry's death the standard of quality was seldom, if ever, maintained. . . . The fact is, Perry and Wilkinson were never in actual partnership. The terms of Perry's will clearly demonstrates this. Here we have at once the secret of the inequality of make, of 'the considerable diversity in the style of copying the model' [noticed by Fleming], and of the difference in the varnish. Responsibility for the inferiority of Perry & Wilkinson's violins must not therefore be saddled upon Thomas Perry. Wilkinson was apparently more artisan than artist, and after Perry's death there was a painful lowering of the standard. Once these facts are grasped there will be a notable appreciation of Perry violins and a corresponding depreciation of those manufactured by Perry & Wilkinson."

VIOLIN AND BOW MAKERS

The importance of Mr. McGoogan's discoveries will be appreciated at its true worth by all admirers of real Perry instruments. Owners of old violins labelled " Perry & Wilkinson " will, however, have a rude shock, for many of them will now learn with painful surprise that the great Perry had absolutely nothing to do with the construction of their treasures. It was high time the truth was discovered, and the artist receive his due, for there can be no two opinions as to the merits of Perry's instruments, they are in the first rank of British violins of the old school. My knowledge of his work is, unfortunately, not very extensive—it is limited to some half-a-dozen violins—but it carries me to a point where I must accept without hesitation the verdict of the Rev. Father Greaven, that Perry was " an artist of the first order." This learned Priest and keen connoisseur has made a special study of Perry's work, and he declares it to be of " careful construction and beautiful finish," and he says the tone of nearly every fiddle he has tried is " wonderfully responsive, sweet, and mellow." We are glad to learn on the same reliable authority that " there is a large number of Perry violins scattered through Ireland." It is to be hoped they are in safe hands.

PETRIE, THOMAS, Brixton : c. 1890. Principally a double bass maker.

PHILIP, WILLIAM, Westfield, Bathgate, N.B. : contemporary. A beginner who already makes a very nice instrument, and who, if he persevere, will probably become a first class craftsman.

PHILIPS, DAVID, Haverfordwest : 1745–1815. A pupil of Henry Whiteside. Amati model, with an exaggerated arch and scoop.

PHILLIPS, JOHN, Ynysybwl, Glamorgan : contemporary. He was born in the parish of Llanpumpsaint, Carmarthenshire, in 1863, and is a joiner and wood carver by trade. He commenced to make violins in 1898 as a hobby, and latterly he has turned his attention seriously to the craft, and contemplates taking violin making and repairing up as a profession. He has great natural abilities, is an adept at all kinds of wood carving, and has strict tastes in all matters artistic. He has made a number of violins on the Strad model, which are of excellent construction, and have a good tone. He will make a splendid addition to the small band of Welsh violin makers.

PHILLIPSON, EDWARD, Norton, Grosmont, Hereford: contemporary. He was born in Alvingham, Lincolnshire, in 1859, and is a Wesleyan evangelist by calling. He has made about twenty violins *en amateur*. He takes a keen interest in every branch of art, is very skilful in the use of keen-edged tools, and makes beautiful instruments.

PICKARD, HANDEL, Leeds: nineteenth century.

PINE, ——, London: nineteenth century.

PLANE, WALTER, Glasgow: 1804–79. Strad model. The workmanship is good, but the varnish is a hard spirit one, and the tone loud and metallic. He is said to have made a few superior instruments, but I have not seen anything by him which could be described as " superior."

POWELL, ROYAL AND THOMAS, London: 1770–1800. They were brothers who did most of their work for William Forster & Son. Careful work, but rather weak tone.

PRESTON, ——, London: c. 1720.

PRESTON, JAMES, —— : 1 have seen his name in catalogues, but know nothing of him.

PRESTON, JOHN, York: 1780–1800. He was capable of good work, but most of his instruments show carelessness. The tone is often very good.

PRICE, ——, London : contemporary. Said to be an excellent bow maker. A pupil of Tubbs.

PRIESTLEY, A. W., Leeds : nineteenth century.

PRIESTNALL, JOHN, Rochdale : 1819–99. Originally a joiner and pattern maker, he became a good maker and a very skilful repairer. He made altogether three hundred violins, thirty violas, six 'cellos, and eight double basses, all of good workmanship and very fair tone. His work has one serious drawback, the varnish is too soft, and has never dried properly—at least it has not dried on a specimen which I see occasionally, and which was made thirty years ago. He stamped his name on the back of his instruments under the button, and the number is punched on the button itself—a very tasteless method.

PYCROFT, ERNEST, Manchester : c. 1874. His fiddles have been advertised from time to time, but I have not seen any of them.

R

RAE, JOHN, Battersea : contemporary. He was born at Macduff, N.B., October 31, 1847, and is the eldest son of James Rae, and a grandson of John Rae, of Forglen, Turriff, a famous maker of bagpipes. He is employed in the Natural History department of the British Museum, and makes violins during spare time. He made his first fiddle as long ago as 1869, and since 1883, when he got his present appointment, he has made two or three new instruments every year. His work is solidly constructed and beautifully finished. Some of his violins are of rather massive proportions, and their plates left rather thick in wood, but the quality of the tone is exceedingly good notwithstanding: I think its quality would be still better if the thickness of the plates were slightly reduced, and the taper slightly increased. Mr.

Rae's instruments have a handsome appearance, and there is a striking boldness of character about them which is very refreshing and pleasing. His wood is magnificent. He has used Californian pine (*Sequoia gigantea*) for the tables of a number of his violins. The blocks were cut from a tree which had reached the height of 276 feet, and which was over thirteen hundred years old when it was cut down in 1872. The "reed" of this pine is very narrow, and of great regularity, and its acoustical qualities are surprisingly good. Facsimile label :—

```
No. 60.
JOHN RAE, Maker,
    LONDON. 1901.
```

RAEBURN, ALEXANDER, Leven, Fife : contemporary. Very good work.

RAEBURN, GEORGE R., West Calder : contemporary. He was born at Largoward, near St. Andrews, in 1846. He has made about seventy instruments on the Strad and Joseph models. The work is good.

RAEBURN, JOHN, Largoward : nineteenth century. He was born in the parish of Carnbee, in 1833, and was the eldest brother of the Raeburns previously mentioned. He made over a hundred violins on various models, of fairly good workmanship and tone.

RAMSAY, WILLIAM, Biggar : contemporary. He has made a few violins on the Strad model.

RAYMAN, JACOB, London : c. 1620–50. He was born in the Tyrol, and came to England about 1620, and worked first in Blackman Street (London), then at Bell Yard, Southwark. In all probability he was the first maker of violins in this country, at any rate, he was the first of whom we have any account. His violins were quaint looking, but the workmanship was very neat (with the exception of the inlaying of the purfling) and the tone was clear, responsive, and silvery.

RAWLINS, ——, London : c. 1770-80.

REED, B., Durham : contemporary.

RICHARDS, EDWIN, London : nineteenth century.

RILEY, HENRY, Birmingham : contemporary. I have not seen his work, but it is said to be very good.

RIMBAULT, H. E., Cardiff : contemporary. A gentleman amateur who has just commenced to make violins. His wide knowledge and skill will doubtless enable him to make beautiful instruments.

RINGWOOD AND WHEATLEY, Dublin : early nineteenth century. Principally dealers, I think, who employed others to make for them.

RITCHIE, ARCHIBALD, Dundee : 1833-1902. He made about a hundred and fifty violins on the model of Joseph Guarnerius, slightly enlarged. The instruments look heavy, although the workmanship is beautifully finished. His instruments have been much praised in certain quarters, but I am not struck with them. If fine cabinet work were all that is necessary to make a fine fiddle, then nothing better than these instruments could be desired. But there is too much body and too little " soul " about them.

ROBERTS, ALEXANDER, Luthermuir, Laurencekirk, N.B., contemporary. Born at Primrosehill, Fettercairn, in 1873. He is a maker of reeds for Highland bagpipes by trade, and a maker of violins during spare time only. He has made about twenty violins, which are beautifully finished, and have a large and telling tone.

ROBERTS, JOHN, Shrewsbury : c. 1690. A rather small violin, on the Stainer model, with very dark varnish, and a small, sweet tone, bearing his label, was through my hands a few years ago.

ROBERTS, LEWIS, Morriston, Swansea. He was born at Morriston in 1868, and died there in 1917. He was the only Welshman whose efforts in violin making have assumed any very definite proportions. The Welsh are a very musical nation, and it is often a puzzle to outsiders why they have so sadly neglected the orchestra and the study of the violin. The explanation probably is that they have devoted all their time to and concentrated all their efforts on the development of vocal music. But a better day has already dawned upon Wales, and the rising generation of Welsh musicians is now turning its attention to instrumentation.

Roberts made a large number of violins, and executed some rather important repairs from time to time. Most of his instruments are on an original model, but for the last two or three years of his life he worked on the Strad model exclusively. In his earlier work he evinced too strong a tendency to depart from the traditional methods, but latterly he had abandoned all eccentricities, and had settled down to serious work. The instruments of the last three years of his life are excellent in every way. Wood, workmanship, varnish, and tone give them a place in the front rank of modern British work. Roberts was of an inventive turn of mind, and had made a very ingenious calipers-drill—a tool which at once drills the plates and determines the graduation of their thicknesses. All the tools specially required for the craft he had made for himself. He was an " original " in every way, and a dreamer of dreams. Whilst working for the future he lived in the past. In spirit he belonged to the days when artists cut their own timber,

VIOLIN AND BOW MAKERS 227

made their own varnish, and sat on three-legged stools producing tone-poems for all time. He won the gold medal in the violin making competition at the Royal National Eisteddfod of Wales held in Neath in 1918. He was without doubt a genius, and his early loss is much to be deplored.

ROGERS, ——, Ballymacarett, Ireland : contemporary. He is mentioned in Father Greaven's list.

ROMNEY, GEORGE, Dalton and London : 1734-1802. This was the celebrated artist, who ranks third in the roll of England's great portrait painters. In early life he was a cabinet maker and wood carver, and he made a number of violins, which he ornamented with carved figures. It would be beside the purpose to give biographical particulars here : these are too well known, but the following facts relative to his violin making will be interesting, and perhaps new to many. They are taken from *George Romney*, by Arthur B. Chamberlain. " To some extent," observes this biographer, " Romney retained his love of the sister art throughout his life. Up to the last he kept a violin of his own making in his studio, and now and then played upon it when thinking out the design for a picture, finding in music, as others have done, a stimulus to his imagination." Mr. Chamberlain also quotes the following paragraph from Cumberland, one of Romney's earlier biographers, with the caution, however, that the tale is an exaggeration. " Smitten also with an embryo passion for the concord of sweet sounds, which he had probably never heard but in his dreams, he conceived the idea of transplanting the arts of Cremona to his native town of Dalton, and began a manufactory of violins, which he disposed of to the rural amateurs, who were, perhaps, as little instructed in the use of these instruments as he had been in the formation of them " (p. 15).

ROOK, JOSEPH, Carlisle : c. 1770-1852. He did not make many instruments. He was appointed vicar-choral at the cathedral, Carlisle, in 1807, which post he held till

1840, when a retiring pension was given to him. A Mr. Herbert Hodson, of 26 Barclay Road, Croydon, Surrey, owned a 'cello of his make in 1912, which he said was well made and had a good tone.

ROSS, DONALD, Edinburgh: 1817 till about 1905. He made about fifty violins on the Maggini model.

ROSS, JOHN, London: c. 1560–1600. A maker of lutes and viols.

ROWLEY, A. G., Cardiff: contemporary. He is not actually a maker, but he has varnished many instruments for other makers with a very beautiful varnish of his own make. He has studied the varnish problem for many years, and though he may not have solved the "riddle of Cremona," he has certainly succeeded in producing a varnish of wonderful lustre and transparency.

RUDDIMAN, JOSEPH, Aberdeen: 1760–1800. I have not seen any of his work. Mr. Alexander Wilson, advocate, of Aberdeen, has a violin of his make, which is said to be of good workmanship and tone.

RYLANDS, JOHN, Bristol: c. 1800. His name has appeared in lists of old instruments.

S

SABY, H. H., Cape Town, S. Africa: contemporary. He was born at Burton Latimer, Northamptonshire, in 1860, and emigrated to South Africa in 1890. He is a pupil of the late W. Calow, the violin maker, of Nottingham, with whom he remained for five years. He is established as a professional maker and repairer at 75 Plein Street, Cape Town, where he has worked up a fine business connection and won for himself a great reputation as a first-class maker and repairer. His violins are said to be beautifully made, and to possess a large, brilliant, and responsive tone. At the Industrial Exhibition held in Cape Town in 1904-5, he was awarded a gold medal for general excellence and for repairs. I have not seen any of his violins, but judging from numerous press and other reports they are of great merit.

SAUNDERS, S., Twickenham : 1840—. He was alive and working a few years ago, but I do not know whether he is alive now. He was an amateur who made a large number of violins of considerable merit, some of which were on the " Long Strad " model. He was awarded a silver medal for an exhibit of four violins at the Surbiton Industrial Exhibition, held in 1889.

SAXON, JOHN, Stockport : nineteenth century.

SCHOLES, ARTHUR, L., Rushden, Northants : contemporary. A maker, repairer, and dealer, who was born at Stamford, Lincolnshire, in 1870, and whose earlier years were spent in journalistic work. He made his first instrument in 1888, and shortly after adopted violin making as a profession. He has not made a large number of instruments, his time being mostly occupied with repairs, of which he always has an abundance in hand. He follows the Strad (Dolphin) and Guarneri patterns, and he has made a few violins on an original model. His work is excellent in every way—material, varnish, and workmanship evincing a thorough knowledge of the craft, and perfect skill in the handling of tools. I have tried only one violin of his make, which was a fine instrument, with a large and brilliant tone. This maker has undoubted abilities, and ought to produce important work. Facsimile label :—

SHAW, JOHN, London : c. 1650. A viol maker.

SHAW, J., Manchester : contemporary.

SHAW, THOMAS, Cove, Scotland : contemporary. An amateur of good average ability.

SHEPHERD, H. G., Brighton : contemporary.

SHEPLEY, GEORGE, Bristol : 1830-40. Poor work.

SHERDON, DANIEL, Gloucester : 1845-60. High arch, and poor work.

SHROSBREE, HENRY JAMES, Adelaide, S. Australia : contemporary. He was born in London in 1858, and followed a seafaring life from 1872 to 1880, voyaging to Adelaide for the second time in the latter year, when he entered the service of Sir E. T. Smith, with whom he remained till his retirement from business. Shortly after, he took up violin making and repairing. Judging from various notices which have appeared in the Australian press from time to time, and from many private letters which I have received, in reference to his work, there can be no doubt that Mr. Shrosbree's instruments reach a very high standard of excellence. It has not been my good fortune to see any of these instruments, and I therefore can express no opinion as to their merits. The editor of *Music* (Adelaide), referring to this maker's success at the Century Exhibition, held in Adelaide, in 1900, remarks thus : " The commendatory references we have from time to time made to Mr. H. J. Shrosbree's skill as a luthier, have been very amply confirmed by the judges for musical instruments . . . the exhibit comprised his Nos. 7 and 8 violins, his recently constructed viola, and some assorted bridges. With their brilliant coatings of oil amber varnish the instruments certainly make a splendid show, and the awards given are as follows : first for violins, first for viola, first for musical appliances (bridges, etc.), and a special prize for the best exhibit of its group." Facsimile label :—

Henry James Shrosbree, faciebat
Adelaide, S. Australia, Anno 18   [H.J.S.]

SIMPSON, JAMES & SON, London : 1780–1800. Probably not actual makers, but merely dealers who employed others to make for them.

SIMPSON, THOMAS, Birmingham : contemporary. Born at Burnley in 1866. He worked at Handsworth for a few years, but is now settled at Birmingham as a professional maker and repairer. He has made a number of violins on an original model, but his later instruments are on the Strad model, and show much better work. The wood is of fine quality, and the workmanship is carefully and beautifully finished. One of his violins which I tried recently had a particularly full and brilliant tone.

SINCLAIR, WILLIAM, New Pitsligo. An amateur who was living a few years ago, and possibly is still living, who had made a good number of violins of fairly good workmanship.

SKEFFINGTON, WILLIAM KIRKLAND, Glasgow : contemporary. Average merit.

SMILLIE, ALEXANDER, Glasgow : contemporary. Born at Hallside, Cambuslang, in 1847. He has worked at various places in Glasgow as a professional maker, repairer, and dealer. He has made a large number of violins, violas, and violoncellos, on the Stradivari and Guarneri models. I have not seen any of his more recently made instruments, but they are said to be superior in every way to his work of ten years ago : if that is so, they must be exceptionally fine. His instruments many years ago ranked, in my opinion, with the best that are made in Great Britain to-day. The wood was of the very best description, and the craftsmanship in every part of the work showed the mind and skill of a born artist. The tone of all his violins which I have tried is very sonorous and brilliant, possessing that subtle something which we call the Italian quality.

Mr. Smillie has never exhibited any of his instruments, the spirit of rivalry being quite foreign to his genial nature and unassuming manner.

Facsimile label :—

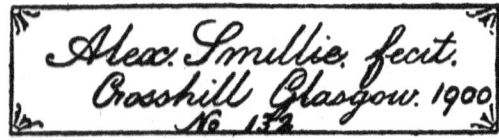

SMITH, ——, Wetherby : contemporary.

SMITH, ALBERT, Tomalosset, Enniscorthy, Ireland : contemporary. An amateur who is said to have made some good instruments.

SMITH, A. E., Maldon : contemporary. I have not seen his later work, but it is said to be very good.

SMITH, ALEX. HOWLAND, Edinburgh : nineteenth century. Stradivari and Guarneri models. Good tone.

SMITH, HENRY, London : c. 1630. A maker of viols.

SMITH, JASPER, London : nineteenth century.

SMITH, JOHN, Glasgow : contemporary. Born at Fauldhouse, Linlithgowshire, in 1859. He worked for some years at Falkirk, and he has lived in different parts of Glasgow, and elsewhere. He works on various models, but chiefly on an original one, which is of very full proportions

VIOLIN AND BOW MAKERS

and rather massive in appearance. The work is beautifully finished and the varnish carefully laid on and well polished. His scrolls are magnificently carved. The tone is large and incisive, and will no doubt be of excellent quality when age and use have mellowed it.

SMITH, JOHN HEY, Burnley : contemporary.

SMITH, JOHN, Whitchurch, Salop : nineteenth century.

SMITH, JOHN, Teddington, Middlesex : contemporary. An amateur who has made a few violins of very good workmanship and tone. He is capable of important work.

SMITH, NATHANIEL, Bristol : 1830–40. Indifferen work.

SMITH, PYE, Hereford : c. 1850. Model and workmanship very good, but tone very thin.

SMITH, THOMAS, London : 1745–90. A pupil and successor of Peter Wamsley. Some writers have bestowed great praise on his violoncellos, but I am of opinion they have never tried them. Such as I have tried had a hard, rasping tone. The workmanship is not bad, although the varnish is rather poor stuff, of a dirty amber, or brownish yellow colour. He used various labels.

SMITH, W. F., Edinburgh : contemporary. Average work.

SMITH, WILLIAM, Hedon : 1780–1805. Poor work.

SMITH, WILLIAM, Leeds : contemporary. Rough work.

SPIERS, STEWART, Ayr : 1805–70. Fair work and tone.

SPICER, JOHN, London: c. 1667. It is not at all certain that he was a violin maker.

SPICER, WILLIAM, London: c. 1860–70.

STANLEY, ROBERT A., Manchester: contemporary. I am not certain whether he works in Manchester at present, but he was there a few years ago. He is a pupil of James Barrow, of Salford, and of James Cole, of Manchester. He has made over two hundred instruments, including violins, violas, 'cellos, and double basses. I have not seen his work of the last ten years, and have no information as to what it is like.

STEPHENS, G. B., Bristol: c. 1780. Very fair work.

STIRRAT, DAVID, Edinburgh: c. 1810–20. This is a magnificent old maker. His work is quite equal to that of Matthew Hardie, and had he lived a few years longer and produced anything like the number of instruments Hardie did, I have little hesitation in saying that the title of "Scottish Stradivari" would have been his and not Hardie's. Mr. Honeyman says that Stirrat followed the model of Stradivari: this may be generally true, but in three instruments which I have seen, the model only approximated to that of the grand Strad. The finest Stirrat fiddle in existence, I think, is owned by Dr. George Raimondi Young, late of 784 Park Avenue, New York, and now of Vevey, Switzerland. The outline of this instrument is pure, and the curves well balanced and very graceful. The principal measurements are :—

Length of body	14 inches.
Width across upper bouts	$6\frac{1}{2}$,,
,, ,, middle ,,	$4\frac{7}{32}$,,
,, ,, lower ,,	$8\frac{1}{16}$,,
Length of sound-holes	3 ,,
,, ,, C's	$3\frac{3}{32}$,,
Depth of ribs $1\frac{1}{4}$ inch diminishing to	$1\frac{3}{16}$,,

VIOLIN AND BOW MAKERS

The workmanship is finished with extreme care and delicacy, and if the fiddle had been covered with the right varnish it would easily pass as an old "Italian." The varnish is evidently a spirit one, very thinly laid on, of a dark reddish-brown tint : it has not penetrated any distance into the wood, and it is not in sufficient thickness to materially affect the tone. The tone is moderately powerful, and wonderfully clear, bright, and mellow, very suitable for solo work in small halls and drawing-rooms. Mr. Honeyman says that Stirrat was " described as a delicate-looking man, with curly hair and thin white hands," and that he died " at an early age, just when he promised to become a greater maker than his master " (Matthew Hardie). That nature had endowed him with some of her choicest gifts is very evident from the few instruments of his make that still remain. It is not certain that he used a label. In the violins I have seen he inscribed his name, place, and date on the bare wood with a hard pencil. I am indebted to the courtesy of Dr. Raimondi Young for the following facsimile of the inscription in his violin.

D Stirrat Fecit
Edinb 1811

STONEMAN, H., Exeter : contemporary. Born in the parish of Zeal Monachorum, in the county of Devon, March 27, 1856, and now working as a professional maker, repairer, and dealer, at 3 Union Terrace, St. Sidwells, Exeter. He was apprenticed to the joinery trade, and worked for an ecclesiastical building firm in Exeter for about twenty-four years, for the last five of which he was their foreman. During spare time he studied the construction of the violin, and did some repairing now and again. He gradually acquired a thorough knowledge of the craft, and resolved to give up his post as foreman joiner and become a violin maker and repairer. This was fifteen years ago. By diligent application he has now reached a high degree of proficiency in his art, and is recognized as the best repairer in the South-West of England. He is undoubtedly a very clever and skilful craftsman. I have seen some of his restorations, and consider them equal to anything done by the most skilled repairers of London or Paris: they are not mere clever joinery work, but restorations in the true sense of the word. He has not made many new instruments, his time being almost entirely occupied with the sister branch of the craft. The few he has made are on the Stradivari model, and are carefully constructed and beautifully finished. Mr. Stoneman is highly respected for the transparency of his character and for his uprightness as a man of business.

STOTT, GEORGE T., Liverpool: contemporary. I have not seen any of his work.

STREETS, JAMES, Sunderland: contemporary. An amateur who produces excellent work. A viola of his make which I saw and tried some years ago might pass for the work of an experienced professional maker.

STRONG, JOHN, Somersetshire: c. 1650. An old viol maker, who is thought to have lived somewhere in the neighbourhood of Bristol.

STRONG, MATTHEW, Huddersfield: nineteenth century.

STURGE, H., Bristol and Huddersfield: 1800–60. A repairer.

T

TARR, WILLIAM, Manchester: 1808–91. Born in Manchester February 21, 1808; died there July 10, 1891, and was buried (with secular rights) in the Southern Cemetery, on St. Swithun's day. He was apprenticed when about sixteen to a cabinet carver, and made such rapid progress and became so expert a workman that at the age of eighteen he purchased his indentures from his employer for £100, and at once commenced work as a journeyman. He commenced violin making as a hobby, but gradually relinquished joinery and took up the craft as a profession. He made doublebasses principally, but devoted a great deal of his time also to repairing. He worked till he was about eighty years of age, and completed two hundred and six basses, besides a number of violins, violas, and 'cellos. His eldest son assisted him in the business till his eighteenth year, when he left home. Another son, Joseph, was also a violin maker, and assisted his father for a time. His youngest son, Shelley, who is in business in Manchester, was a skilful maker, and helped the old man for many years. Tarr, it is said, built a number of organs, and took out several patents for his inventions in the organ line.

On the occasion of a certain musical festival held in Dublin, where Tarr was one of the performers, all of the nine basses in the orchestra were of his make. He was an excellent musician, and was for twelve years one of the bassists at the "Gentlemen's Concerts," Manchester. He was for some time organist of a church in New Orleans, where he lived during a few years' stay in the United States. During the latter part of his life he became a prominent socialist, secularist, and anti-vaccinator.

He was a conscientious and a diligent worker, and for the long stretch of sixty years was devoted uninterruptedly and whole-heartedly to his art. He certainly was the most prolific double bass maker we have had in this country.

TAYLOR, B., London: c. 1750. Very fair work.

TAYLOR, EDWARD, Hull: nineteenth century.

TENNANT, JAMES, Lesmahagow: nineteenth century.

THOMAS, WATKIN, Swansea: 1849 to about 1908. He made about sixty or seventy violins, a few violas, and one or two 'cellos. He was capable of good work, and some of his instruments have a very good tone. He was very erratic, and would never settle down to steady work.

THOMPSON, ——, Manchester: nineteenth century.

THOMPSON, ROBERT, London: 1749–64. He worked at the sign of the "Bass-violin," in St. Paul's Churchyard. Rather ordinary work on the Stainer model.

THOMPSON, CHARLES & SAMUEL, London: c. 1780. Sons of the preceding, and his successors in business. Chiefly dealers.

THORLEY, N., Failsworth, Manchester: c. 1800–30 or later. He made several very good 'cellos, besides other instruments. He was a member of Hallé's orchestra.

THORLEY, T., Manchester: nineteenth century. A son of the preceding. He made a number of violins and a few 'cellos. Fairly good work.

THORNE, W. H., Tottenham: contemporary. An amateur who has made only a few violins, some with very peculiar sound holes.

THORNLEY, ——, Oldham: nineteenth century.

THOROWGOOD, HENRY, London: c. 1760. No instruments of his are known.

TIFFIN, MILLER, Carlisle: contemporary.

VIOLIN BY TOBIN.

To face p. 239.

TILLEY, THOMAS, London : c. 1770.

TOBIN, RICHARD, Dublin and London : 1777-1841. A pupil of Thomas Perry, and an artist every whit as great as his master, if only he had his full due. Nearly all his finest instruments, however, are either without labels, or (as is oftener the case) have somebody else's labels in them, so that the poor maker has been robbed of the credit that justly belongs to him. Tobin never was, apparently, in a position to set up business on his own account, and he was often in very straitened circumstances, whether through his own neglect and folly, or through lack of patronage, or what, it is impossible now to say. He was employed by Perry, by Betts, and by others, and when not so employed made a few instruments which he disposed of to the trade. He became an apprentice of Perry somewhere about 1800-2, and remained with him about eleven years. He went to London in 1813, and found his way to the workshop of " Old " Betts, with whom he remained for most of the time till his (Betts') death in 1823. Betts discovered in Tobin a craftsman after his own heart, and both acknowledged and recompensed his superior abilities.

The few instruments which have been recognized as the undoubted work of Tobin are acknowledged to be of a very high order of merit—i.e. " very high " relatively to the work of the old English school. I know of three Tobin violins, of the grand Strad model, which I consider to be superior in point of workmanship to anything ever made in this country. These have had very little playing, and their tone is consequently somewhat undeveloped : with careful handling for a few years, I am confident they would reveal tonal qualities of exceptional beauty. In all matters except the varnish I consider these instruments to be entitled to a place beside the old Italian violins. The varnish also is very good, *particularly* good for that period (1820-40), but of course it has not the " fire " of the old Italian varnish. No varnish of the old English period ever has that suffused, golden glow—that limpid fire of amber which the Cremonese varnish has, and it was hardly to be expected that one British artist should succeed where *every* other British artist had failed. I am not sure that Tobin's varnish was always of his own making, it varies both in colour and pâte. While working for others he would naturally use his employer's varnish.

Hart said very many years ago that " in cutting a scroll [Tobin] was unequalled amongst English makers." The observation is perfectly just, but it has possibly taken the eye of the connoisseur away from other beautiful features of Tobin's work, and the more so since every subsequent writer on old British violins has repeated the remark parrot-like.

Tobin's scrolls are not finer than his outline, his curves, or his sound-holes. Any one who has carefully examined a fine example of his art, and who has the capacity to appreciate subtle differences of style, will have observed how the curves of the plates " melt " and " flow " into the gentle channel near the edges. I saw quite recently a fine orange-red " Tobin," and when I looked at its surfaces through its beautiful varnish I could not but think that Hogarth's " line of beauty " and Burns' " lily dipped in wine " were both in the back of that fiddle—the one in the form, and the other in the colour.

Sandys and Forster say that Tobin during the latter part of his life kept a shop in West Street, Soho. I have searched old directories and records in vain for any evidence of this, and I do not think it is correct. If he had a shop at all, it was evidently of so modest a pretence as to altogether escape the attention of directory compilers. He possibly sold a few fiddle oddments, and exposed one or two of his instruments in the window for sale, but that could hardly be called " keeping a shop." Whatever it was that he " kept," it failed to keep him, poor man, for he ended his days in the Shoreditch poorhouse. Like the great John Dodd and Matthew Hardie, he found rest and peace in a pauper's grave.

JAMES TUBBS.

To face p. 241.

VIOLIN AND BOW MAKERS

TOLMIE, G., Hanwell : contemporary. A gentleman amateur who has made a few violins of excellent workmanship and tone. One of his instruments which I tried about a year ago had a beautiful tone.

TORRING, J., London : 1800–10. He repaired chiefly.

TRIMNELL, JOSEPH HENRY, Birmingham : 1840–1904. Average ability.

TRINGHAM, HENRY, Shrewsbury : 1835–1860. Model and workmanship very fair, but tone hard and metallic.

TROTMAN, WILLIAM, Hereford : c. 1850. Small Amati model.

TRUEMAN, RICHARD, Bath : 1820–30. A pretty little instrument of his make on the A. and H. Amati model, which I saw a few years ago, had a sweet tone.

TUBBS, JAMES & SON, London : contemporary. James Tubbs is a son of William Tubbs, a bow maker, and was born in Rupert Court, March 25, 1835. His name has been a " household " word among artists and bow collectors for a generation or more, and Tubbs has long won for himself the title of " the Modern British Tourte." He is a pupil of his father, with whom he remained working till about 1860, in which year he commenced business on his own account in Church Street, Soho, where he remained till 1864. From Church Street he removed to High Street, Marylebone, and from there to King Street, Soho, where he worked for a few years. In 1872 he removed to his present address, 94 Wardour Street, and here he has " laboured and toiled " for upwards of forty years, producing those gems of the bow maker's art for which the name of Tubbs has so long been famous. He is in his eighty-fifth year, but still hale and hearty in spite of his great age, and in the full possession of all his faculties. He was busy at work on a violin bow when

I called upon him on August 5, last year (1919), and seemed to be almost as active and as keen as he was twenty-five years ago, when I first made his acquaintance. He certainly looks good for another ten years' work. He is a man of medium height, of rather spare but wiry figure, very shrewd and somewhat reticent and incommunicative in his manner. He seldom speaks except when spoken to, and his answers are usually brief and categorical. The enthusiast or scribbler who enters the little shop at 94 Wardour Street, with the intention of " drawing " its occupant is certain to go away a disappointed man. Tubbs is invulnerable, and criticism or praise are equally lost upon him. On one point only is it possible to rouse his susceptibility : if you confuse his name with that of any other bow maker of the name of Tubbs, you are likely to drop in for a warm time of it. He is a " character," is James Tubbs. He is a man of the good old school, plain, simple, straightforward, with a rather crusty exterior, but with a solid heart and plenty of sober sense. He is very different from the typical business man of to-day, who is essentially a man of the world, with often a slice of the flesh and the devil thrown in.

Up to about six or seven years ago, Mr. Tubbs made at the rate of seven to ten new bows per month. He must therefore have made altogether between four and five thousand bows, of one sort and another. These are all of uniform excellence as regards workmanship and finish, though they possibly may not be of the same excellence as regards material. In so large a number it would be extraordinary if the wood were absolutely of the same high standard of perfection. But the best of these bows (and a large percentage of them have the very finest material) are, in my opinion, equal to the bows of François Tourte, Voirin, Peccate, Henry, or any other great bow maker, past or present. Opinions differ, of course, but that is my honest opinion. To appreciate the fine qualities of a Tubbs bow one must be accustomed to the use of it. One who has used a French bow for a number of years does not take kindly to a " Tubbs " at first : there is something about the " feel " of it (as the expression goes) which puzzles him, and he loses, or imagines that he loses, perfect control over the movements of his bow arm. When I read (or heard some artist or other remark) something to this effect years ago I thought it could hardly be possible, but when I tried the experiment for myself I found it was possible enough. The fact is, the balance of a Tubbs bow is rather different from that of any other bow, and therefore affects the muscular action of the arm differently.

But there is not the slightest doubt about it, the balance of a " Tubbs " is scientifically arranged—that is to say, it is the correct balance for an arm of good average strength, and whose muscles have developed normally. Mr. Tubbs makes his bows on the principle of proportion and balance laid down by the late W. S. B. Woolhouse, the eminent mathematician and well-known musical enthusiast, who held that the primary essential of a perfect bow is that its weight and proportions (diameters) are so arranged that the stick vibrates with absolute uniformity throughout its whole length. Woolhouse's contribution to the science of bow making is very valuable, but I am rather inclined to think that it tended to obscure the importance of another great factor in the making of a good bow, viz. the putting in of the " spring " or *cambre*. To determine the depth and sweep of the curve is a much more difficult problem than to determine and arrange the graduation of diameters. A gauge will help to obtain the correct proportions, but the eye and the feeling of resistance alone must fix upon the quantity and sweep of the curve.

Mr. Tubbs was assisted for many years by his son Alfred, a very skilful workman and an excellent repairer, who died in November, 1912. He has no assistant now, and is therefore not able to make many new bows, and he is obliged to curtail the amount of repairs he undertakes. He obtained a gold medal for an exhibit of bows at the Inventions Exhibition, London, 1885.

TUBBS, WILLIAM, London : c. 1814-1878. Father of the preceding. He made many bows, principally for the dealers, and his work was said to be very good. He was a son of Thomas Tubbs, also a bow maker. There were, and there are to-day, several other members of the Tubbs family connected with the bow-making branch of the craft, but I know nothing of them or their work.

TURNER, WILLIAM, London : c. 1650. A maker of viols.

TUSON, ROBERT, Gravestown : contemporary.

TWEEDALE, CHARLES L., Weston, Otley, Yorks : contemporary. He is the vicar of Weston, but since he advertises his violins for sale he is treated here as a quasi-professional maker, and not as a mere amateur. He was born at Stainland, near Halifax, and is a son of Dr. Thomas Tweedale, surgeon, and of Mary, daughter of Charles Oates, an engineer, of Cranshawborth, Rossendale. Both his grandsires were amateur violin makers, and one of them, Mr. Benjamin Tweedale, made several violins of excellent workmanship and tone, and was an enthusiastic devotee of the violin and the leader of all the oratorios and concerts in his neighbourhood. Mr. Tweedale has been interested from his youth in the arts, crafts, and sciences, and it was his father's intention to make an engineer of him. Mr. Tweedale senior died in 1885, and young Tweedale turned his energies into another channel. At that time he became deeply interested in astronomy, and he ground and polished the specula for his own reflecting telescopes up to ten inches in diameter. With these instruments he did a good deal of work, and independently discovered the triple tailed comet of 1886 (comet *f*). Just about this period one of Benjamin Tweedale's violins came into his possession, and he taught himself to play upon it. He soon became more interested in its construction than in playing, and he procured Heron-Allen's book, and under the charm of that work commenced to make a fiddle, and he did not rest

VIOLIN AND BOW MAKERS

satisfied till he had finished two. All scientific and research work was now laid aside, for it was suddenly resolved that he should enter Durham University and study for the Church. In due course he graduated at Durham, and was ordained to the curacy of Hyson Green, Nottingham, in 1891. In 1901 he became vicar of Weston, Otley, and in 1908 he re-commenced his violin researches, which, however, he had never completely relinquished. The varnish problem came in for a large share of attention, and Mr. Tweedale claims to have discovered an oil varnish " which is equal in all respects to that of the great Cremonese luthiers."

He has had in his hands for the purpose of study and comparison several fine " Strads," such as the " Tuscan," " Cessol," " Amherst," " Prince," " Paganini," and a number of " Josephs," and he claims that he is " now able to make instruments which are worthy to compare with these in tone, and equal to the very best of them in varnish." Whether Mr. Tweedale's varnish is " equal in all respects " to the Cremonese varnish is a matter upon which there may be more than one opinion, but there can be no differences of opinion, I think, as to the quality of his more recent varnish : it is of excellent pâte and of wonderful " fire " and transparency. The varnish he made some years ago is not for a moment to be compared with it.

He has made a large number of violins—some on the Strad, Joseph, and Maggini lines, but the greater number on an original model. The outline of the original model is full, and bold, suggestive rather of masculine strength than of feminine gracefulness and delicacy. The scroll and soundholes are also very original in design, and are evidence (if evidence were wanting) of the strong, clear-thinking brain, and of the skilful hand which is able to carry out the dictates of that brain. All the work is beautifully finished, both inside and outside, even to the minutest detail. The tone of his later instruments is of a very fine quality : it is large, responsive, and brilliant, and perfectly equal on all the strings.

In addition to his artistic work, and the care of a country parish, Mr. Tweedale has contributed many articles on scientific and psychical subjects to various magazines and papers. He has made a notable contribution to psychical research in his book: "Man's Survival after Death"—a work which has run into several editions, and has had a wide circulation.

Facsimile label :—

TWEEDY, J., Acklington : contemporary.

TWEMLOW, S. P., Sandbach, Cheshire : contemporary. An amateur who has made a number of violins of beautiful workmanship and tone. He is well-to-do, and therefore able to procure the very best material, and to devote an abundance of time to the construction of each instrument. He is preparing for the press a work on violin making.

U

URQUHART, ALEXANDER, Invergordon: contemporary. An amateur who turns out an occasional violin of good workmanship and tone.

URQUHART, DONALD, Tain, N.B., contemporary. Born at Balblair, near Invergordon, in 1859. He has made a considerable number of violins on the grand Strad model, which are of very beautiful construction, with a moderately powerful, sweet, and responsive tone. He is the maker of a fine oil varnish, a large stock of which he has recently disposed of to Mr. William Glenister, of London.

URQUHART, THOMAS, London: 1650–80. One of our early old makers, the best part of whose work is the varnish, which very closely resembles the Italian varnish. I have seen one violin of his make, which was much arched, and had a sweet but small tone.

V

VAUGHAN, DAVID ROBERT, Chester: contemporary. Strad model; fairly good work.

VICKERS, RICHARD, Bath: c. 1870. Very fair workmanship, but poor model.

VIOLIN MAKERS' GUILD. This is a Guild or school of violin making established at 35 South End Road, Hampstead, London, N.W. Its full title is " The British Violin-Makers' Guild," and it is described in the pamphlet explanatory of its object as " The only *all British* manufactory producing violins, violas, violoncellos, and basses at competitive Continental prices." Its managing director, Mr. Albert J. Roberts, in a letter in the press writes that " arrangements are being made for the employment of disabled soldiers and sailors," and that "there are also vacancies for improvers and a few articled pupils desirous of learning the art of violin-making under the guidance of a skilled staff of English, French, and Russian instructors, now engaged." I visited this institution, or factory, in August of the year 1915, when the managing director was good enough to take me over the workshop, and to explain to me that the Guild had two definite objects in view: (1) to teach violin making, and (2) to produce a high-class factory violin at a price that would enable them (the Guild) to compete successfully with the foreigner. Every patriot will agree that the objects are very sensible and praise-worthy. There is not a shadow of doubt about it, the factory fiddle has come to stay. The connoisseur may fling his scorn and utter his malediction, but the British public will smile at him and purchase its thirty shilling fiddle. Well, since there must be factory fiddles, let those used in Britain, I say, be of British manufacture. I express myself thus in all sincerity, firm believer in universal brotherhood though I be, for my sense of brotherhood does not bid me love my neighbour (the foreigner) *better* than myself (i.e. my own nation).

The time is propitious for the founding of an industry of this description, and all its promoters need to make it a success is organization, concentration, co-operation, and a reasonable belief in themselves.

VOYLE, BENJAMIN, Swansea: 1860–70. Average merit.

VOYSEY, HUBERT, Hereford: c. 1840. I quite recently saw a kit with his label in it.

W

WADE, JOSEPH, Leeds: nineteenth century.

WADE, WILLIAM, Leeds: nineteenth century.

VIOLIN AND BOW MAKERS

WALKER, H. J., Whitby : contemporary. His work is said to be fairly good.

WALKER, HECTOR M., Liverpool : contemporary. Some years ago he made a few violins experimentally, for the purpose of testing certain theories, but I do not know whether he makes now.

WALKER, J., Birmingham : contemporary. Born at Brailsford, in 1876. He works at 8 Broomfields, Solihull, as a professional maker and repairer. He has not made a large number of instruments, most of his time being occupied with repairs. His instruments are carefully finished, and covered with a beautiful amber oil varnish of his own make. He is said to be an excellent repairer.

WALKER, WILLIAM, Mid-Calder : contemporary. An amateur who has made a good number of violins of excellent workmanship and beautiful tone. He follows the Stradivari and Guarneri models, and shows such great ability and skill that it is a pity he does not devote his whole time to the craft.

WALTON, WILLIAM, Preston : contemporary. Born at Longton in 1860. He follows the Stradivari and Guarneri models, and has also made a number of violins on an original model. His work is of a high order, and finished with extraordinary care. His scrolls are of a vigorous design and carved very beautifully. The tone is large, brilliant, and perfectly equal and responsive. His work places him in line with our first-class professional makers.

WAMSLEY, PETER, London : 1715–51. An old maker whose work has been much praised by some, and whose violoncellos at one time were held in considerable esteem. I cannot say that I particularly like his work, nearly all the instruments of his make (especially the violins) that I have seen being worked much too thin in the plates.

The finest " Wamsley " that I am acquainted with is a viola, dated 1734, owned by the Messrs. George Withers and Sons.

WARD, ——, Dublin : c. 1750–1800. A fine violin of his make, on a model closely approximating to that of the grand Strad, is in the Dublin museum. He was an artist of undoubted ability, and it is a pity that little or nothing is known of him. Father Greaven mentions him, but is unable to give any particulars.

WARDLAW, RICHARD, Cardiff : 1890–1900. An amateur of average ability.

WARRICK, A., Leeds : contemporary. Born at Reading in 1863. He is a pupil of Mr. G. A. Chanot, of Manchester, with whom he served an apprenticeship of six years, from 1884 to 1890. He works on various models, but chiefly on the two principal classical ones. He has made a large number of instruments of all sizes, and he has an extensive repairing business. He uses excellent material, and the work is beautifully finished throughout. The varnish is of his own make, and has much the same characteristics as the varnish traditionally associated with the house of Chanot. It is made in four colours : yellow, reddish-yellow, brown-red, and ruby. He was awarded the sole gold medal for a case of violins at the Leeds International Exhibition in 1895.

WARRICK, REGINALD, Northampton : 1880–1902. An amateur of average ability.

WATSON, FRANK, Rochdale : contemporary. Born at Rochdale in 1866, where he has been established for about twenty-five years as a professional maker and repairer. He has made about a hundred and fifty violins, and a few violas and violoncellos. The work is carefully finished throughout, and the tone is powerful, and very good for orchestral purposes. He is said to be a very skilful repairer.

WATSON, JOHN, Lerwick, Shetland : contemporary. A Presbyterian clergyman who has made about fifty violins of good workmanship and tone. The outline of his instruments is rather quaint, otherwise the work is faultless. Mr. Watson was obliged to retire from the active work of the ministry last year through failing health.

WATT, ALEXANDER STOCKS, Inverkeithing : 1859 to about 1906, or a little later. He made a few instruments of beautiful workmanship. A copy of the " Cessol " Strad was a wonderfully faithful facsimile of the original. He was a man of an ingenious and inventive turn of mind.

WEAVER, SAMUEL, London : 1780–1800. Ordinary work.

WHITAKER, HENRY, Plymouth : c. 1875.

WHITE, JOHN, Camerton, Somerset : c. 1840–50. He made a number of violins and violoncellos of good average merit, some of which were in use in village churches in the neighbourhood of Camerton before the advent of the harmonium or small organ.

WHITEHEAD, ——, Cork : c. 1800–30. A maker of kits.

WHITELAW, JAMES, Glasgow : 1852–1904. The celebrated discoverer of the amber oil varnish which bears his name. (*Vide* Introduction.)

WHITESIDE, HENRY, Liverpool and Solva, Pembrokeshire : 1749–1824. He was the builder of the first

Smalls lighthouse, and made a large number of musical instruments, including spinets, harpsichords, and violins. One of his violins, which is on a model approaching to that of Stradivari, is in my possession: it has a beech back, and a powerful but rather hard tone. He was a remarkable man and a clever craftsman. He died at Solva in 1824, and was buried at Whitchurch, Pembrokeshire.

WHITMARSH, EMMANUEL, London: nineteenth century. A prolific maker. There is, or was very recently, a maker of this name in London, but I do not think he is the Whitmarsh whose work was largely advertised many years ago.

WHITTAKER, BUTTON &, Leeds: 1805–30. Chiefly dealers.

WIGAN, DAVID, Shrewsbury: 1890–1904. An amateur.

WIGHTMAN, GEORGE, London: c. 1760.

WILKIN, G. H., Hull: contemporary. An amateur.

WILKINSON, S. B., Leeds. I am not certain whether he is now living: I have come across his name somewhere, but can give no particulars.

WILKINSON, WILLIAM, Dublin: c. 1818 to about 1839. He was a son-in-law of Thomas Perry, and carried on business under the name of "Perry and Wilkinson," although Perry had absolutely no hand in the making of the instruments which bear the dual name (*vide* "Thomas Perry"). The instruments which are labelled "Perry and Wilkinson," and which were really the work of Wilkinson or of his assistants, are much inferior to the work of Thomas Perry.

WILKS, ALFRED, Manchester: 1890–1904. An amateur.

To face p. 253.

VIOLIN AND BOW MAKERS

WILLIAMS, ALFRED, Cheltenham: 1840 till about 1910, or a little later. He made a large number of violins on various models.

WILLIAMS, BENJAMIN, Aberavon: 1768–1839. He made about eighty violins on the Duke-Amati model. Very good workmanship. Tone rather small but of good quality.

WILLIAMS, O. R., Manchester.

WILSON, ——, Whitby: c. 1820.

WILSON, J. J. T., London: contemporary. A bow maker, who works principally for the trade. He worked for some time with James Tubbs, and later with C. E. Tubbs. I do not know that I have seen any of his bows, but they are said to be very good.

WILSON, JAMES L., Greenock: contemporary. An amateur who has produced excellent work. He won a gold medal for an exhibit of violins at the Greenock Exhibition held in 1893. His instruments have a beautiful tone.

WILTON, JAMES, Whitby. I do not know whether he is alive, but he was working up to eight or ten years ago.

WISE, CHRISTOPHER, London: c. 1656. Chiefly a maker of viols.

WITHERS, EDWARD, London: 1808–75. He was born in London, December 23, 1808, and died there December 19, 1875. He bought the business of R. & W. Davis, 31 Coventry Street, Haymarket, in 1843, and set up in that year as a professional maker and repairer, although he had had little previous training. He soon became an expert craftsman, and long before the end of his career was recognized as one of the best makers England had produced in the nineteenth century up to that time. He followed the Stradivari and Guarneri models exclusively, and made a large number of instruments, including violins, violas, and violoncellos. The set of instruments known as the "Wither's quartet," now in the possession of the Messrs. Withers, of Wardour Street, are among the finest instruments ever made in this country. One of the violins of this set has been sold and re-sold twice for the sum of £50 : its purchaser on one occasion being Mr. L. d'Egville, who presented it to Wilhelmj. Its companion violin was sold at first for £30, but it realised later no less than £120—so the late Mr. E. Withers informed me. That seems an enormous sum for an English fiddle of the nineteenth century. The tenor was sold for £40, and the violoncello for £150.

Maucotel and Boullangier worked under Edward Withers at one time : these were clever workmen, and were of great assistance to the Englishman at a time when the fame of his instruments had created a greater demand for his work than he, working alone, could supply. Withers died at the age of sixty-seven, and was buried in Brompton Cemetery. Facsimile label :—

WITHERS, EDWARD AND SONS, London. Mr. Edward Withers, the father, was born in London, October 22, 1844, and died there, May 10, 1915. He was the eldest son of the preceding Edward Withers, and was trained by his father, and by Jack Lott. He commenced business at 31 Coventry Street, in 1856, which he removed a few years later to the present address of the firm, 22 Wardour Street. He worked with his father for about twenty-five years,

Edward Withers

To face p. 254.

during which time he made a large number of new instruments, and executed nearly all the principal repairs that were entrusted to the firm. Like his father, he copied exclusively the two principal models, and never attempted in any way to modify the measurements, outline, and curves of Stradivari and Guarneri, believing that the evolution of violin models had reached its culminating point with these two masters. He made altogether about three hundred instruments, including violins, violas, and violoncellos. All these are made of very choice wood, and constructed with the utmost care. The work is beautifully finished, and the varnish is of excellent quality and rich appearance. On June 1, 1893, he was appointed by Royal Warrant violin maker to H.R.H. the late Duke of Saxe-Coburg-Gotha, then Duke of Edinburgh.

Mr. Withers played the violin, viola, and 'cello, and was passionately devoted to classical music. He frequently had quartet and symphony parties at his private residence, " Elmwood," Atkins Road, Clapham Park. His sons, who now carry on the business, are: Edward Sidney Munns, born in 1870, Sidney Bernard, born in 1873, and Douglas Sidney, born in 1879. The three have received a thorough grounding and practical training in their art, and are clever craftsmen. Facsimile label:—

WITHERS, GEORGE AND SONS, London: contemporary. Mr. George Withers is a son of Edward Withers, senior, and a brother of the late Edward Withers, of Wardour

Street. He and his sons are dealers in a large way of business, whose establishment at 22 Leicester Square is familiar to every connoisseur and *virtuoso* in the country. All of them are practical violin makers, but Mr. Withers, senior, has neither made nor repaired any instruments these many years, the business occupying the whole of his time. His two sons (who assist him in the business) received their training in Mirecourt, and one of them, Mr. Guarnerius Withers, is an excellent craftsman, and has made a few violins quite recently.

This firm is justly celebrated for its long, honorable, and successful record : its reputation is second to none. To have business dealings with the Messrs. Withers once is to esteem them for ever after as men who are actuated by the highest principles.

WINRAM, JAMES, Edinburgh : contemporary. A clever amateur maker and professional teacher of the violin who has made a number of beautiful instruments. He is a born artist, and would doubtless make his mark as a professional maker.

WOOD, G, F., London : nineteenth century. Very good work.

WOODING, J. T., Swansea : contemporary. He is said to be a good maker and an excellent repairer. I have not seen any of his work, and cannot express an opinion as to its merits.

WOODNEY, H., Manchester : nineteenth century.

WOODWARD, ——, Birmingham : c. 1820. I am not certain, however, as to his period, and I know nothing about his work.

WORDEN, JAMES, Preston : 1839 to about 1908, or a year or two later. He was a descendant of the Wordens of old Worden Hall, and his mother was descended from the

VIOLIN AND BOW MAKERS 257

Plessingtons, of the Dimples, an old Lancashire family, who gave to the Roman Catholics their last British martyr—the Rev. J. Plessington, who was executed in the year 1678.

He made about sixty instruments, on various models. The work is good and careful all over, and the tone of a quality which makes it very suitable for orchestral purposes.

WORNUM, ——, London : c. 1794. Nothing is known of him.

WRIGHT, DANIEL, London : c. 1745.

WRIGHT, EBENEZER, South Shields : nineteenth century. Average ability.

Y

YATES, RICHARD. He worked in Manchester ten years ago, but I do not know whether he is still there, or whether he is still making violins. The only violins of his make which I have seen were early efforts, but they showed much ability.

YOOLE, WILLIAM, St. Andrews : 1806–68. He received some instructions from Matthew Hardie, and was at one time a sort of collaborator with Tom Hardie, but only as an amateur. He was Town Clerk of St. Andrews.

YOUNG, JAMES, Edinburgh : c. 1880–1904.

YOUNG, JOHN, London : c. 1700. No instruments of his have been seen, but we learn from the curious verses of Purcell that he was a maker.

YOUNG, G. RAIMONDI, Vevey, Switzerland. A well-known scientist and medical doctor who has made about a dozen violins of beautiful workmanship and tone. He is a keen connoisseur, and an enthusiast in all matters appertaining to the violin. He hopes to devote a great deal of time in Switzerland to his beloved hobby of violin making. His knowledge and wonderful skill are a sufficient guarantee of the excellence of his future work.

YOUNGMAN, M., Halifax. He worked there ten years ago, but I do not know whether he is there now. His work was carefully finished, and one of his violins which I tried had a very good tone.

PART III

A DICTIONARY OF VIOLIN AND BOW MAKERS CONTINUED

A List of Present-Day Makers, and a few Old Makers recently discovered.

A DICTIONARY OF VIOLIN AND BOW MAKERS

ALLWOOD, ——, Sheffield; c. 1800. He is said to have been an excellent craftsman.

ANGELL, S. E. He lived at 29 Gillingham Road, Cricklewood, London, N.W., and died there November 26, 1918. He made a number of instruments, and was considered a good workman.

AUBREY, PHILIP, Gloucester; c. 1830–50. Poor material and very ordinary work.

BARRETT, KERSHAW, Oxenhope, Yorks. Uses excellent material and follows the Strad model mostly. Good workmanship: varnish of a light golden brown colour of good quality. He is particularly successful in obtaining a large, responsive, and mellow tone.

BEAMISH, JOHN, London. An excellent amateur, who is working for the Peasant Arts Guild, which has its headquarters at 17 Duke Street, Manchester Square. He commenced to make violins as a hobby only a year or two ago, but intends to devote much time to it in future, and ought to succeed well, since he is an adept in the use of keen-edged tools.

BEE, F. C., Shiremoor, Northumberland. Contemporary.

BERRY, PETER, Kirkcaldy, N.B., where he was born in 1879. He works on an original model, and has made a number of instruments of beautiful workmanship. The design of his scroll is original, and the button is cut in the form of a shoe. The material is excellent, and the varnish, which is an oil one of a dark golden brown tint, is of good quality. The tone is moderately powerful, of a reedy quality, even, and very responsive. The maker is a talented amateur.

BIRCH, THOMAS, Hereford; c. 1850. Average ability.

BIRD, RICHMOND HENRY, Liverpool. He was born at Walsall, Staffordshire, in 1869, and has been employed for the last six years by the Messrs. Rushworth and Dreaper to do their violin repairs, and to make their high-class instruments to order. Up to the present (1919) he has made a hundred violins, nine violas, and eighteen violoncellos, following usually the Stradivari or Guarneri model. The workmanship is beautiful, every detail of the work both inside and outside being finished with the utmost accuracy, and pointing unmistakably to the master mind and the cunning hand. Particular attention is paid to the graduation of the thicknesses of the plates, the maker being of the opinion that the secret of the Italian masters lies in that part of the work. Mr. Bird maintains that after long meditation and innumerable experiments he has finally unravelled the mystery of the Italian tone, and affirms confidently that he can reproduce accurately the tone of any particular instrument of the classical period. That is a bold claim to advance, and will probably evoke rebuke if not ridicule from the critics. But whatever theory (or "fad," as some would call it) this maker may hold, and whatever the critics may say, it is certain that he is in the front rank of modern British violin makers, and that his work will bear comparison with the best that has been produced in modern times. He is certainly right in his fundamental principle that the best modern work is that which most accurately reproduces the salient features of the best work of the Italian masters. Acting on this principle, Mr. Bird sets out to copy as accurately as his knowledge and skill enable him, the grand instruments of Joseph and Antonio. And well does he accomplish the task. I recently examined two violins of his make, one varnished and one " in the white," which were exact reproductions, as far as wood and workmanship went, of a Strad of the grand period, and it must be admitted that they were instruments which I think the white-aproned master himself would have readily admitted to the fellowship of his own. The tone was powerful, brilliant, even, and reedy. It had fine carrying power, and an inexhaustible reserve, since it did not give out or " break " even with the vigorous use of a 'cello bow.

BLIGHT, R., Exeter : c. 1830. Very good work.

BROWN, J., West Marsh, near Great Grimsby. He was alive and working a few years since.

BUXTON, HENRY, Chester : c. 1845. Stainer model ; poor work.

BUXTON, JAMES, Bristol : c. 1830. A repairer, and probably a maker of no particular repute. A few years ago I saw an old violin bearing a partially obliterated label which had a name like Buxton, or something similar, of Bristol.

BYRON, HUMPHRY, Oxford : c. 1800-20. A violin recently seen bore the label : " Humphry Byron, fecit in Oxon. 1810," and was on the Amati model, varnished golden brown. It was well made and had a sweet tone.

BYRTH, WALTER, Nottingham : c. 1800. Whether he was a maker or only a repairer it is impossible to say.

BYTTLE, J., Swansea : c. 1850. Probably only a repairer.

BYWATER, HENRY, Bristol : c. 1800. A rather nice looking violin was recently picked up in a curiosity shop bearing the label : " Made by Henry Bywater, in Bristol," without a date. The maker had evidently the work of Richard Duke in his mind, and the varnish was very similar to and quite as good as that used by Duke, but the tone was not equal to the workmanship, and certainly not to be compared with that of the old English maker.

COAD, ALBERT, Redruth, Cornwall : contemporary. He was born at Camborne, Cornwall, in 1884, and is now established at Mount Pleasant, Redruth Highway, Redruth, as a professional maker. As far as I am aware he is the only Cornish maker now living and working in his native county. Cornishmen like their first cousins the Welsh are by instinct and temperament an art-loving people, but like them also have neglected to a great extent the art of violin making. How to account for this neglect—a neglect which amounts to aberrancy—is more than I care to attempt. The efforts of this maker (if they meet with the success they deserve) will go a long way towards supplying the short-comings of Cornwall. Mr. Coad is a disciple of the late Walter H. Mayson, of Manchester, and has adopted that celebrated maker's outline, arching, and thicknesses, and his work shows that " the spirit of the master doth rest on the disciple." He uses handsome wood of the finest quality, and makes only four or five instruments per year, devoting much time and the greatest care to the construction of each one. The work is beautifully finished, every detail evincing the good taste of the born artist and the perfect skill of the trained craftsman. Some connoisseurs would perhaps find fault with this maker's work on the score of excessive thickness in the plates, and I have no doubt the thickness might be very slightly reduced without injury to the robustness and brilliancy of the tone. But it is always safer to err on the side of excess of thickness than otherwise : there is a remedy for that, but there is no remedy for deficiency of timber. Many instruments of the modern French school are too thin in the plates ; they sound clear and responsive now, but these qualities are obtained at the expense of " stamina," and the instruments will have been played out a hundred years hence. Mr. Coad is particularly successful in obtaining fine tonal results. The tone of one of his violins which I tried recently was large, brilliant, and very easy to produce : it had the clear " ring " of a first-class old instrument, and was exceptionally free from the harshness which usually mars the tone of a new fiddle. Work of the description produced by this maker is bound to come to the front and to win recognition.

The label is hand-written, and each instrument has an inscription written on the back on the bare wood.

CLARK, WILLIAM, Exeter : c. 1800–20. Several violins of his make have been seen, bearing a written label. They were unpurfled, but were otherwise well made, and had a good tone.

COCKCROFT, ——, Rochdale : c. 1860.

COCKMAN, F. G., London : contemporary. He works at 31 Springcroft Avenue, East Finchley, but whether as an amateur or a professional maker I cannot say.

COLLINGWOOD, JOSEPH, London : 1725–1750. He worked at the " Golden Spectacles," London Bridge, and labelled his instruments : " Joseph Collingwood, Londini," adding the date. He made a large number of instruments on the Stainer, Strad, Amati, and a few on the Joseph models. This is another old maker who has received scant justice, or no justice at all, at the hands of connoisseurs and writers on the violin. The reason is not far to seek : Collingwood's labels have been extracted wholesale from his violins, and other labels, bearing more imposing names, have been inserted in their place. Collingwood's best work is in every way worthy of a place beside the finest work of Banks, Forster, Duke, and Parker.

Charles Challenger, Esq., of Tiverton, St. Andrew's Park, Bristol, had an Amati copy by Collingwood, covered with an orange-coloured oil varnish of great lustre and transparency, and with a beautiful tone, which equalled, if it did not surpass, the very best work which ever came from the hands of Benjamin Banks.

"One swallow does not make a summer," and perhaps to have made one fine violin does not constitute a man a violin maker, but it certainly shows what he is capable of. But the fame of Collingwood does not rest on the merit of the solitary example just named; there are other fine specimens of his handiwork in the country. Dr. Broad, of Almonsbury, Gloucestershire, has, or had, one. This gentleman, who is a keen connoisseur, has seen several of Collingwood's fiddles from time to time, and says they were all beautifully made, possessing a remarkably sweet and mellow tone. A few years back a fine Amati copy, with golden brown varnish, was knocked down at Puttick & Simpson's for £35. This specimen was in Collingwood's best style, and it had all the characteristics of Italian work. More than likely by now it has had its legitimate label removed, and one bearing a *clarum et venerabile nomen* inserted instead.

CONKERTON, E. R., Newark: contemporary. Has made some excellent violins and violas.

DAVIES, VINCENT, Erwood: contemporary. According to reliable report, he has made several beautiful instruments, but I have not seen any of his work.

DAVY, WILLIAM, Bolton, Lancashire. A litterateur who devotes his spare moments to the making of violins and violas, and has produced some instruments with a wonderfully fine tone. His outline and model are original, showing a marked divergence from the traditional type, but there is nothing outré or grotesque about them. Mr. Davy does not aim at a high degree of finish, but concentrates his knowledge and skill on producing instruments with a grand, rich, and mellow tone.

DIXON, ALFRED T., London : contemporary. A violinist who makes violins *en amateur*. I have not seen any of his work, but it is said to be excellent.

DUNCAN, JAMES, Cluny, Aberdeenshire, where he was born, in 1871. He has made up to date twenty-nine violins and one double-bass. A violin which I examined recently was on an original model, but most of his instruments are on the Joseph model, after Honeyman's drawings. The workmanship is much above the average, and the material used is selected with great care. He uses varnish of his own make, which is an oil one, of good quality, and perfectly transparent. The tone of the instrument I tried was large, rich, and free.

DUNLOP, ALEXANDER, Broxham, Linlithgowshire : contemporary. Strad model slightly modified. Good material, varnish, and workmanship. I have seen only one specimen of his work, and this had a beautiful tone.

EVANS, ISAAC PROBYN, Merthyr Tydfil : contemporary. He has made a few violins on the Amati and Guarneri models. He is a keen connoisseur and a good 'cellist.

FARRELL, WILLIAM JAMES, London : contemporary. He was born in South Shields in 1870 ; and he now works at 181 Caledonian Road, where he carries on the business of making and repairing, and trades as Farrell & Co., dealing in violin wood, accessories, etc. As a youth he showed aptitude for the use of keen-edged tools, and a predilection for wood carving, so that when he decided later on to take up violin making as a hobby, he found that he required very little instruction in the technical part of the craft. He has a sound, practical knowledge of timber, which he has gleaned during his travels abroad, and more especially during a sojourn in the forests of West Africa, for which he paid dearly, having four times contracted malaria fever. He works principally on the Strad and Guarneri models, but his instruments cannot be described as " copies " in the strict sense of the word, since they show departures from the classical models in several little matters of detail, such as, e.g., the scroll, which is of an entirely different pattern from the classical scroll, and, indeed, from any scroll I have ever seen before. The wood used by Mr. Farrell, as was naturally to be expected, is of the finest description, and the varnish, which is of orange tint, is also of excellent quality. The tone of the violin I tried was robust, responsive, even, and carried well. Mr. Farrell is a keen artist, and has in preparation a work on violin construction, in which he deals principally with the vexed question of " How to reproduce the Italian tone."

FEAR, HARRY, Handsworth, Birmingham: contemporary. He was born at Brixton in 1878, and commenced to make violins *en amateur* in 1912, since when he has completed about a dozen instruments. He is particularly successful in obtaining a rich, mellow tone.

FISHER, GEORGE, Cheltenham: c. 1820. I saw recently a violin bearing this name and date, which had rather a good tone.

FLETCHER, JOSEPH, Hitchin, Herts: 1810–25. A violin bearing this label was fairly well made and had a good tone.

FOUCHER, FELIX, London: 1888–1917. Son and pupil of Mons. Georges Foucher, a French maker and expert who has been resident in London for many years. He lived at 25 Wingate Road, Ravenscourt Park, W. On March 20,

FELIX FOUCHER.

To face p. 269.

VIOLIN AND BOW MAKERS

1916, he enlisted in the East Surrey Regiment, and was sent to France ten weeks later, where he was killed in action on August 24, 1917. He made two hundred and fifty violins and two violoncellos. The workmanship, more especially of his later instruments, is beautiful, evincing the artist mind and the trained hand in every turn of the chisel and gouge. The number of instruments he completed is very large for one so young, but there is not the slightest evidence of hurry in any of the violins of his make that I have seen. He was a born artist, and by his early death Britain has lost one who would have greatly helped to bring *lutherie* to the highest degree of perfection in this country. I recently had the opportunity of seeing and trying three of his violins; one was a magnificent copy of a Gagliano, and another an exact copy of a B. S. Fendt, but not (I observed with satisfaction) bearing a fraudulent label. The imitation was clever enough in the case of the latter to deceive (had such been its intention) an experienced connoisseur. Wood and varnish had been matched to perfection, and marks of wear reproduced most minutely. To my mind the time and energy expended on a facsimile reproduction of this kind are wasted, and the result serves no purpose other than as a demonstration of cleverness. Extremely clever young Foucher was without a doubt, and it is gratifying to think that he did not spend many of his precious moments (moments that were all-too-brief, alas) in wanton exhibitions of mere cleverness, but that he consecrated the best part of his time to the production of genuinely artistic and unsophisticated work.

Facsimile of label :—

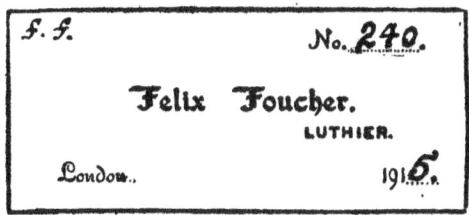

FOUCHER, GEORGES, London: contemporary. Brother of the preceding. I have not seen any of his work, but he is said to be a promising young artist.

FOX, ISAAC, Canterbury: contemporary. He was born in Loath, Lincolnshire, in 1856, and is established at 4 Upper Bridge Street, Canterbury, as a gun, rifle, and cartridge manufacturer. He has made violins and violas for many years, as a hobby, and his work reaches a high standard of excellence. He uses very beautiful wood, and the workmanship and tone are exceedingly good.

FOX, RICHARD, Enfield Town, London: contemporary. He is established at 10 Fyfield Road as a pianoforte dealer and tuner, and makes violins during leisure time. His instruments are said to be excellent, both as regards workmanship and tone. I have not seen any of his work, but I have seen specimens of his varnish, which is beautifully brilliant, and of the very finest quality. He has experimented in violin varnish for a long number of years, and he has certainly succeeded in producing a mixture of rare excellence.

FULTON, HENRY, Liverpool: c. 1800. A very well made violoncello with this label was recently for sale in a second-hand shop in one of the arcades in Liverpool.

GOFTON, ROBERT, Whitby Bay: 1844–90. He made about thirty violins and a number of banjos. He was a clever craftsman, and some of his instruments show beautiful work. He was a cabinet maker by trade, and made instruments during spare time. One who knew him describes his work in a quaint manner thus: "He could make a lovely fiddle, and when he had finished it you would just think it had grown on a tree."

GRAHAM, R., Cadoxton, Barry: contemporary. He is a native of Brompton, Cumberland, and a pupil of James

VIOLIN AND BOW MAKERS

Meek, of Carlisle. He has made only a few violins, which show excellent workmanship, and evince undoubted talent for the craft.

GRAY, JOHN, Sunderland: contemporary. I have not seen any of his work, but it is said to be excellent.

GREENWOOD, G. W., Rochdale : contemporary. He was born in Rochdale on March 4, 1885. He is a professional maker, and a pupil of T. E. Hesketh, the well-known violin maker of Manchester, with whom he served a five years' apprenticeship. He has not made many instruments as yet, his time being taken up with repairs, but he hopes to devote himself to the more interesting (if less profitable) side of the craft in future. The workmanship of the one example of his work which I have seen was magnificent, every part of the instrument being beautifully finished. The tone was firm, responsive, and of the reedy quality which is only found in high-class fiddles. This maker ought to produce work that will help materially to enhance the fame of the rising generation of British violin makers.

GRIFFITHS, A. V., London : contemporary. He is said to have made some excellent instruments.

GUNTER, HENRY, Scarborough : c. 1850. Fair work, but poor wood and harsh tone.

HANCOCK, GEORGE, Stoke-on-Trent : contemporary. He was born in Hanley, Staffordshire, in the year 1851. He commenced as a professional repairer in 1886, but did not make his first violin till 1909, since when he has completed about a dozen instruments. He follows the Strad and Joseph models, and a specimen of his work which I saw and tried recently was of beautiful workmanship and had a very fine tone. This maker is a born artist, and it is a pity that his other business does not allow him to devote more time to that of making.

HARROD, ROBERT, Exeter: c. 1784. A violin was recently seen bearing his label: " Made and sold by Robert Harrod from London. In St. Peter's Churchyard, Exon. 1784."

HARVEY, E. VICTOR, Dinas Powis: contemporary. He is a son of Mr. E. Harvey, the violin maker, of Penarth, and a very promising beginner.

HARVEY, EUGENE, Dinas Powis: contemporary. A brother of the preceding, and a talented and promising beginner.

HAY, JAMES, Guildford, Surrey: contemporary. He was born at Farm of Hilton, Forfarshire, April 23, 1869, and has been trained as an electrical and mechanical engineer, in which profession he is now acting as a consultant. An amateur of great ability and skill, who has made several lovely instruments on an original model.

HAYNES, H. C., Southsea: contemporary. He was born at Great Malvern, in 1867, and is now established at " Bonniecot," Goldsmith Avenue, Southsea, as a professional maker and restorer. He comes of a musical stock, and has taken a keen interest in music, musicians and instruments, from his youth up. He is a brother to the well-known Prof. Battison Haynes, sometime examiner to the Royal College of Music, and the Royal Academy of Music, and a nephew of William Haynes, the widely known organ recitalist. He has worked professionally as a violin maker and restorer for twenty-five years, and has made a considerable number of violins, but his time is principally taken up with repairs. His model is original, approximating to that of Joseph Guarnerius. The workmanship is good, but Mr. Haynes' chief aim is perfection of tone rather than elegance of construction, and it must be admitted that he is remarkably successful in obtaining a large, even, responsive, and sweet tone.

HAXTON, GEORGE, Glasgow : contemporary. He was born at Kingskettle, Fifeshire, October 19, 1878, and began to make violins about ten years ago, following the Strad and Joseph models. Up to the present he has completed thirty-five instruments, of excellent workmanship and tone. A Joseph copy recently seen by me was beautifully finished, and had a large, rich, and mellow tone. This maker is a born artist, and in the front rank of Scotland's present day luthiers.

HENDERSON, JOHN, Broxburn, Linlithgowshire : contemporary. He was born at Dundas, in the parish of Dalmeny, Linlithgowshire, on November 13, 1842, and has been established at Janefield Cottage, Broxburn, for a long period as a professional maker and repairer. He is a man of unique personality, and possessed of astonishing versatility. A literary friend has furnished me with the following account of him : " His first connection with craftsmanship was as a blacksmith's apprentice, but about nine months sufficed to quench his aspirations in that direction. He next tried farming, and became an expert ploughman. In the year 1861 he won the second prize at the Mid and West Lothian ploughing competition, and in the same year he won the first prize at a similar competition at Currie. His next venture was as a pit engineman, and after about eight years at this work he obtained employment with the Oakland Oil Co. as engineer. Afterwards he served with the Broxburn Oil Co. for thirty-two years, but becoming possessed of extensive property he retired some years ago, since when he has devoted the greater part of his time to violin making and repairing : but not all, for he is also an expert florist. His violins are noted more for their wonderful tone than for their workmanship. They have obtained first honours at various industrial exhibitions held in Edinburgh and Glasgow for their tone. Mackenzie Murdoch, the ' Scottish Paganini,' Mr. Will Findlay, Mr. Andrew Bartholomew, and other celebrated Scottish artists, have played upon them, and pronounced them to be equal to the best modern instruments for tone. Although advanced in years he is surprisingly youthful, and brimming over with pawky humour, good sense, and the milk of human kindness."

HODGSON, ——, Alverstone : c. 1877. His name has appeared recently in advertisements.

HOYLE, EDWARD, Todmorden, Yorkshire : contemporary. He was born at Carr-house Fold, Cross-stone, Todmorden, April 17, 1841. He was trained as a cabinet maker, and began to make violins in 1881, since when he has completed seventy-three, following various models according to the dictates of his fancy. He uses a varnish of his own make, which is an oil one, of various shades, but mostly of dark brown, and of good quality. The workmanship, as was naturally to be expected in the case of one who had been trained in the use of edged tools, shows nothing of the 'prentice hand, but is highly finished throughout. The tone is powerful, and of good quality—even, free, bright, and pleasing.

HUMPHREYS, ROBERT, Timberland, near Lincoln : contemporary. He was born in the year 1859, and began to make violins in 1888. He follows the Strad and Joseph models, and turns out three or four instruments every year, which are of excellent workmanship and have a large and telling tone. He is very careful in the selection of his material, and every detail of the work is accurately finished. Age and careful use will greatly improve his instruments.

IRWIN, E. J., Bradford, Yorkshire : contemporary. He was born in Bradford in 1875, and commenced to make violins in 1913. He has made about twenty instruments, all of good, honest, solid workmanship, and varnished with Anderson's amber oil varnish. The tone is very good.

J'ANSON, EDWARD POPPLEWELL, Leeds and Manchester : c. 1840–75, or a little later, perhaps. Unfortunately, there is no certainty as to when and where he was born, nor as to his period of work, date and place of death, etc. In some books he is said to have learnt his craft from William Booth, junior, on what authority I do not know. It does not matter much where he learnt or from whom, since he was undoubtedly an extremely clever artist, if not a genius, and would have shaped his destiny under almost any circumstances. The great man, be he philosopher, poet, artist, or what not, moulds his environment and develops even by antagonism : he can say with Topsy : " I 'spect I growed. Don't think nobody never made me." There can be no doubt as to the ability of J'anson, the instruments that still have his label in them (few though they be in number) bear abundant testimony to his consummate skill. Mr. Charles Holt, of Leicester, a keen and an experienced connoisseur, who owns a fine example of his art, writes : " The most perfect J'anson fiddle I have ever seen, and certainly one of the finest instruments I have seen in my life (and I have seen not a few) was that sold at a sale at Puttick & Simpson's in 1908. It was dated ' Leeds 1854,' and was knocked down to a dealer at a very high figure. I dare assert that that fiddle was the grandest that English art has ever produced." And with regard to the specimen that he himself owns, Mr. Holt writes : " It is beautifully made, and its tone is extraordinarily large and at the same time ravishingly sweet. I recently bought what is probably the finest Gennaro Gagliano in existence, in immaculate condition, and gave two hundred pounds for it, but the J'anson puts it absolutely out of court. I have examples of Maggini, Grancino, Andreas Guarnerius, Ceruti, etc., and have been a fiddle fancier for upwards of thirty years, yet saw I never a fiddle (except the very best of Stradivari or Giuseppe Guarneri) to come up to the J'anson for grandeur and purity of tone." Mr. Holt was good enough to send this violin down for my inspection a little while ago, and I certainly am obliged to confess myself in agreement with him. The conviction has been growing upon me of late that if we only possessed as many examples of the work of Tobin, J'anson,

Collingwood, and one or two others, as we do of the work of Banks, Duke, Forster, Parker, etc., that we should have to revise our estimate of the relative merits of our English makers. Doubtless there are a goodly number of Tobins, J'ansons, etc, in existence, but they have lost their identity, and are " sailing about under the Italian flag." Once upon a time it was said that " the poor ye have always with you " : to the devotees of the fiddle it would be more appropriate to say, " the rogue ye have always with you." Of course, it must not be forgotten that the majority of the instruments of such men as Tobin have borne false labels from the start, that is to say, they have carried a trade label, or the employer's label, and not that of the actual maker. Misappropriation is another besetting sin of the fiddle trade. Some of the finest of our present day artists are lost to their own generation and to posterity because in the struggle for existence they have " to knuckle to," and sell their birthright for a mess of pottage to their more fortunate brethren ; in plain words, they are obliged to sell their instruments unlabelled to the trade.

The label in Mr. Holt's violin runs :—

Edward P. I'anson. Fecit. Manchester, Anno 1872.

The two last figures are filled in with a pen.

JERMY, ARTHUR, Kingsland, London : contemporary. He is a professional maker and repairer, and is said to be a clever artist. I regret I cannot say anything about his work, as I have not seen any of his instruments. He was born at Old Ford, London, in 1867, and has been established at 6 Crossway, Kingsland, for a number of years.

JERVIS, FRANK, Belfast : c. 1800. This is another old maker about whom little or nothing is known. Two

EDWARD KEENAN.

To face p. 277.

violins bearing his label have been recently seen, one of which was on the Amati model, very well made, and with a beautiful tone. The varnish was of excellent quality, and of a dark golden brown colour, lustrous and transparent. It was evidently the work of one who was a master of the craft.

KEENAN, EDWARD, Dublin : contemporary. He was, born in the village of Clonolvy, in the parish of Ardcath, Meath, Ireland, on the 18th of July, 1876, but his parents belonged to Dublin, where Keenan has also lived from his infancy. He lives at 5 Spencer Street, North Strand, and is a professional maker and repairer. At the age of sixteen he was apprenticed to a large firm of coach builders, and he progressed so rapidly that at twenty-four he was appointed foreman wheeler to the Messrs. Potter & Co., North Wall, Dublin, who have a large export trade in wheels of every description. He was married at the age of twenty, and has seven children living. He commenced to make violins as a hobby at an early age, and the mysteries of the craft exercised so weird an influence over him that he felt irresistibly drawn more and more towards violin making as a profession. He read all the literature on the subject that he could get hold of, and made a point of " interviewing " every fine fiddle inside or that passed through Dublin, so that he gradually stored up a mass of information that enabled him, by-and-by, to wield gouge and callipers to some purpose. He succeeded in producing a passable instrument almost from the start. In his studies he has received material assistance from Robert Cathcart, Esq., of Lurganbrae, Shankill, Co. Dublin, whose profound knowledge of the subject, and wide experience as a connoisseur, have proved a good substitute for a regular apprenticeship at an *atelier*. Mr. Cathcart had in his keeping during the period of the war a fine Strad, of the golden period, and he was good enough to furnish Mr. Keenan with an accurate set of tracings of this instrument a few years ago, from which he (Keenan) now makes all his

T

beautiful Strad copies. The owner of this particular Strad is Captain Joshua Watson, of Herbert Park, Dublin, who entrusted it to the care of Mr. Cathcart till the end of the war. Three years ago Mr. Keenan made a copy of the Strad for Captain Watson, and concerning this fiddle Mr. Cathcart writes me : " It has the best tone of all that he has ever made. I had it for a couple of weeks before Captain Watson was demobilised, and I found I could pick it up immediately after playing on the Strad for some time, and play on it with pleasure, and I think that a very severe test, especially as the Strad (called the ' Vieuxtemps-Hause ' in one of the old documents connected with it) is a magnificent instrument and in perfect condition." I recently had here for inspection another copy of this Strad, made by Mr. Keenan for Captain Oakley, of S. Africa, and in my honest opinion the instrument summed up in itself all the excellent qualities that a copy can ever claim to possess. The art of the copyist cannot possibly, I think, reach greater perfection than it has reached in this instance. Material, varnish, finish, and tone proclaimed it to be *ne plus ultra*. This is not extravagant, but just praise. The luthier's art has been under a cloud in Ireland for well-nigh a century, but the strong rays of the sun have been piercing through the cloud during the last few years, and already the art is shaking her wings and preparing for another flight. The home of Celtic art, the land of the Perrys, of Tobin, Delaney, Dollard, Molyneux, etc., is yet capable of noble things. There is even now a considerable number of native violin makers, some of them men of great talent and skill, and it is not hazardous to prophesy that the Emerald Isle will have her own school of violin making before many more decades have passed.

Mr. Keenan has made a few violins on the Joseph model, and several on an original model, and he won the first prize with one of these at an exhibition held in 1913 in connection with the Royal Dublin Society. But it is since he adopted the Strad model that he has made the great strides which have brought him so far towards the summit of his ambition, and he will be well advised if he adheres to this model to the end of his journey. It is to be hoped that he will be patronised sufficiently well in his native land to enable him to dispense with repairing and devote the whole of his time to making.

Facsimile of label :—

MADE BY
∴ **EDWARD KEENAN,** ∴
DUBLIN.
ANNO 19/8...

KNIGHT, FRANK R., Reigate : contemporary. He was born in 1870, and commenced to make violins in 1917. A violin I recently examined showed that he had made wonderful progress in the art in a short space of time. The instrument had a fine tone, due principally, I think, to the very choice quality of the pine in the table.

LAMB, JOHN, Shiremoor, Newcastle-on-Tyne : 1823–1903. He made a considerable number of violins, of various models. Some of his better class work is not without merit.

LAMB, JOHN, Shiremoor : contemporary. Son of the preceding John Lamb, born in 1855. He has made about thirty violins and two violas, on no particular model.

LEADER, JAMES HENRY, Bristol : c. 1830–40. I recently saw a quaint-looking old fiddle bearing this label : it was well made, of good material, and had a very fair tone.

LEAKE, H., Huntley : c. 1820. A rather crude looking old fiddle, with a very good tone, had his MS. label in it. The material was excellent, a fact which probably accounted for the good tone.

LEE, PERCY, London : contemporary. He is established at 6 Ashford House, Ashford Road, N.W., as a professional maker, and viola player, and is considered by some of the principal London dealers to be one of the ablest representatives of the modern British school of violin making. He was born in Huddersfield in the year 1871, and is the fourth son of the late Mr. Joseph Lee, woollen merchant, and sometime organist and choirmaster of St. John's Church, of that town. He was educated at the private academy of Mr. W. E. Thomas, a Welshman, whose school at that time enjoyed a high reputation in the district. He came to London at the age of seventeen, when he was apprenticed to the firm of Messrs. George Rogers and Sons, pianoforte makers, where he got his first insight into the mysteries of fiddle construction, and became interested in the study of acoustics. Soon after he had served his apprenticeship he joined the ranks of the musical profession as a viola player, and discarded pianoforte making. He next took a course of instruction in violin making at the warehouse of Messrs. Haynes, of Grays Inn Road, and soon acquired a high degree of proficiency in the craft. His output of instruments is not great : having more than one string to his bow he is not entirely dependent on making, and is able to devote extra time and care to the construction of each fiddle. The bulk of his production consists of violas, for the making of which he (as a viola player) considers he has special aptitude and fitness.

In the opinion of artistes who play upon Mr. Lee's violas the instruments possess a remarkably fine tone, and are magnificently made and beautifully finished.

Mr. Lee has recently turned his attention to mediaeval and pre-renaissance instruments. A *viol d'amour* which he finished about six months ago, and which is figured here, is worthy in every way to be placed beside the finest example extant of the old viol maker's art. Mr. Henry Saint-George, who was perhaps our greatest living authority on these old instruments, spoke very highly of it.

VIOL D'AMOUR BY LEE.

To face p. 280.

VIOLIN AND BOW MAKERS

It may be remarked here that an effort has been made within these last few years to revive certain mediaeval and post-mediaeval types of stringed instruments, but the effort, I think, is only a passing whim, and can result in no real advantage. Crazes of the kind break our every now and again. In Wales we have tried hard to revive interest in the triple harp, and we have even tried to revive the clumsy *crŵth*, but what availeth it, the hand of the clock will not be put back! Haweis very pertinently remarks that " there is something inexorable about the consensus of posterity. Individuals may chafe under it, and writers may try to reverse its verdict. You even have crazes for the revival of neglected poets, painters, and musicians, but you will never succeed in pushing from their pedestals the great gods whom posterity has once decided to bow down to." And if this is true of individual men and things, how much more true is it of types, which represent the maximum effort of nature and art, and which are being eternally evolved from the less to the more perfect ? Violin makers should not take a plunge back into mediaevalism, but should endeavour to catch a glimpse of the age to come and see visions of the fiddle that is to be—unless, indeed, they think the fiddle type is already perfect. That Mr. Lee is an artist of exceptional talent is manifest, and posterity will thank him if he devotes his time and energy to the construction of high-class violas. He has ample scope in this direction for his powers. To begin with he might profitably devote some time to the study of the problem of dimension and cubic capacity, for, strange as it may seem, there is yet a diversity of opinion among the best makers as to what the length, widths, and depth of the perfect viola should be. The matter has been settled long ago as far as the other instruments are concerned, but both makers and players are in as fidgetty a mood as ever about the viola.

LIGHT, GEORGE, Exeter. Period probably the last quarter of the eighteenth century. Only one or two violins bearing his label have been seen, but these showed very careful work, and had a sweet and mellow tone, lacking in power.

LINDSAY, WILLIAM HENRY, Cardiff : contemporary. He has made only one or two instruments.

LOCK, GEORGE HERBERT, M.A., Shrewsbury : contemporary. He was born at Dorchester in 1850, was at Cambridge from 1869 to 1873, and since that date has lived in Shrewsbury, where he was mathematical master (at the well-known Shrewsbury School) from 1873 to 1904, when he retired.

He has made violins as a hobby for many years, and has completed fifty-one instruments altogether, including two violas and three 'cellos. The workmanship is excellent, and the tone large, brilliant, and remarkably responsive. He is a very clever amateur.

LONSDALE, W. P., Preston : early part of the nineteenth century.

MARDON, J. C., Exeter : c. 1850. It is not certain whether he was a maker, or only a repairer.

MATHER, ——, Swanwick : early part of the eighteenth century. A 'cello of his make has been seen, which was of handsome wood, well made, and had a very fine tone.

M'NEILL, JOHN, Edinburgh : contemporary. He was born at Tranent, Haddingtonshire, in 1848, and made his first violin about twenty years ago, since when he has completed twenty-two instruments. His time is principally taken up with repairs, and he greatly regrets that he has not had the opportunity to perfect himself in the art of making, albeit he has made some good fiddles, which have a powerful and responsive tone, very useful for orchestral purposes. M'Neill is said to be a skilful repairer.

VIOLIN AND BOW MAKERS 283

MILLINGTON, ERNEST, Borrowash : contemporary. A clever amateur who has made a few instruments by way of experiment, with the object of discovering, if possible, the secret of the Italian tone.

MOWBRAY, DAVID C., Leith : contemporary. Born at Melrose in 1868. Commenced to make violins eight years ago, and has completed several on the Strad and Joseph models, but devotes most of his time to repairing. An excellent craftsman, that would eventually produce important work if he devoted all his time to making.

MURRAY, ALEXANDER, Morpeth. Period, about the middle of the nineteenth century. He made a considerable number of violins, one of which is owned by Councillor Lawson, of Newbiggin-by-the-Sea, which is said to have a good tone.

NANCE, S. E., Penarth, Glamorgan : contemporary. A native of Padstow, Cornwall, who settled down in business in Wales many years ago. He is keenly interested in the theory of violin making, and has made about forty instruments on an altogether original pattern.

NELSON, GEORGE, North Seaton, near Blyth, in Northumberland : contemporary. I have not seen any of his work, but I have reliable evidence that it is of considerable merit, and that some of his violins have a remarkably fine tone. Unfortunately he has been an invalid for a long time and unable to work.

NOON, T. M., Cardiff : contemporary. An amateur who has made a splendid beginning.

OPIE, A. J., Portsmouth : contemporary. This very clever amateur is by training a scientist, but by nature an artist, and is the first of the name who for the last five generations has not been trained as an artist. He is employed by the Admiralty as a specialist in testing and designing the various forms of fighting ships, both above and below the water, and by the greatest good fortune he has been trained under Froude, the first and leading authority in the world on the mathematics of naval architecture. He has made a number of violins on an original model, which are of beautiful workmanship and have a very fine tone.

PAGE, ARTHUR LEWIS, Uxbridge : contemporary. He was born at Midhurst, W. Sussex, in 1879, and commenced to make violins in 1912. He follows the " grand " Strad model, using material of excellent quality, and a varnish which looks like Whitelaw's, of golden or orange red colour. He has made only a few violins as yet, but hopes to produce them more rapidly in future. The work is excellent, and the tone large, brilliant, and responsive.

RICHARDSON, ARTHUR, Crediton, Devon : contemporary. He was born at Stavely, Derbyshire, in 1882, and he now lives and works as a professional maker at Butts Park Cottage, Park Road, Crediton. After receiving a good education he was apprenticed to the wood-carving and pattern-making trade, and when he had finished his training he was acknowledged to be an exceptionally intelligent and clever craftsman. Before he settled down at Crediton a few years ago, he travelled about a great deal, in the pursuit of his calling, and he made it a point to study works of art of every description, wherever he went, including painting, sculpture, architecture, and especially wood carvings. He had rare opportunities, and made the fullest use of them. In addition to being an expert wood carver, he has displayed great talent as a wax modeller, and some of his original designs are works of art. Needless to say, he is also a good draughtsman.

This kind of early training, based upon a sound general education, is, I verily believe, the best possible introduction to the art and craft of violin making. I consider it to be superior to a regular apprenticeship served in an *atelier*, after the Continental fashion, which usually begins at the age of fourteen, or even earlier in many instances, with the scantiest knowledge of even the rudiments of science, and with barely the skill to draw straight lines and simple curves. Violin making, it should be borne in mind, is a science and an art combined. A science teaches us to know, and an art to do. It is a science in so far as it investigates the necessary principles and forms of construction, and thus teaches us to understand how the principles are discovered and the knowledge of them applied : it is an art when it is occupied in framing a number of practical rules, and in giving to material certain definite forms. It is a delusion to think that violin making is only a kind of glorified carpentry or cabinet making. Many violin makers regard it as such, with the result that they never (except perhaps by accident) produce a great violin—a violin which is at once a work of art and a great musical instrument. When a violin maker tells me that his chief ambition is to make a fiddle that is beautiful to look at, I cannot help thinking that his knowledge of the craft is somewhere in the neighbourhood of zero. Another tells me that he simply works for tone, and cares nothing for appearance, and I hear something whisper to me : " He has not the skill to make a thing of beauty, but he would if he could." The conclusion of the whole matter, and my apology for this digression, is this : let him who aspires to be the Stradivari or the Guarneri of the future train his brain to think, his eye to see, and his hands to do.

Mr. Richardson went through a long course of rigorous training, and the result is manifest both in the fine tone and in the graceful lines of his instruments. As to tone, the result of the Cobbett competition, in which Mr. Richardson's violin won the first prize, is sufficient guarantee of excellence. And the workmanship is equal to the tone. One notable feature of the construction is the careful graduation of the thicknesses of the plates. Another is the discrimination shown as to the proper quantity of wood that should be left in the plates. Mr. Richardson works his plates neither too thin nor too thick. To work them too thin is, of course, a fatal mistake, but there is a school of violin makers to-day which apparently thinks it impossible to err on the side of thickness. It cannot be too strongly insisted upon that it is a big mistake to leave too much wood. A well-known writer on the violin has been preaching the thick plate doctrine so indefatigably that he has converted a host of makers to his views, many of them against their reason, but he has won no converts among the cognoscenti, and the error of the doctrine is sufficiently demonstrated in its practice. Reason and experience abundantly confirm the verdict pronounced by Hyacinth Abele long ago : " If the wood is too thick, the tone will be poor and without any *ringing* quality ; if the wood is too thin, the tone will be hollow and *tubby* " [" The Violin and its Story," in " The Strad " Library, p. 98].

Mr. Richardson has two models : the grand Strad, and a model of his own, which may be described as the grand Strad slightly modified in outline. Every detail of his work is finished with elaborate care, and there is that grandeur, refinement, and what the French call *état de repos*, about the completed instrument, which gives it a distinct individuality, and is very pleasing to the eye of the connoisseur.

This maker is on the sunny side of forty, and therefore a comparatively young man, and I venture to predict that, given health and a little encouragement, he will produce work that will not only contribute to maintain the traditions, but will raise the status of the craft in Britain.

RITCHIE, ALEXANDER, London : contemporary. An amateur who has made only a few instruments, but whose work shows such extraordinary talent that it commands attention. I recently examined a specimen of it, and entered the following remarks in my notebook :—" A most faithful and accurate copy of the grand Strad model. Excellent material, beautiful workmanship, varnish a soft, elastic, transparent, and brilliant mixture—very similar to Urquhart's varnish. Tone large, reedy, responsive and ringing. A born artist, and as dexterous a craftsman as any now

VIOLIN AND BOW MAKERS 287

living." He was born of Scottish parents in the year 1888, at Battersea, in the county of London, and now resides at 34 Surrey Lane, Battersea Park, S.W. He is an engineer by profession, a clever draughtsman, a violinist of repute, and a man of solid learning. It is to be hoped he will make many fiddles.

ROBINSON, WILLIAM, London : contemporary. He works as a professional maker, and violin case maker, at 68 Rochdale Road, Plumstead, S.E. His life story, related in his own words, has a touch of pathos and quaintness about it that makes it interesting. He says : " I was born in the village of Avebury, Wiltshire, in the year 1873, but am much younger than my years would suggest. My father died when I was two years of age, leaving a widow and four children to fend for themselves. We were poor, so that I had to labour on a farm at an early age : sometimes I was sent to mind the sheep on the downs, but never went without pieces of wood and my pocket knife, to make toys with, and nicknacks. I spent my coppers, not on sweets, but on the empty boxes which had contained them : these 1 converted into rustic fiddles, for the country lads to play on. I toiled through weary years up to manhood, and dreamed of the time when I should make a real fiddle, and I am happy that I have lived to see my dreams come true." Mr. Robinson was apprenticed to the saddlery trade, and he followed this occupation till recently. He has designed and makes a speciality of a beautiful kind of solid leather violin case, for which he gets more orders than he can execute. His violins (of which there is not a large number as yet) are beautifully constructed, and players think highly of their tonal qualities. Mr. Towry Piper, in an article devoted to him in *The Strad* for April, 1919, concludes his remarks thus : " I cannot help regarding this maker as quite unusually gifted. He is still in the prime of life, and if he continues to produce work of this class he should go far, and obtain wide recognition in the fiddle maker's calling." I thoroughly agree with this eminent expert.

ROGERS, GEORGE, Conlig, Co. Down, Ireland : contemporary. An excellent member of the small but growing band of modern Irish makers. He has made a number of fine instruments on the Stradivari model. It is worthy of remark that the majority of Irish makers have a decided preference for the Strad model, whereas Scottish makers have a penchant for the Joseph model. Perhaps the national temperament has something to do with the respective choice. The Irish are fervid, sympathetic, and responsive; the Scotch dour, persistent, and practical. With the exception of Italy there is no soil in the world more rich in art productibility than Ireland. The country which produced the fine old artists of a century ago is capable of even greater things, and when the Emerald Isle is regenerated and its sorrows forgotten, the melody of fiddles that are yet unmade will gladden the land. Artists of the type of Mr. Rogers will hasten the coming of the new age.

SIMPSON, FRANK THOMAS, Dunmow, Essex : contemporary. Born in the parish of Great Saling, Essex, in 1887. He works on the Strad model, also on an original model, with flat arching, and other differentiating characteristics. He is particularly careful in the selection of his material, and has had the rare good fortune to pick up choice bits of maple and pine—where, it is difficult to imagine, in these days of timber famine. The thicknesses are very carefully graduated, and the work is carefully finished and beautifully varnished. The tone is large and telling. He is a very capable craftsman, and if he were to adhere to the Strad model, and to copy every detail scrupulously, he would produce fine work.

SOWERBY, A. L., Manchester : contemporary. He has made violins *en amateur* for a number of years, and has lately opened business at 87 Fitz George Street, as a professional maker and repairer. I have not seen any of his more recent work, but his earlier work evinced a very special aptitude for the craft, and augured well for a successful career. Mr. Sowerby has a thorough knowledge of the history of the craft, and of the principles of fiddle construction, and there is no reason why he should not make his mark.

STEDMAN, ROYSTON, Leyton, Essex : period, about the middle of last century. Mr. Charles Holt, of Leicester, reports having seen a viola of his make, which was of excellent workmanship, and had a very fine tone.

STOCKDALE, WILLIAM, Acklington, Northumberland : contemporary. He has made a number of violins on various models, the later ones being on that of Guarneri. I have not seen any of them.

STURDY, ALFRED. An old fiddle, ascribed to the middle of last century, had this name on a label, without date or name of place.

TAYLOR, STEPHEN OLIVER, Leicester : contemporary. I am indebted to Mr. Charles Holt, the violin connoisseur, of Leicester, for particulars respecting this maker, and I take the opportunity here of thanking him for his valuable assistance. Mr. Holt writes : " Regarding Stephen Oliver Taylor, I must first of all say that he is the son of Mr. Stephen Taylor, the well-known organ builder, and that he is himself an organ builder first, and a violoncello maker after. But he is, nevertheless, a consummate artist. He has been brought up from childhood among fiddles, and all kinds of woods, etc. His 'cellos are really the finest things in the way of new instruments that I have seen or heard. They are built on the lines of Giuseppe Guarneri's violins, with the long Gothic sound-holes, and the effect is very striking, altogether harmonious, and pleasing to the eye. I have played on several of these 'cellos. They are all made of beautifully figured wood—in fact, it is extremely handsome in the back and ribs—and their appearance is grand and majestic. The tone is all that could be desired—full, round, and as mellow as that of any old instrument I have met with. The scrolls, too, are quite remarkable for their bold, yet exquisite carving ; in fine, the conception of the whole design is the quintessence of vigour and elegance."

Mr. Taylor has secured a large stock of extremely old wood, of the finest acoustical qualities, figure, and grain, and he husbands it with the greatest care, and values it above rubies. It seems that he does not make to sell, nor can he be prevailed upon to part with any of his work : he loves the art for its own sake.

TAYLOR, ROBERT, Leicester : contemporary. He is a professional maker and repairer, and has his workshop at 5 Ann Street. Mr. Holt writes respecting him : " He is not related to Mr. Stephen Oliver Taylor, mentioned above, and has not had the same advantage of being trained to woodwork, albeit he is a splendid craftsman, and is turning out some excellent fiddles. He pays special attention to that very important part of fiddle construction, viz., the graduation of the thicknesses of the plates, and his success in obtaining a good tone is to be attributed largely to his sound knowledge of timber, and of the principles of acoustics. I have been able to offer him advice, from time to time, during the various stages of the work, and I must say that I have found him to be a most intelligent, diligent, and patient worker. He is full of enthusiasm for his art, and I certainly think he ought to reach a high standard of excellence."

Mr. Taylor submitted a violin for my inspection some time ago, and a careful trial of this instrument enables me to endorse the foregoing remarks. There was very little in the workmanship to justify criticism, and the tone was exceptionally good.

THOMPSON, ——, Felkington, Northumberland,

VIOLIN AND BOW MAKERS

TILLER, C. W., Boscombe, Bournemouth: contemporary. An exceptionally clever amateur, who has made several violins, the last of which, finished a year ago, was of very fine workmanship and tone. He is a joiner by trade, but he shows such talent that it is a pity he is not a professional maker.

TYE, J., London: period, about the middle of last century. A decent workman, but his sound-holes are the most absurdly grotesque of all that I have ever seen. His label runs : " Made by J. Tye, 37 Agnes Street, York Road, Lambeth, London."

WALKER, HENRY, Stoke-on-Trent: contemporary. Born in Leeds, in 1876. A modeller by profession, and he has made a 'cello, a viola, and several violins as a hobby, which are said to be good.

WILD, FRANK, Rochdale, Lancashire: contemporary. He was born in Rochdale in 1869, and is a tool maker by trade, and makes and repairs violins only during spare time. He has completed about a dozen instruments on the Amati-Strad, and grand Strad models, the later ones of which are of excellent workmanship, with a large, bright, even, and responsive tone. He is a very enthusiastic and capable craftsman.

WILLIAMS, R. J., Llandudno, N. Wales: contemporary. A very clever amateur who has made about thirty instruments, including violins, violas, and one 'cello. He won the silver medal for the second best violin at the Royal National Eisteddfod of Wales, held in Neath in 1918.

WILSON, FRED, Chelmsford: contemporary. A well-to-do, enthusiastic amateur who has made a number of violins of exquisite workmanship and beautiful tone.

WILSON, JAMES, Belkington, Scottish Borders. Towards the end of last century. He made several violins on the long Strad model.

WILLIAMS, THOMAS, Edgbaston, Birmingham : contemporary. He was born at Langley Green, Worcestershire, in 1864, and lives now at 93 Lee Bank Road, Edgbaston. Although he considers himself only an amateur maker, his work reaches a high standard of excellence, and would bring no discredit to the best professional maker in the country. His last effort is a facsimile of a Lorenzo and Tommaso Carcassi, and is a very clever bit of work. He is a born artist, and it is a pity he does not take up the work professionally.

WITHERS, JOSEPH, London : contemporary. The life story of this " Grand Old Man of the Gouge " should be given as it is related by himself in a letter to me, dated March 18, 1919. He says : " I was born at Poplar, London East, on the 28th of May, 1838, and was the only boy in a family of seven children. My father and mother were born in London, as were also my grandfather, grandmother, and great-grandmother, on my father's side. My mother's people were Scotch, hailing from Aberdeen, At the age of seven I was sent to a day school, which I attended till I was fourteen, when I was apprenticed to my father, who was a shipwright, working for Messrs. Green at their shipbuilding yard at Blackwall. I worked at first on gunboats which were being built for the government at the time of the Crimean war, and I also worked on the first armour-plated vessels ever constructed. On August 1, 1860, my father met with a fatal accident, and my mother and young sister then had no one to look to for support but me, so I had to take my father's place in the home. I kept on working at my trade in the shipyard till 1879. I commenced to make violins as a hobby at the age of eighteen, and received some instruction from a maker named Lambert, who had worked with James Brown, of Spitalfields. In the year just named I exhibited a violin at the Westminster Industrial Exhibition, and was awarded the first prize for musical instruments. This Exhibition was on a large scale, and was held in a

VIOLIN AND BOW MAKERS 293

temporary building in Queen Victoria Street, Westminster, from May 1 till September. The judges spoke so highly of my violin that I thought it afforded me a favourable opportunity to start as a professional maker. I acted on the impulse, and set up business at 158 Caledonian Road, N., and I am pleased to say I have never had cause to regret it. From the time I started my career as a professional maker I never missed an opportunity to improve my knowledge of the violin, and I diligently applied myself to the acquiring of perfect skill in the use of the tools peculiar to the craft. I was a regular visitor at the great Exhibition of stringed instruments held at South Kensington in 1872, and paid the closest attention to the famous fiddles gathered together there. The ' Messie ' Strad fascinated me above all the other instruments ; it held me spell-bound, and it was with difficulty that I could tear myself away from it. That fiddle has pursued me all through my life since I first saw it, and haunted me in all my dreams. I have worked at my fiddles under its spell, and have tried to catch some of its spirit in order to imprison it in my work. Up to the present I have made about a hundred and fifty violins, twelve violas, and a few violoncellos. I am now nearly eighty-one years of age, but my sight is as clear, and my hand as steady, as they were fifty years ago, thanks to the life I have lived, without alcohol or tobacco in any shape or form. The number of instruments I have made is small, considering the long years I have laboured, but that is because I have been busily occupied with repairs all the time. I shall not make many more fiddles : my material has been used up, and my work has been done."

The last violin made by Mr. Withers is on the table before me now, and as I look at its pure outline and graceful curves I can but admire and wonder. The scroll is of bold design, symmetrical, with easy flowing lines, and justly proportioned to the body of the instrument, whilst the purfling is inlaid unbrokenly and evenly without a tremor. One looks in vain for the slightest evidence of old age in any little detail

U

of the work. The tone has a rich reedy quality that is not often heard in a new instrument, and it is sweet, even, and perfectly responsive.

Facsimile of label:

Made by
JOSEPH WITHERS,
Aged 80 Years.
London, A. D. 1918 .

WORTHINGTON, JOHN, Hereford : c. 1820. Exaggerated Stainer model ; fair workmanship and tone.

WOULDHAVE, ——, North Shields : c. 1870. I am not certain whether he was an actual maker, or merely a dealer. Some of the instruments which have his label are well made.

WRIGHT, PETER, Gloucester : c. 1840–50. Probably only a repairer.

APPENDICES

Appendix A

THE FRONTISPIECE

The magnificent quartet of old English instruments shown in the frontispiece is owned by J. E. Smith, Esq., of Bayswater, London. The violins are by Daniel Parker and Richard Duke, the viola by Benjamin Banks, and the violoncello by " Old " William Forster. The instruments are typical examples of the old English school, and in excellent condition. The Parker violin is, I think, one of the most superb specimens of this fine old maker's work in existence. I have seen altogether about twenty of his fiddles, but none that would quite match this one. It is of the Long Strad model, with a lovely orange-red varnish of excellent quality. It has the quaint droop of the upper corners so characteristic of Parker in his happy moments. It is figured here by itself as an example of the " craft-poetry " of British genius. The other instruments of this set are also each notable in its own way, but space will not allow of a detailed description. The quartet must be seen before its excellence can be fully appreciated.

Appendix B

BIBLIOGRAPHY

The following is a list of some of the more important English books on the violin, and is intended as a guide to the student who is desirous of acquiring a fairly wide and accurate knowledge of the instrument and its literature. The author has in preparation, and hopes to publish shortly, *A Complete Bibliography of the Violin*, including British and Foreign works, as well as " Violin Schools " and books of instruction.

BROADHOUSE, JOHN. Facts about Fiddles. Violins old and new. London, n.d. (1879) : W. Reeves. 8vo. pamphlet.

DAVIDSON, PETER. The Violin: Its Construction theoretically and practically treated, etc. London : F. Pitman. Edinburgh, Glasgow, Dundee, 1881. Small 8vo.

[There were four editions of this work, the first of which was published in 1871. It is now very scarce.]

ENGEL, CARL. Researches into the Early History of the Violin Family. London, 1883 : Novello, Ewer & Co. 8vo.

FÉTIS, FRANÇOIS JOSEPH. Notice of Anthony Stradivari the celebrated Violin-maker, known by the name of Stradivarius. Preceded by Historical and Critical Researches on the Origin and Transformations of Bow Instruments, and followed by a Theoretical Analysis of the

APPENDIX B 299

Bow, and remarks on François Tourte, the author of its final improvements. Translated by John Bishop, of Cheltenham. London, 1864 : R. Cocks. Large 8vo.

FLEMING, JAMES M. Old Violins and their Makers : Including some References to those of Modern Times. Illustrated with facsimile of tickets, sound-holes, etc. London, 1883 : L. Upcott Gill. Cr. 8vo.

FLEMING, JAMES M. The Fiddle Fancier's Guide : A Manual of Information regarding Violins, Violas, Basses, and Bows of Classical and Modern Times ; together with Biographical Notices and Portraits of the most famous Performers on these Instruments. London, 1892. Haynes, Foucher & Co. 8vo.

GROVE, SIR GEORGE. A Dictionary of Music and Musicians. Edition 1912, edited by J. A. Fuller Maitland, M.A., F.S.A. London, Macmillan & Co., 5 volumes. [There are several important articles on the violin, violin makers, violin literature, etc.]

HART, GEORGE. The Violin : Its Famous Makers and their Imitators. With numerous wood engravings from photographs of the works of Stradivari, Guarneri, Amati, and others. London, 1875 : Dulan & Schott. Large post 4to.
Second edition, greatly enlarged, 1884.
New edition, 1909. Large post 4to.
There are also four Popular Editions of this work : Cr. 8vo. [This is the most important and reliable of all the books treating on the violins of the various schools of the classical period, but it scarcely touches on modern work.]

HAWEIS, REV. H. R. Old Violins. In the " Collector Series." London, 1898 : George Redway. [A very instructive and interesting book.]

APPENDIX B

HERON-ALLEN, EDWARD. Violin-Making, as it Was and Is : being a Historical, Theoretical, and Practical Treatise on the Science and Art of Violin-Making, for the use of Violin Makers and Players, Amateur and Professional. With upwards of 200 Illustrations by the Author. Preceded by an Essay on the Violin and its Position as a Musical Instrument. London, 1885 : Ward, Lock, Bowden, & Co. Demy 8vo. [This is the best book on violin-making that has ever appeared in any language.]

HILL, W. E. & SONS. Antonio Stradivari : His Life and Work. London, 1902. 4to.
Second edition, 1909, 8vo.
[This fine monograph will remain for all time the Standard work on Stradivari.]

HILL, W. E. & SONS. Gio. Paolo Maggini : His Life and Work. London, 1892. 4to.

HONEYMAN, WM. C. The Violin : How to Choose One. Edinburgh, 1893 : E. Köhler & Son. Cr. 8vo.

HONEYMAN, WM. C. Scottish Violin Makers : Past and Present. Edinburgh, 1899 : E. Köhler & Son. Cr. 8vo.

READE, CHARLES. A Lost Art Revived. Cremona Violin and Varnish. Four letters descriptive of those exhibited in 1872 at the South Kensington Museum, also giving the data for producing the true varnishes used by the great Cremonese makers. Reprinted from the *Pall Mall Gazette* by George H. M. Muntz, Birchfield.
Gloucester, 1873 : John Bellowes. Large 8vo pamphlet.

SANDYS, WILLIAM, AND FORSTER, SIMON ANDREW. The History of the Violin and other Instruments played on with the Bow, from the remotest times to the present. Also an account of the principal makers,

APPENDIX B

English and Foreign, with numerous illustrations. London, 1864 : J. R. Smith, Addison and Lucas. Demy 8vo.

STOEVING, PAUL. The Story of the Violin. London, 1904 : The Walter Scott Publishing Co., Ltd.

" THE STRAD " LIBRARY. About a dozen or more exceptionally useful handbooks have been issued in this series. London : " The Strad " office.

Appendix C

THE WELSH CRWTH

That the *crwth* (*crwth* proper, as distinguished from *crwth trithant*, or three-stringed *crwth*) was a popular instrument in Wales for hundreds of years is abundantly evident from the numerous references to it in the Welsh bardic remains. The bulk of these references belong to the fifteenth and sixteenth centuries, a good number to the seventeenth, and a few to the first half of the eighteenth century. I have made a long and diligent search for references to the *crwth* in the literature and unpublished manuscripts of the seventeenth and eighteenth centuries, and I hope before long to publish the result of this interesting labour in a volume on the Musical Instruments of the Welsh. Mr. Heron-Allen is correct in his statement that "the *crwth* existed in Wales to comparatively recent times," but is in error when he says that it disappeared about the year 1801. There was a family of *crwth* players in the Gwaun valley, near Fishguard, living down to 1827. The last member of the family, who was called *Shams y Crwthwr* (Demetian dialect—James the *crwth* player) died at an advanced age in the year named, and was buried in the churchyard of Llanuchllwydog. There was a *crwth* player, bearing the bardic name of *y Crwthwr Mwyn* (the meek *crwth* player) at Carmarthen in 1810. There were several eminent *crwth* players scattered about Wales back in the middle of the eighteenth century. Here is a list of *crwth* makers, most of whom were also performers upon the instrument :—

Dafydd ap Shôn Forus, Trefnewydd, c. 1690.

APPENDIX C

Dafydd Sion, Gwrecsam, c. 1700.
Dafydd ap Roberts, Trallwm, c. 1675.
Dafydd Emwnt, Melin Ifan Dda, c. 1680.
Dafydd Ifan, Trefriw, c. 1700.
Shôn Offeiriad, Aberhonddu (John the Priest, Brecon), c. 1670.
William Rhŷs, Llanymddyfri, c. 1680.
Shôn Grythor, Abertawy, c. 1690.
Tomos Morgan, Caerfyrddin, c. 1675.

I have discovered the names of only two makers of the eighteenth century, Richard Williams, and Richard Evans, both of Anglesey, but probably some of the above lived on through its first quarter, if not longer. Gradually the " wee fiddle " found its way to the Welsh hills, and drove out its quaint but cumbersome cousin, the *crŵth*. It was a case of the survival of the fitter. The native instrument had disappeared completely by about 1830. Most of the *crythau* in use in the eighteenth century were probably made in the previous century, and many of them were possibly much older, so that it is not surprising to find that only a few of them are now extant. One of these is in the South Kensington Museum, another is owned by Sir John Williams, Bart., M.D., a third was the proprety of the late Colonel C. Wynn-Finch, and is at Voelas Hall, North Wales, and a fourth is in the Municipal Museum at Warrington. Of these by far the most perfect and interesting specimen is the one at Voelas Hall. The late Alderman Edward Samuelson, of Liverpool, in a little pamphlet which he printed for private distribution in 1892, gives an interesting account of it. He says : " On closely examining it, I arrived at the conclusion that it had originally been strung with wire, judging from the minuteness of the holes in the tailpiece and the iron string-wrests resembling those of a lyre or harp. It seems probable that it had been manipulated in a manner similar to the latter instrument, for it was at first designed to carry twelve strings, though some subsequent owner had modified it by filling up the holes of half-a-dozen of the string-wrests. Further evidence is found in the bridge, constructed to carry twelve strings, nearly level and very low. The tail-piece and finger-board appear to have been introduced after the strings were reduced in number. There is a traditional record of a certain Crwthyr [*sic* : it should be *crythor*] named Morgan, who is said to have played on this instrument, in Carnarvon or at Newborough, early in the present century, but there is no record of *how* he played it, and, in the absence of any mark showing friction at the part where the chin usually rests, I am disposed to think that, if used as a bowed instrument, it was played from the knee, after the manner of the viol da gamba or viol d'amour, and in that case there would be no difficulty in playing *pizzicato* passages on the two harp strings appended at the side of the finger-board, and about which there seems to be much mystery. The available information is, however, so slight that I am not disposed to dogmatise, and it is quite possible to hold either that it was played in the way I describe, or that it was played in a manner resembling the guitar—an instrument which we will do well to remember was immensely popular throughout England early in last century, and indeed, until the all-devouring pianoforte drove it from the field. One thing I am pretty sure of is, that the *crŵth*, in its original form, was not held and played in the same way as the modern violin."

The Voelas Hall *crŵth* is figured in " Musical Instruments : Historique, Rare, and Unique," by A. J. Hipkins.

An instrument somewhat resembling the *crŵth* is still in use among the Basques of the Pyrenees. The late T. H. Thomas, the well-known artist and antiquarian, of Cardiff, saw a strolling minstrel boy in the streets of Mentone in the summer of 1880 playing upon what looked like a *crŵth*, but minus the wings. The minstrel played the accompaniment to a quaint, plaintive melody which was sung by a little girl with a lovely voice.

A serious attempt was made years ago by Alderman Samuelson (already referred to) and others who were

APPENDIX C

interested in Welsh musical instruments, to revive the *crwth*. The Alderman gives an account of his efforts in the pamphlet just quoted from : " It seemed to me," he writes, " after my study of the ancient *crwth*, that it possessed features which it would be worth my while to attempt to reproduce in such a modified form as would render it suitable to modern use. So I commissioned a practical violin maker, in the person of my young friend John Byrom, of Liverpool, a former pupil of G. A. Chanot, a musical instrument maker of some eminence, to construct for me an instrument on the lines of *yr hen grwth Cymreig*, less rude in outward form, yet in essentials the same. He has carried out his instructions skilfully, and here is the result. It has a compass equal to the violin and the tenor combined, and has a tone which may be described as approximating to that of the viol d'amour or viol da gamba. It is capable of great range of style and effect, and lends itself admirably, for example, to such compositions as Stradella's ' Chanson d'Eglise ' (*Pieta Signore*), already arranged for violin, harp, and organ ; etc. . . . and many other compositions of a similar character. In short, here is one of our old national musical instruments reconstructed, capable of effective use in modern music, and only wanting enthusiastic young Welsh musicians to make it their own. I hope sincerely that some such may be led by my experiment to give it a trial."

This hope, earnestly and confidently expressed, was never realized, and the strenuous effort to revive one of the old national instruments of Wales came to nothing.

Appendix D

LEGENDARY ORIGIN OF STRINGED INSTRUMENTS

Keltic legends about the origin and development of stringed instruments have escaped the attention of writers on the violin, and yet they are as interesting in themselves, and as valuable to the antiquarian, as are the legends of ancient Greece, Egypt, or India. In addition to the mythological stories given in chapter V the following are noteworthy: they are taken from the "History of Down and Connor," by the Rev. Father James O'Laverty, P.P., M.R.I.A

(1) "There once lived a man, Cuil, and his wife, Canochlach Wor, and the wife conceived a hatred to him, and she was fleeing from him through woods and wildernesses, and he was always following her. One day the woman came to the seashore of Camus [Professor O'Curry thinks this is the mouth of the Bann], and she heard the wind making music through the sinews of a whale's skeleton, and the sweet sounds lulled her into a deep sleep. Her husband, perceiving the effect of sweet sounds, cut a tree in the woods and formed from it a musical instrument (*cruit* or *clairseach*) and put strings on it, in imitation of the sinews of the whale's skeleton. Thus he formed an instrument to calm the angry temper of his wife, and that, says the legend, was the origin of stringed instruments.

(2) "The *cruit*, or *clairseach*, was invented, as saith the legend, by Daghda, the great King or demi-god of the

APPENDIX D

Tuatha-de-Danaan, who ruled about eighteen hundred years before the Incarnation. This instrument was capable of giving forth three classes of music—one sort which would put the audience to cry, lament, and shed tears; another sort which caused them to laugh with their mouths so wide open that all but their lungs were visible; and the third cast them into a deep sleep from that hour till the same hour next day."

The following is a characteristic legend, which, according to Professor O'Curry, belongs to the earliest Gaelic mythology.

(3) "And it came to pass that Fraech went to solicit the hand of the princess Findaber, the daughter of the queen Maev, of Connaught. He obtained from his fairy aunt a retinue, among whom were three players of the *cruit* (or *clairseach*), each with the appearance of a king, both as to his dress and his arms and steed. And this was the condition of these musical instruments: there were bags of the skins of otters about them, ornamented with coral (*partaing*), with an ornamentation of gold and silver over that, lined with snow-white roebuck skins, and these again overlaid with black-grey strips of skin and linen cloths as white as the swan's coat, wrapped around the strings. The *cruits* (or *clairseachs*) were of gold, and silver, and bronze, with figures of serpents, and birds, and greyhounds upon them."

(4) There is a legend of an Irish saint who made a stringed instrument, to which he added a string at every new moon, till he had obtained a perfect instrument of thirteen strings, upon which "he made sweet sounds and gave praise unto God."

This is the legendary way of accounting for the development of stringed instruments. There are two or three similar stories relative to the saints in Welsh folk-lore.

(5) Here is a characteristic story, of a different type, from the folk-lore of South Pembrokeshire ("Little England beyond Wales"). There lived an old couple at a place called Sudden Pits, who rose from the depth of poverty to a

high degree of affluence in one night, and this is how the happy change came about. At a late hour one winter night, when the goodman of the house had retired to rest, his wife heard somebody approach the door and suddenly strike up on a fiddle. The music was sad and weird, like the soughing of the wind in the chimney: it gradually grew louder and louder, till the very house shook with the storm of sounds. The old man came down and timidly opened the door. There, a few paces away, stood a minstrel, a small man with long hair and beard as white as wool, playing upon a very large fiddle, and tearing away at the strings with a monstrous bow, as though he were bent upon waking the dead that slept in the churchyard near by. At last he stopped, and beckoned to the goodman to fetch a mattock, making motions with his bow to convey his meaning. The goodman, with fear in his heart and trembling in every limb, brought the mattock and proceeded to dig at a spot indicated by the strange little man, who stood by, occasionally grinning and showing a mouthful of large, phosphorescent teeth. After digging hard for an hour or more, he came upon a large iron chest, which, upon being opened, was found to be filled with gold coin and precious stones. The little man, no sooner than he beheld the treasure, whipped his fiddle to his chin and struck up a martial strain, which increased in volume and velocity till the very bell in the church tower rang, and the trees shook, and doors and windows rattled. The commotion had not lasted a minute when, tearing down the hill, there came a carriage drawn by two huge boars, and driven by two monster greyhounds: into this the minstrel jumped and galloped away, leaving the mystified old couple to the enjoyment of their wealth.

There are several versions of this fairy tale, all differing in detail, but relating practically the same thing, about the fiddle.

Appendix E

VIOLIN FATIGUE

In my remarks on the preservation of instruments I have laid stress on the importance of giving valuable old violins periods of rest. The question has been discussed time and again whether old fiddles ever get " played out," and it has been answered with equal confidence affirmatively and negatively. The question is really one which can be determined tentatively. The Messrs. Hill (whose unrivalled opportunities for the study of old instruments claim for them a respectful hearing at all times), asseverate that it is possible to wear out the tone of old violins. I will again quote their words :—" To close—one most earnest word. Instruments by continual use are apt to become weary. They may even virtually be killed. Give them rests. We feel it a duty to urge most strongly that fine instruments should not be brought to premature death by ceaseless use." (*Antonio Stradivari : His Life and Work*, p. 239).

The Rev. H. R. Haweis appears to hold the same view. He says : " The witchery of the violin for collectors is perhaps more difficult to explain. Very often these fanciers don't play, and still more often they seem to have an objection to other people stringing up their treasures and playing on them. It is the construction, not so much the sound of the violin, that deprives the collector of his senses ; but we ought to be very thankful to these monomaniacs, for without them there would be few masterpieces still extant ; through them the violin goes into a period of Devachan, or enforced rest." (*Old Violins*, p. 11.)

APPENDIX E

Mr. Paul Stoeving is emphatic on the matter; he says: "I should like in this connection to vindicate the rich amateur and violin collector, who is commonly chidden because of his withholding such priceless treasures from the hands of the professional, who can put them to better—viz., their proper use. Save for such temporary confinement, consider how few of these old instruments would have stood the continual, merciless strain and strife of professional life to which they are now subjected. I do not know whether it is a real fact, but it is affirmed that some of the best Stradivari violins have already been played out, worked to death, left a mere wreck of their former self as far as tone is concerned. I can almost believe it, for I know from experience that a violin, when played on for hours at a stretch, will get tired, and the voice husky like an over-worked singer; only rest will restore the tone to its usual brightness and responsiveness." The late Dr. Joseph Joachim in a letter to me dated from Gastein, August 13, 1898, writes: "It is an undoubted fact that old violins if over-played become fatigued. I find it necessary to keep three or four in use, so as to give my favourite instrument periodical rests. *Why* continual playing should produce fatigue is more than I can say; there are many theories about the mystery, but no satisfactory solution."

I have corresponded with several eminent professors and *virtuosi* on the subject, and one and all are agreed that old violins become weary if over-worked. Experience seems, therefore, to leave no doubt at all about the matter.

Now, here are some very difficult and interesting problems to solve. Why should over-work produce fatigue in dead matter?—Why, indeed, should it be called *over*-work, if the instrument with which it is produced, or on which it is performed, is dead? What are the determining factors of fatigue? Where is the boundary line of reasonable work? Why does rest restore the tone—i.e., where the harm is not irreparable? At what point of over-work does the injury to the tone become irreparable? What is

APPENDIX E 311

it that happens at that point ? And, finally, why is restoration impossible when a certain stage of fatigue has been reached ?

These, and many more such problems, are awaiting solution.

It would be well if, in tackling these questions, scientists endeavoured to satisfy themselves first on the most vital of them, viz., Why should over-work produce fatigue or weariness in dead matter (violins) ?

In current theories it seems to be taken for granted that thereis a fundamental difference between living and " dead " cells, and that, therefore, the question of violin fatigue is not one of exhausted vitality or of subtle electrical conditions, but one of purely physical change. But may it not be that too much has been taken for granted, and that, consequently, enquirers after the truth have set off on the wrong track ? Is there really a fundamental distinction between what we term " living " and " dead " matter, or, if you prefer, between matter and mind ? Is not the hylozoistic view more rational " that mind of some kind exists not only in man and the higher and lower animals, not only in the protists present and past, not only in the colloids, crystalloids and chemical compounds antecedent to the latter, but in the very molecules and atoms themselves ? " Perhaps the poet who sang that—

"Winds, waves, and flames, trees, reeds, and rocks
All live ; all are instinct with soul "

had a truer conception of the constitution of the universe than he who regards mind and matter as antitheses.

There are innumerable facts which suggest that the difference between living and non-living matter is not one of kind but merely of degree, such as e.g., the affinity in chemical composition between hæmoglobin and chlorophyll, the uniform effect of actinic rays in the so-called three kingdoms of nature, etc.

There would be no harm done if theorists tried another

APPENDIX E

track. If for " cellular incohesion " they substitute " decentralization of mind " they might arrive at some sort of agreement, and bring us at least a little nearer to a solution of the mystery. As bearing on this fascinating subject, I would refer the reader to a very lucid article in the pages of *The Hibbert Journal*, vol. xiii, No 3—" Mind and Matter : A hylozoistic view," by Fleet-Surgeon C. Marsh Beadnell, R.N., where he will find a long passage on memory in the inorganic world.

Appendix F

WOOD AND TONE

It is remarkable how little we know about the tone qualities of various kinds of wood. Hundreds of thousands of experiments have been conducted with a view to (a) a re-discovery of the Italian varnish, or (b) the discovery of a good substitute; but comparatively few with the object of arriving at a fuller and more accurate knowledge of the sound properties of timber. For a generation or more it has been taken for granted that the only suitable kinds of wood for violin making are maple and pine. Not a few luthiers, I suspect, appear to be oblivious of so elementary a fact as that the names " maple " and " pine " are species terms, each including a large number of varieties. There are between fifty and sixty varieties of maple (*acer*), and quite a long list of varieties of pine (*pinus*)—twenty-eight in the United States alone—and if we add the firs (*abies*) the number is very considerable indeed.

Which variety of maple, and which of pine, did the Italian masters use? I do not think the question, simple though it appear, can be answered with anything like certainty. M. Mangin observes that the old masters used a kind of pine called " azarole " (which another French writer, M. Simontre, identifies with *pinus epicea*), but where does he get his information from?

In standard theoretical works the whole subject is dismissed summarily by saying that the best maple for violin making grows on the southern slopes of the Carpathians and in some parts of the Eastern Alps, and that the best pine comes from Silesia, La Valteline, Les Grisons, Le Simmenthal, etc.

The fact is, nobody knows where the best varieties of maple and pine grow, nor even what are the best varieties. Indeed, I do not think sufficient is known on the subject of violin acoustics to warrant even the belief that maple and pine are the best possible woods for tone. We have fallen into the pernicious habit of taking too many things for granted, whereas in strict scientific inquiry nothing should be taken for granted. Within the area covered by this subject there remains an unknown region, waiting the advent of a curious explorer. Dr. Felix Savant did splendid work, but he only just entered the borderland.

I am well aware that violin makers have from time to time tried various kinds of wood, and that experiments have been made with different metals, glass, leather, etc., but sporadic tests and experiments by unlettered men are not likely to lead to any great discovery. The subject demands a deep and persistent scientific study, extending over many years and over many countries. Woods from all parts of the world, from different soils, of different varieties, and of different species, ought to be tried in endless combinations, the results being carefully tabulated, to enable us to arrive at definite results. This is, of course, largely a question of time and money, but an abundance of both has been sacrificed in the pursuit of that *ignis fatuus*, the Italian varnish.

Appendix G

ON THE USE OF THE NAMES "FIDDLE" AND "VIOLIN"

Within recent years the word *fiddle* has fallen almost completely out of use in polite speech, and writers also show a tendency to discard it. Some people use the word to designate instruments of an inferior class, reserving the word *violin* for those of the better sort, or for classical instruments. *Fiddler* and *violinist* are treated in the same way, except that the former appears to have even a greater stigma attached to it than has the word *fiddle*. There is a fashion in the use of words even as there is in ladies' hats, but in the case of the names under discussion it signifies nothing really to the historian and etymologist, for both words mean precisely the same thing. In all probability they come from the same root.

Fiddle is the modern form of the O.E. *fidele* and *fithele*; A.S. *fiðele*, and sometimes *viðele*. The word is akin to the Danish *vedel*, O.H.G. *fiedel*, M.G. *fiedel*, and Icel. *fiðdla*. All these forms appear to be ultimately connected with the late Latin *vitula*, which is of uncertain origin, but which in all probability comes from the early Latin *vitulari*, to celebrate a festival, originally to sacrifice a calf. [*Vitulus*—a bull-calf; *vitula*—a cow-calf]. Vitula was the goddess among the Romans who presided over festivals and rejoicings. *Violin* (with all its Romance equivalents) is the Italian diminutive of *viola*, derived from *viol*, which (according to the accepted etymology) is also derived from *vitula*, just like *fiddle. Veal* [O.E. *veel*, O.F. *veel*, M.F. *veau*] and *vellum, vituline*, are, of course, cognate words.

The disappearance of *t* in *viol* (*viola* and *viula*) is in accordance with one of the sound-laws which govern the passage of popular spoken Latin into the Romance dialects, whereby a medial consonant between two vowels is generally syncopated, as, e.g., *magistrum* in modern French becomes *maître*; *securum* = *sûr*; *rotundum* = *rond*, etc.

If the above be the correct etymology of the words *fiddle* and *violin* (and the weight of scholarship is in its favour), it seems a hard fate which has overtaken the former name. There is no reason why *fiddle* should fall into disfavour. Let us hope that another generation will have a truer appreciation of history and a keener sense of the fitness of things.

The poor word *crowd* has had to go by the board long ago, but it was quite a respectable word, being related to the Gaelic *cruit* and the Welsh *crŵth*.

It is remarkable how, in the growth of language, names and words which once were considered fitting and polite have come to indicate something which is offensive; take e.g., the words gossip, vulgar, clown, pagan, silly, etc. If to the list of degraded words must eventually be added the word *fiddle*, that will be when ignorance is allowed to sit in judgment at the gates of elegance.

Appendix H

CLIMATE AND TONE

That climate has a great deal to do with the quality of the tone of violins is a fact that does not appear to need demonstration, nevertheless it has been questioned. My own observations, extending over a quarter of a century, and the testimony of others who have interested themselves in the subject, enable me to say very explicitly that the fiddle (unlike the great Samuel Johnson) is much affected by the weather. Two things establish the fact :—(1) 'A damp or variable climate affects detrimentally the tone of old instruments. There is nothing (unless it be accident or theft) that artistes who own fine old fiddles so much dread as damp, murky weather, and the foul, over-heated atmosphere of a concert room. Dr. Joachim once told me that his Strad positively refused to sing in a humid room. The more perfect the constitution of the fiddle, and the sweeter its voice, the more is it affected by climatic changes. For this reason it is probable that we rarely or never in this country hear the great Strad and Joseph at their best.

(2) A warm climate helps to mature new instruments. I have seen instruments that were made by British makers twenty to twenty-five years ago, which had been for a number of years in a warm climate—some in India, some in British East Africa, Egypt, and Italy—the tone of which had matured wonderfully. It will suffice to name one instance. In the year 1895 the late James Hardie, of Edinburgh, made specially to my order a fine violin on the Maggini model : he made also a similar instrument to the

order of a gentleman who went in that year to East Africa, taking the fiddle with him. Some time ago this latter instrument came into my possession, and I had the opportunity to judge of the effect of nearly twenty years of tropical heat on the constitution and tone of the fiddle. It was very marked: the wood had aged in appearance, the glint of the varnish had been much softened, and the tone had developed a maturity which an existence of fifty years in England would not have given it. There is now a vast difference in the tone of these two Hardie fiddles.

Can we in this country, is the question, with our grey sky and grumpy climate, ever hope to impart to our new fiddles a full and perfect maturity? I fear not. We can import wood from Alpine hill and Croatian dale; we can reproduce the graceful lines of Strad or Joseph; we may yet succeed in adorning our work with Cremona ruby; but one thing remains for ever beyond our grasp—the maturing warmth of the generous climate of the fair land of Italy.

www.ingramcontent.com/pod-product-compliance
Lightning Source LLC
Chambersburg PA
CBHW021828220426
43663CB00005B/170